UNIX®
U S E R'S
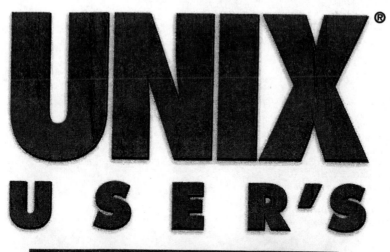

INTERACTIVE WORKBOOK

JOHN McMULLEN

Pearson
Education

Prentice Hall PTR
Upper Saddle River, NJ 07458
http://www.phptr.com

ISBN 0-13-099820-6

90000

9 780130 998200

Editorial/production supervision: *Joanne Anzalone*
Acquisitions editor: *Mark L. Taub*
Development editor: *Ralph Moore*
Marketing manager: *Dan Rush*
Manufacturing manager: *Alexis R. Heydt*
Editorial assistant: *Audri Anna Bazlan*
Cover design director: *Jerry Votta*
Cover designer: *Anthony Gemmellaro*
Art director: *Gail Cocker-Bogusz*
Series design: *Meryl Poweski*
Web site project manager: *Yvette Raven*

©1999 Prentice Hall PTR
Prentice-Hall, Inc.
A Pearson Education Company
Upper Saddle River, NJ 07458

Prentice Hall books are widely used by corporations and government agencies
for training, marketing, and resale.

The publisher offers discounts on this book when ordered in bulk quantities.
For more information, contact: Corporate Sales Department, Phone: 800-382-3419;
Fax: 201-236-7141; E-mail: corpsales@prenhall.com; or write: Prentice Hall PTR,
Corp. Sales Dept., One Lake Street, Upper Saddle River, NJ 07458.

Printed in the United States of America
10 9 8 7 6 5 4 3 2

ISBN   0-13-099820-6

Prentice-Hall International (UK) Limited,London
Prentice-Hall of Australia Pty. Limited, Sydney
Prentice-Hall Canada Inc., Toronto
Prentice-Hall Hispanoamericana, S.A., Mexico
Prentice-Hall of India Private Limited, New Delhi
Prentice-Hall of Japan, Inc., Tokyo
Pearson Education Asia Pte. Ltd., Singapore
Editora Prentice-Hall do Brasil, Ltda., Rio de Janeiro

Dedication

To Bethany (because now we know her name) and Sandi;
and with thanks to Ralph and Jeff and Jim for helping, and
extra thanks to Stephe, for letting me do this.

CONTENTS

FROM THE EDITOR

Prentice Hall's Interactive Workbooks are designed to get you up and running fast, with just the information you need, when you need it.

We are certain that you will find our unique approach to learning simple and straightforward. Every chapter of every Interactive Workbook begins with a list of clearly defined Learning Objectives. A series of labs make up the heart of each chapter. Each lab is designed to teach you specific skills in the form of exercises. You perform these exercises at your computer and answer pointed questions about what you observe. Your answers will lead to further discussion and exploration. Each lab then ends with multiple-choice Self-Review Questions, to reinforce what you've learned. Finally, we have included Test Your Thinking projects at the end of each chapter. These projects challenge you to synthesize all of the skills you've acquired in the chapter.

Our goal is to make learning engaging, and to make you a more productive learner.

And you are not alone. Each book is integrated with its own "Companion Website." The website is a place where you can find more detailed information about the concepts discussed in the Workbook, additional Self-Review Questions to further refine your understanding of the material, and perhaps most importantly, where you can find a community of other Interactive Workbook users working to acquire the same set of skills that you are.

All of the Companion Websites for our Interactive Workbooks can be found at http://www.phptr.com/phptrinteractive.

Mark L. Taub
Editor-in-Chief
Prentice Hall PTR Interactive

INTRODUCTION

Welcome to yet another introductory UNIX book. I'm glad you picked this one up, because I think you'll find it a bit different, and worth your time.

Why is this book different? Well, it's one of the practical books, for starters. It concentrates on things you can do to learn to use UNIX. Every chapter is full of exercises and answers; every chapter ends with a project that makes use of what you've covered.

And this book is supported in a way that others aren't. You're not alone in working on this book. If something in the book is giving you trouble, you can exchange solutions or hints with other readers (or me, even), just by going to the Web site or the newsgroup (more on those in a moment).

There are three important topics that are not covered in this book, simply because every system (even every office!) does things differently. The topics are electronic mail, the World Wide Web, and Usenet news. There are other books that describe these topics in all their variety.

WHO THIS BOOK IS FOR

This is a book for people who want to learn to use a UNIX computer system. It's not about programming, databases, Web surfing, or even popular networked shoot'em-up games. Before you can do those things, you need to know the things in this book. This is a book of basics and tricks that you'll need.

It's helpful if you've seen a computer (such as a PC) before, but it's not absolutely necessary. (Is there anyone left who hasn't seen a computer?)

WHAT IS UNIX?

There are two answers to this.

1.   UNIX is a concurrent multitasking, multiuser computer-operating system. What does that mean?

An operating system controls the computer's resources, distributing those resources among the different programs running on the computer. (On any UNIX system you use, there will always be more than one program running.) Although an operating system is itself a program, it isn't a program in the usual sense—you don't use the operating system the way you would use a word processor or a drafting program or a game. (By the way, the desire to play a game called "Space War" was one reason why the UNIX operating system was created, back in 1969.) Instead, the operating system provides the framework so the other programs can make use of the computer.

To put it another way, if your spreadsheet is a car that gets you from here ("Here are the numbers") to there ("There are the answers"), then the operating system is the superstructure supporting that trip. It's the laws ("Right turn allowed on red light") and the control devices (one-way streets, and traffic lights). With those laws and support structures, thousands or millions of cars can share the roadways. Without the superstructure, collisions are inevitable.

Multitasking means that more than one user-program can be run at once. (On a UNIX system, you can drive two cars at once, or drive a car and a skateboard.) And concurrent multiuser simply means that more than one user can use the machine at the same time. As with roads, you won't notice the effect until many users are using the system at once: too many users slow down everyone's trip.

2. The second answer is that UNIX is a registered trademark, licensed exclusively by The Open Group. That means that only systems that have passed certain tests given by The Open Group are allowed to call themselves UNIX systems. Since that testing (called "branding") costs oodles of money, there are a number of less expensive systems that look just like UNIX systems but aren't legally allowed to call themselves UNIX systems. Kind of like knowing how to drive but not being allowed to test for your license. (This includes systems such as LINUX and systems that conform to the POSIX standards.)

In this book, I'm referring specifically to the Solaris operating system, which is a UNIX system, but almost everything I say is applicable to all of those other systems.

If you think you already know everything in this book, maybe you're right. Consider reading one of the other Interactive Workbooks—there's a list of the series in the front of this book.

WHAT YOU'LL NEED

You'll need access to a UNIX computer system. This means you need a *shell account*, and access to a terminal or a computer.

You'll also need a pen or pencil and some paper. This book asks questions and expects you to answer them.

Each chapter should take an hour or two; the early chapters take less time than the later chapters (and the chapter on the vi text editor will take the longest of all).

HOW THIS BOOK IS ORGANIZED

Each chapter contains a brief introduction and a series of Labs, and ends with a project that makes use of the information in the chapter. Suggested answers to the projects are found on the Web site, not in this book.

Each Lab is organized in a similar way. After a brief introduction, there are a set of exercises and questions. (If you do the exercises, you can answer the questions.) After the questions for the Lab come the answers, and after the answers there's a multiple-choice quiz on the Lab. (Answers to the multiple-choice quizzes are in Appendix A.)

As to the order of the chapters... you don't have to work on them in order. Obviously, I think you should; I put them in the order that makes the most sense to me. For example, if you're using a system with X Windows installed, you might want to do Chapter 13, "X Window System," right after you finish Chapter 2, "The Command Line." It's your book now and you can use it as you please.

Some of the chapters fall into natural groups, and I *do* suggest you do the groups in sequence.

You should work through Chapters 1-4 in sequence. They introduce the basic commands and concepts you'll use throughout the rest of the book.

Chapters 5 and 6 ("Finding Help" and "Emergency Recovery") teach you how to find information when you need it, and how to recover from the kinds of minor emergencies you might encounter.

Chapters 7 and 8 ("Finding Files" and "Regular Expressions") work together well. Honesty compels me to tell you that you could probably live your entire life without learning regular expressions, but I think they're well worth the effort. They make working with text much easier.

You should do Chapter 9, "The vi Editor," because the vi editor is on every UNIX system. Even if you later go on to another editor later you should know at least how to exit the vi editor.

Chapters 10 and 11 ("Working with Text Files" and "Printing Text Files") work together.

Chapter 12 introduces a number of shortcuts and tricks to join commands together and to run more than one command at a time.

Chapter 13, "The X Window System," describes the graphic user interface available with many UNIX systems.

CONVENTIONS USED IN THIS BOOK

The following typographical conventions are followed in this book:

`cp file1 file2`	A command you should enter into the computer
`$ echo $LOGNAME`	
`johnmc`	An example of output from the computer
yourname	Either an emphasized or defined word, or a placeholder, a word you should replace with a suitable value.

You should be able to identify the questions in each section. There are also a few icons that help you locate important information: one for Advice, one for Tips, and one for the Web companion.

ABOUT THE WEB COMPANION

This book has a companion Web site, located at:

```
http://www.phptr.com/phptrinteractive
```

Think of the Web site as a student lounge, where you can go and find the answers to the projects or just chat with other students about the course or topics of interest. There's even a corner where the author (that would be me) presents items that didn't get into the book or answers questions or just possibly corrects a mistake.

Visit the Web site periodically to share and discuss your answers.

ABOUT THE AUTHOR

John McMullen has been paid to be a biologist, an actor, a bookstore clerk, an inventory clerk, a software trainer, a fiction writer, and a lumber-yard guy. (Sometimes he was only paid once, but it was the principle of the thing.)

None of those jobs lasted as long as being a technical writer, which he has done for more than ten years. Right now, he is the Senior Technical Writer for Softway Systems, proud makers of Interix for Windows NT (end of commercial). He has used UNIX systems since his university days, which are getting to be a long time ago.

He lives in southern Ontario, Canada, with his lovely and talented wife and his lovely and talented daughter and a dog. This is his second book.

CHAPTER 1

YOUR FIRST SESSION

 Any complete encounter with the computer system is a session. In any session, you get in, get on with it, and get out. The basics are simple.

A session on a UNIX computer system always has the same basic structure:

1. You identify yourself to the system by providing a name (your log-in name) and a password to prove your identity. This is called logging in. (The fact that you have started a session is actually logged—recorded—in the system's records.) When the system has confirmed your identity, you are logged in. The system lets you know by providing a command prompt, either a dollar sign ($) or a percent sign (%).

2. You issue commands.

3. When you are finished, you end the session by logging out. The usual command to leave the session is exit.

L A B   1.1

LOGGING IN

LAB OBJECTIVES

After this lab, you will be able to:

✓ Log In
✓ Identify Your Terminal Type

Before you can perform this lab, you need an account on a UNIX system and a computer terminal connected to that system. When you get your account, you will also get your log-in name and your password. If you don't get a password, you don't need it to log in.

YOUR ACCOUNT

Your account is your relationship with the system. Like a banking account or a commercial account with a parts supplier, your computer account grants you certain rights in the system. Instead of 30 days of credit, you have permission to use the resources of the computer. To use the system, you need a computer-friendly identification and a way of proving that you are the person who should be using that identification.

Your identifier is your log-in name (also called a user name or a log-in ID). On a PC, you don't need any kind of identification. A PC is designed for a single user. While someone may borrow your PC, it's essentially "yours"—you own the files on it, you make use of it, and if a file gets deleted, it's because you deleted it. On a system with more than one user (such as a

UNIX system), you need to be able to label things: this file is yours, that file is hers or this program that is running is yours, that program is his.

Some accounts are for jobs, not people. Every UNIX system has a special account for the system administrator, *who keeps the computer system running. The system administrator, or* superuser, *has the authority to do anything; his or her log-in name is usually "root."*

Your log-in name is assigned to you (although the system administrator may ask you what name you want). Your log-in name may be some variant on your name or it may be arbitrary; it depends on how many users there are, and on the system administrator's policy. For example, I have had the log-in names "john," "jhmcmullen," "t4sm," and "johnmc." (At that office, they started with the user's first name and added letters; the company already had a "john" and a "johnm.")

Both log-in names and passwords are case sensitive. If your log-in name is "dana," the system probably won't recognize you as user "Dana" or "DAna."

LOGGING IN

When the system is ready for you to log in, it presents a log-in prompt. The prompt can be a large box with spaces for your log-in name and password, or it can be a line that simply says:

```
login:
```

■ FOR EXAMPLE:

No matter which it is, type your log-in name, press the Enter key, type your password, and then press Enter again.

```
login: jordan
password: ######
```

If you make a mistake, try to backspace over it and fix it. If it still doesn't work, try again.

The Backspace key may not work as you expect during the log-in. On some systems, the Delete key erases the previous character.

Once you have entered your password, the `login` command starts your shell program. As the shell program starts up, it may display more text or it may not.

■ FOR EXAMPLE:

A sample log-in is shown here:

```
login: jordan
password:
TERM (AT386)
Last login: 03/29/98 15:32:21
March 31, 1998: The system will be unavailable from
midnight to 6:00 am for filesystem maintenance.
$
```

In this example, there is an extra prompt: The TERM prompt is asking for the terminal type. (Different types of terminals use different control codes to display characters on the screen.) The information in parentheses, AT386, is the *default* value. Accept the default value (by pressing the Enter key). You can always change it later.

After you've logged in, you can see the name of your terminal type by typing the command `echo $TERM` and then press the Enter key. (You must press the Enter key after all commands in UNIX.)

The information about "filesystem maintenance" is news from the person who administers the system. In this example, it wouldn't be important to you unless you were planning on working through the night. You could ignore this message.

The last line is the *command prompt*, and it indicates that the system is ready to take your orders. Although you can change it, the first time you log in, your command prompt will be either $ or %.

There will also be a *cursor*. A cursor is an indicator that shows you where the next letter will be displayed. It may be an underline or a rectangle; it may flash or be a solid color.

 Every UNIX system is different; no book can cover all the possible variations and still be carried by human beings. You may need to ask someone at your site about how it's all set up for you. This is especially true for this chapter.

LAB 1.1 EXERCISES

1.1.1 LOG IN

Log in with your user ID.

a) Are you prompted for a password? If not, why not?

_____

_____

b) Why is your password not displayed as you type it?

_____

_____

c) Are you asked for any other information?

_____

_____

If so, what is it? Is a default value provided?

_____

_____

d) What is your command prompt?

_____

_____

e) What does it mean?

_____

_____

1.1.2 IDENTIFY YOUR TERMINAL TYPE

Type the following commands and record the result (if any). Remember to press the Enter key at the end of each command line.

```
echo $TERM
tset -r
```

a) What are the results of `echo $TERM`?

_____

_____

b) What are the results of `tset -r`?

_____

_____

LAB 1.1 EXERCISE ANSWERS

 This section gives you some suggested answers to the questions in Lab 1.1, with discussions related to those answers. Your answers may vary, but the most important thing is whether or not your answers work. Use these discussions to analyze differences between your answers and those presented here.

If you have alternative answers to the questions in these exercises you are encouraged to post your answers and discuss them at the companion Web site for this book, located at:

`http://www.phptr.com/phptrinteractive`

1.1.1 ANSWERS

Log in with your user ID.

a) Are you prompted for a password? If not, why not?

Answer: You should be prompted for your password. If you're not, it's because your account was set up without one.

Your password proves your identity to the system. No one should know your password, not even your system administrator. (If you ever forget your password, your system administrator can give you a new one, which you should then change, so no one else knows your password.) While a password is not always necessary, it is a good idea to have one.

If you have trouble logging in in the first place, refer to Table 1.1 for some possible solutions.

Table 1.1 ■ Troubleshooting Log In

Problem	Possible Reason	Fix
There's no log-in prompt	The terminal may have gone into an energy-saving mode where the screen is blank.	Press Enter on the keyboard or, if there is a mouse, wiggle the mouse.
	The previous user didn't log out, so the terminal is still in his or her session.	If there is already a command prompt on the screen, type `exit`. If there is clearly something on the screen (pictures), try holding down the right mouse button.
	The terminal isn't turned on.	Is any part of the screen glowing? If not, look for an on/off switch. Try turning the terminal on.
You get the message *login incorrect*	You've made a mistake typing either your log-in name or your password. Remember: log-in names and passwords are case sensitive. Upper and lowercase letters are different.	Log in again.
After logging in, all letters are capitals and there are backslashes (\) before some letters	You typed your log-in name in all capital letters.	Release the Caps Lock key, type `exit`, and log in again.

b) Why is your password not displayed as you type it?

Answer: For security reasons, to prevent someone else from reading it and impersonating you.

The system does not display your password. It may show nothing, or (as in our example) it may display some other character. This is for security reasons. Your password proves your identity to the computer. If your password were displayed ("echoed") to the screen, someone could read it over your shoulder and impersonate you.

c) Are you asked for any other information? If so, what is it? Is a default value provided?

Answer: Answers will be different for each system.

The most common request—almost the only request—for "other information" is your terminal type. UNIX systems can use many different types of terminals, and what looks good on one terminal may look terrible on another.

Because you may not know what your terminal type is, a default value is usually provided in brackets. This is the value that will be used if you simply press Enter to continue. The default value is configured as the most common terminal type available for the system (if the system administrator knows what that is).

Most programs that ask you to provide information will indicate the default value.

d) What is your command prompt?

Answer: Answers will be different for each user; probably one of $ or %.

Because you can set your own prompt, your prompt *could* be nearly anything. (I know a programmer whose command prompt is, "Command me, master.") However, the default prompt depends on which shell program you use. Some shell programs use $ as the command prompt, and others use %. (When the system administrator is logged in as "root," the command prompt is #. This is to remind the administrator that he or she is acting as "root" and must be cautious.)

e) What does it mean?

The computer system is ready to accept orders.

TERMINALS

The terminal is how you communicate with the computer. Unlike a PC, a UNIX system can have more than one user at a time. Because it's not practical to have them all sitting at the same desk sharing the keyboard and screen, UNIX systems have more than one keyboard and screen attached. Each keyboard–screen combination is called a *terminal*.

It's important to remember that the terminal is not necessarily the computer—it's just a way to communicate with the computer. It's like a phone for talking to the computer (the very first UNIX terminals were teletype machines operating across phone lines). Usually, turning off the terminal will not have an effect on the UNIX system itself, although it will probably end your session.

Each type of terminal has its own commands for writing letters on the screen. (You don't have to be concerned with what those commands are, but you do have to know that there are different types of terminals.) Each type of terminal has its own name, which is stored in a variable called TERM. (The name stored in TERM varies between terminal types. That's why it's a variable.)

The four common possibilities are:

- You may have a terminal with a screen and a keyboard. This is the simplest setup, and the "original" UNIX system working environment. All of the other terminal types provide ways to *emulate* (imitate) this kind of terminal, often called a "dumb terminal." The name stored in TERM is usually related to the name and model of the terminals. (Hewlett-Packard terminals have names beginning with "hp." Volker-Craig terminals have names beginning with "vc." If there is no default name, try "vt100."
- You may have a PC running a terminal program that makes it behave like a terminal. This is almost identical to the previous situation. Check the documentation for the terminal program to learn which kind of terminal it emulates. Otherwise, it's probably "vt100."
- You may have an X terminal. An X terminal is a UNIX terminal running the X Window System (see Chapter 13, "X Window Systems"). You can identify an X terminal by the mouse attached.
- You may have a UNIX workstation. A workstation is a complete UNIX computer system that is connected to another larger system. With a workstation, you don't need to share computing time with other people. If you are using a UNIX

workstation, it will almost certainly be running the X Window System. See the "Instant X" section that follows. The name stored in TERM is "xterm."

Turning off an X workstation will turn off your machine and will have other bad consequences as well. **Don't do it.**

For the purposes of this workbook, you can ignore the fact that you have an X terminal or an X workstation. Almost all of the labs will be done in a program called xterm, which is a program that behaves like a dumb terminal. You will need to know how to start xterm, which is discussed in the next section, "Instant X." The name stored in TERM is "xterm."

INSTANT X

If you're using an X terminal and there's no command prompt, you need to start the xterm program. I cannot guarantee these hints will help; you may need to ask your system administrator or some other user for help.

I assume you know what it means to click or double-click a mouse button and select an item. If you do not, go to Chapter 13, "X Window Systems," for descriptions..

If there is an icon (picture) labeled xterm, position the pointer over it and click the left mouse button twice, rapidly.

Or: Position the pointer over the background (that is, not on any of the little pictures) and press the left mouse button once. This usually displays a menu—that is, a list of options. You want an xterm program, which is probably labeled "xterm," "shell," or "console."

1.1.2 ANSWERS

Type the following commands and record the results.

a)   What are the results of echo $TERM?

Answer:The result depends on the individual.

**LAB
1.1**

This command shows the name stored in the TERM variable. The echo command repeats whatever you type after the command. Putting "$" before the word "TERM" means that echo should print the value stored *in* TERM, not the word "TERM."

Two possible results are shown here:

```
$ echo TERM
TERM
$ echo $TERM
vt100
```

In the first command, the "$" was left off the beginning of TERM, so the echo command repeated the word "TERM." In the second command, the word was "$TERM" instead of "TERM" and the echo command printed the information stored in TERM. The value of TERM was "vt100." If you try the command on a machine running X Windows, it will print "xterm."

b)   What are the results of tset -r?

Answer:You will either get a terminal name (which should be identical to the value you got in Question a), or you'll get an error message.

An easier way to find out what kind of terminal you have is the tset command, but not all systems have it. To display your terminal type, type tset -r and press Enter. The system will either display your terminal type or an error message, like this:

```
$ tset -r
tset: command not found
```

If you get the error message, your system doesn't have tset installed.

LAB 1.1 SELF-REVIEW QUESTIONS

To test your progress, you should be able to answer the following questions.

1) Two people on the same UNIX computer can have the same log-in name.
   a) _____True
   b) _____False

2) Each type of terminal has its own name.
   a) _____True
   b) _____False

3) All users have passwords.
   a) _____True
   b) _____False

   Quiz answers appear in Appendix A, Lab 1.1.

LAB 1.2

CHANGING YOUR PASSWORD

LAB OBJECTIVES

After this lab, you will be able to:

✓ Choose a Password

✓ Change Your Password

Your files and information on a UNIX system are as private as your password. Anyone who knows your password can impersonate you—as far as the computer is concerned, the impersonator *is* you. The impersonator can read or change or remove any of your files or directories.

The key to keeping out impersonators is keeping your password secret and difficult to guess.

 People who break into systems are "crackers," by the way; to UNIX users, the word "hacker" means a clever programmer in general.

A good password should be at least six letters long. It should contain upper- and lowercase letters and punctuation marks. It shouldn't be something the cracker will try.

To guess your password, a cracker will try:

- Every word in the dictionary.
- The names and birthdays of everyone the cracker knows you care about.
- The password your system administrator used to set up your account; many people never change their passwords.

The command to change your password is `passwd`. When you run `passwd`, the command asks for your old password (to prove you're really you), your new password, and then your new password *again* (in case you made a typing mistake).

LAB 1.2 EXERCISES

1.2.1 CHOOSE A PASSWORD

Judge each of the following passwords as suitable or not suitable. If not suitable, give a reason why.

a) u2 _____

_____

b) 2bAg4st _____

_____

c) Your middle name _____

_____

d) I'mnNlf8r _____

_____

e) Jan012001 _____

_____

**LAB
1.2**

1.2.2 CHANGE YOUR PASSWORD

a) Change your password by using the `passwd` command.

_____

_____

LAB 1.2 EXERCISE ANSWERS

 This section gives you some suggested answers to the questions in Lab 1.2, with discussions related to those answers. Your answers may vary, but the most important thing is whether or not your answers work. Use these discussions to analyze differences between your answers and those presented here.

If you have alternative answers to the questions in these exercises, you are encouraged to post your answers and discuss them at the companion Web site for this book, located at:

`http://www.phptr.com/phptrinteractive`

If this concern with security seems obsessive, remember that UNIX is a multiuser operating system. The security that keeps unwanted people out also keeps others from accidentally removing your files. Remember too that UNIX systems are often used on college and university campuses, where pranks are a way of life.

Although UNIX systems can be very secure, they aren't necessarily the most secure systems around. The policies set by the system administrator determine whether your system has extremely good security or lax security. The bottom line is: It's a good idea to change your password periodically.

1.2.1 ANSWERS

Judge each of the following passwords as suitable or not suitable. If not suitable, give a reason why.

a) u2

Answer: Not suitable. Too short, and it's the name of a band.

b) 2bAg4st

Answer: Suitable, although some systems might require 8 characters instead of 7.

c) Your middle name

Answer: Not suitable. Could be guessed.

d) I'mnNlf8r

Answer: Suitable. It's long, and it contains upper and lowercase letters and punctuation. Although it spells a phrase ("I'm in an elevator"), the phrase isn't particularly significant.

e) Jan012001

Answer: Not suitable. Dates can be guessed, especially one like this which might be significant.

Keeping your password secret is the key to controlling access to your account and your files. Your job is to make it difficult for the cracker to guess your password. The best way to do that is to choose something that isn't obvious.

So, you can see that a *bad* password is:

- Short, such as "Abc"
- A word or common abbreviation
- A vanity license plate, such as "2HOT4U"
- All lowercase, such as "hoagie"
- A number, phrase, or date that's significant in your life
- The same for each account you have

A *good* password is:

- Long
- Not a word, phrase, or vanity license plate
- Composed of upper- and lowercase letters, digits, and punctuation
- Different for every account

**LAB
1.2**

Unfortunately, this also may mean it will be difficult to remember. If you can avoid it, don't write it down. If you forget your password, contact your system administrator.

Some systems allow you to insert control characters (such as backspaces) in your passwords. Some don't. I advise against it, simply because the way to produce control characters can vary from one terminal to another; you don't want to move to a new terminal and then discover you cannot log in.

1.2.2 ANSWERS

a) Change your password by using the `passwd` command.

Answer: Answers depend on the individual and the individual's system.

Some systems have special restrictions on changing your password. For example:

- You *must* change your password if you haven't changed it for some time.
- You *cannot* change your password if you have changed it recently (usually the last 24 hrs.).
- Your password must be at least six characters long (some systems require eight).
- Your password must contain at least two letters and at least one nonalphabetic character.
- Your new password must be different from your log-in name and your old password.

Your system may have any or all of these restrictions.

LAB 1.2 SELF-REVIEW QUESTIONS

To test your progress, you should be able to answer the following questions.

1) Two people on the same UNIX computer can have the same password.
   a) _____True
   b) _____False

2) Any user can use `passwd` to change someone else's password.
   a) _____True
   b) _____False

Quiz answers appear in Appendix A, Lab 1.2.

L A B   1.3

BASIC COMMANDS

LAB OBJECTIVES

After this lab, you will be able to:

✓ Identify Your Shell's Purpose

✓ Identify Your Current Directory

✓ Change Directories

✓ List the Contents of a Directory

Once you have logged in, what have you logged in *to*? There are two answers to that:

1. **Your shell:** The program you use to give commands to the computer.
2. **Your home directory:** The space on the computer reserved for you.

YOUR SHELL

Whenever you're using UNIX, you're using a shell program.

It's called a shell because it wraps around the operating system, much like a shell does. It's also called a shell because UNIX programmers are fond of wordplay: The actual operating system program is called the *kernel*, and a shell, naturally, coats a kernel. Your shell program protects you from the raw intricacies of the operating system. (It also protects the operating system from you.)

A shell program does three things for you:

- It interprets your commands.
- It stores information for you.
- It runs programs for you.

Shells may have many more features, but all shells do these three things.

You can discover which program is your shell by using the command ps and then pressing the Enter key. The output is a list of all of the programs you're running. Normally, this is your shell and the ps command.

■ *FOR EXAMPLE:*

```
$ ps
   PID  CLS PRI TTY       TIME COMD
   1381   TS  70 pts000   0:00 ksh
   1393   TS  59 pts000   0:00 ps
```

The last word on each line is the name of the command (COMD is short for command). Of the two programs listed, you know your shell isn't ps, so it must be ksh.

IDENTIFY YOUR CURRENT DIRECTORY

Whenever you're logged into a UNIX system, you're considered to have a *working directory.* You are "in" this directory. When you give a command that has a file's name in it, the shell tries to find that file in the directory you're in, unless you specify otherwise.

The command to print your current working directory is pwd (for print working directory).

■ *FOR EXAMPLE:*

```
$ pwd
/home/jordan
```

The working directory is /home/jordan, which means the directory jordan inside the directory home. (The directory home is said to be the *parent directory* of jordan, because jordan is contained inside home.)

CHANGE DIRECTORIES

You can change your working directory using the cd command (for change directory).

■ *FOR EXAMPLE:*

To change your working directory to /home, use the command cd /home:

```
$ pwd
/home/jordan
$ cd /home
$ pwd
/home
```

You can also give the cd command some special directory names, as outlined in Table 1.2.

Table 1.2 ■ cd Command Directory Names

	The command cd (with no directory at all) moves you to your home directory.
-	The command cd - returns you to your previous directory. This does not work in the Bourne Shell.
..	The command cd .. moves you to the parent directory of your current directory.

LIST THE CONTENTS OF A DIRECTORY

Once you have changed directories, you can see what files are in the working directory with the command ls (for list). To see what files are in another directory, type the directory name after the ls. Normally, the ls command doesn't distinguish between files and directories; in later chapters, you'll see options to show which are files and which are directories.

UNIX commands don't give a lot of extra information. If you give a command and the system responds with another command prompt, that means the program ran but there was nothing for it to do. If the program starts but you don't get another command prompt, then the command is still running. Wait a few minutes. If you still don't get a command prompt, try typing Control-D (hold down the Control or Ctrl key while you press the D key).

■ *FOR EXAMPLE:*

LAB 1.3

This command shows there are no files or directories visible in your current working directory:

```
$ ls
$
```

In the directory .., there are files or directories:

```
$ ls ..
bev     chris     dana     jordan     leslie
$
```

The parent directory of your current working directory (the directory ..) contains the files or directories *bev, chris, dana, jordan* and *leslie*.

LAB 1.3 EXERCISES

1.3.1 IDENTIFY YOUR SHELL'S PURPOSE

Enter the command:

```
ps
```

a) What is a shell program? _____

_____

b) Name two things a shell program does for you. _____

_____

c) What command-line shell program are you using? _____

_____

d) Can you run a shell inside a shell program?

_____

1.3.2 IDENTIFY YOUR CURRENT DIRECTORY

In your home directory, type the following command:

```
pwd
```

Then press the Enter key.

a) What is your home directory? _____

_____

b) What is the parent directory? _____

_____

c) What is the root directory? _____

_____

d) Do all users have their own home directories?

_____

1.3.3 CHANGE DIRECTORIES

Enter each of the commands that follow and then use `pwd` to display your working directory.

a) `cd ..`

_____

b) `cd -`

_____

c) `cd /`

_____

d) `cd`

_____

1.3.4 LIST THE CONTENTS OF A DIRECTORY

a) When you give the command `ls`, what directory is being listed?

_____

_____

b) When you give the command `ls /`, what directory is being listed?

_____

_____

LAB 1.3 EXERCISE ANSWERS

This section gives you some suggested answers to the questions in Lab 1.3, with discussions related to those answers. Your answers may vary, but the most important thing is whether or not your answers work. Use these discussions to analyze differences between your answers and those presented here.

If you have alternative answers to the questions in these exercises, you are encouraged to post your answers and discuss them at the companion Web site for this book, located at:

```
http://www.phptr.com/phptrinteractive
```

Your shell is your operating environment. It's the program you use to do all your work on a UNIX system.

There are different shell programs available, and you could change to a new one if you want. (Perhaps one shell has a feature you like more than another.) Some people have an almost religious zeal about their choice of shells. For a beginner, though, the differences between shells are barely noticeable.

Because your shell is running whenever you're logged in, you can discover what your shell is by listing the programs you have running with the ps command.

If you want to use the Korn Shell (the one used in this book), you can ask your system administrator to make the Korn Shell your log-in shell (the shell you get when you log in).

There may be reasons why you cannot have the Korn Shell as your log-in shell. It may not be on your system, for example. Or, there may be corporate requirements to use a different shell.

You can try out another shell with the command exec shell-name.
For example, exec /bin/ksh *replaces your current shell with* /bin/
ksh, *for this session only.*

1.3.1 Answers

a) What is a shell program?

Answer: The program you use to give commands to the computer.

A shell program is sometimes called a "command interpreter" because that's what it does: It takes your commands and turns them into orders that the UNIX operating system can carry out.

For every command, there are three stages:

- You type the command. By pressing Enter, you tell the system that the command is ready.
- The shell examines the command and interprets it.
- After it has "translated" any special commands or terms, the shell runs the command.

b) Name two things a shell program does for you.

Answer: Any two of the following: It interprets your commands, it stores information for you, it runs programs for you.

The shell interprets commands for you. It has to interpret the command because the shell regards certain characters as special, and treats them specially. It transforms them (or interprets them) before starting the command. This is what happened when you typed echo $TERM: The $ character told the shell to turn "$TERM" into "the value that is stored in TERM."

In that case, the shell was also storing information about your terminal type. When it runs a program, the shell uses stored information about where programs are kept. For example, when you typed passwd in the previous Lab, the shell searched all the places where commands are kept, looking for a program named passwd.

Besides information such as your terminal type, the shell stores other information about your session. Most of this information is to be used by other programs (a program may need to know how big your screen is, for example, so it can draw things properly). You can also add information such as short forms for commands you use often or information to be used by other programs.

After the program is found, the shell starts it for you. As soon as the program finishes, the shell asks you for another command by printing a new command prompt.

c) What command-line shell program are you using?

Answer: The answer depends on the individual.

Table 1.3 shows possible results.

Table 1.3 ■ Possible Shells

/bin/bash	Bourne-Again Shell	This is the shell that tries to combine most of the nice features of the C Shell and the Bourne Shell. The authors of this shell picked different nice features. Not all systems have bash installed.
/bin/csh	C Shell	The C Shell is a more user-friendly shell than the Bourne Shell (which isn't actually saying much). Most of the features that the C Shell introduced are found in the other two shells listed here. The C Shell uses % as its command prompt, so you can easily tell if you are using the C Shell. The ps command reports the C Shell as csh. (There are some other versions of the C Shell, but they all have names ending in csh.) It's possible there are systems without a C Shell installed, but they're very rare.
		The built-in commands of the C Shell are very different from those in sh and ksh.
/bin/ksh	Korn Shell	This was written by David Korn in the 1980s. Korn was trying to combine most of the features of the C Shell and the Bourne Shell; he also made sure that the Korn Shell does everything the POSIX Shell does. Not all systems have the Korn Shell installed, but it may be the most popular shell right now.

Table 1.3 ■ Possible Shells (Continued)

/bin/sh	Bourne shell or POSIX shell	The Bourne Shell was the first widely used shell, written by Steve Bourne in 1979. The Bourne Shell has none of the features that later shells have. It's used mostly to run scripts of commands. All UNIX systems have a Bourne Shell installed. If you are using the Bourne Shell, consider changing to one of the other shells.
		The POSIX Shell is the shell described by the POSIX.2 international standard. The POSIX Shell is the Bourne Shell with features such as command history added. Even if `echo $SHELL` reports `/bin/sh`, it's unlikely you have the POSIX Shell; not all systems have a POSIX Shell installed, although it is becoming more common.

LAB 1.3

These shells are all command-line shells: You type the commands and press Enter. There are other kinds of shells. If you're using the X Window system, the entire graphic environment is your shell, and you run other shells (such as `xterm`) inside that shell. Instead of giving commands with words, you give commands with the mouse.

d)   Can you run a shell inside a shell program?

Answer: Yes.

Although the shell is a big, complicated program, there's nothing magical about it. A shell can run another shell.

In fact, many programs on UNIX are actually *scripts*, lists of commands for a particular shell. The shell goes through the script, running the commands one after another, like an actor reading his lines. (Sometimes the first command is another shell, which runs the rest of the commands.) A script can also be called a command file, a shell program, or a shell procedure.

1.3.2 ANSWERS

a) What is your home directory?

Answer: This answer depends on the individual. The rest of the answers will assume it is `/usr/chris.`

When you log in, you always start in your home directory.

b) What is the parent directory?

Answer: `/usr`

A parent has children. In this case, the "child" of `/usr` is `chris`, the current directory.

c) What is the root directory?

Answer: `/`

The root directory is always `/`.

d) Do all users have their own home directories?

Answer: No.

A user doesn't have to have a unique home directory. Some log-in names are for specific administration tasks. For instance, the "sys" identity is used for some administrative programs, but its home directory is the root directory. However, a regular user should always have a home directory.

1.3.3 ANSWERS

Enter each of the commands that follow and then use `pwd` to display your working directory.
These answers assume you started in your home directory of `/usr/chris`:

a) `cd ..`

Answer: `/usr`

The `..` directory is always the parent of your current directory.

b) cd -

Answer: /usr/chris

The – name is special to the cd command. When you provide - as the directory name, the cd command moves you back to the previous directory. In this case, you started in /usr/chris, and you returned to /usr/chris.

c) cd /

Answer: /.

The cd/ command takes you to the root directory.

d) cd

Answer: /usr/chris

When you don't name a directory, the cd command takes you to your home directory.

1.3.4 ANSWERS

a) When you give the command ls, what directory is being listed?

Answer:Your working directory.

Unless you tell it otherwise, the ls command prints the contents of your working directory. This default saves a lot of typing.

b) When you give the command ls /, what directory is being listed?

Answer:The directory / —the root directory.

When you specify a directory name, the ls command prints the contents of that directory. You can actually name more than one directory, and ls will print the contents of each of those directories.

LAB 1.3 SELF-REVIEW QUESTIONS

To test your progress, you should be able to answer the following questions.

1)   You do not need a shell program.
   a) _____True
   b) _____False

2)   The `ls` command shows you the contents of a directory.
   a) _____True
   b) _____False

3)   All files and directories are contained in the root directory.
   a) _____True
   b) _____False

4)   In the following table, match the command to its task.

a) cd ..	i) Print working directory
b) cd -	ii) Change to parent directory
c) pwd	iii) Return to home directory
d) cd	iv) Return to previous directory

Quiz answers appear in Appendix A, Lab 1.3.

LAB   1.4

LOGGING OUT

+--+
| **LAB OBJECTIVES** |
| |
| After this lab, you will be able to: |
| |
| ✓ Log Out |
+--+

To end your UNIX session, type the command `exit`. When you log out, the system ends any programs you have running and performs some other cleanup. It may even display an exit message.

Some shells have other commands that will also log you out. Most shells exit if you press Control-D (hold down the Control key and then press the D key). If you are using the C Shell, you can exit using the command `logout`.

In the X Window System, exiting your command-line shell (in `xterm`) doesn't exit you from your session, it just ends that shell program and the `xterm` program.

To log out from an X Window System, you must find the appropriate menu item. It is usually named "logout" or "end session" or something similar.

LAB 1.4 EXERCISES

1.4.1 LOG OUT

Log out by typing the following command:

```
exit
```

a) What happens when you log out?

_____

_____

LAB 1.4 EXERCISE ANSWERS

This section gives you some suggested answers to the questions in Lab 1.4, with discussions related to those answers. Your answers may vary, but the most important thing is whether or not your answers work. Use these discussions to analyze differences between your answers and those presented here.

If you have alternative answers to the questions in these exercises, you are encouraged to post your answers and discuss them at the companion Web site for this book, located at:

http://www.phptr.com/phptrinteractive

1.4.1 ANSWERS

a) What happens when you log out?

Answer: Your session ends and the log-in prompt returns.

When you type exit, the shell does the following:

- Cleans up. It ends any programs you have running.
- It may run some commands. Most shells can automatically run commands before exiting, so you may see a message such as "Thank you."
- Records the fact that you have exited in the system log.

Once the shell has finished, the log-in prompt comes back. (In fact, the login command is the command that starts your shell for you.)

**LAB
1.4**

LAB 1.4 SELF-REVIEW QUESTIONS

To test your progress, you should be able to answer the following questions.

1) Your shell continues running after you log out.
   a) _____True
   b) _____False

2) Which of the following lets you log out?
   a) _____Control-D
   b) _____logout
   c) _____quit
   d) _____end
   e) _____bye

Quiz answers appear in Appendix A, Lab 1.4.

CHAPTER 1

TEST YOUR THINKING

 The projects in this section are meant to have you utilize all of the skills you have acquired throughout this chapter. The answers to these projects can be found at the companion Web site to this book, located at:

`http://www.phptr.com/phptrinteractive`

Visit the Web site periodically to share and discuss your answers.

1) The shell runs commands for you. What program starts the shell?

2) If you had more than one terminal, could you be logged in more than once?

3) Identify some features of UNIX that make it secure.

C H A P T E R 2

THE COMMAND LINE

 One of the features of UNIX that makes it confusing to learn yet power-ful once it is learned is the tool-oriented nature of the commands. The commands are written to work together. Once you understand the commands and how they work, you can link commands together to create new compound commands.

Because commands can be joined, UNIX is a very flexible working environment. The commands are written to work together. Each of the common utilities is a specialist. The `ls` command lists files—but it can list files in hundreds of different ways, depending on which options you have given it.

A command can have a dozen options, each of which changes its behavior in a slightly different way. To understand these, there is a short form, called the *command synopsis*.

But because there can be so many slightly different ways to assemble a command so it does just what you want, you must understand the structure of the command. Then you can understand the "magic" characters that are not part of the command itself: the characters that can be used to link commands together.

L A B   2.1

THE STRUCTURE OF A COMMAND

LAB OBJECTIVES

After this lab, you will be able to:

✓ Identify the Parts of a Command

✓ Interpret Options and Operands

✓ Read a Usage Line

The shell interprets all command lines you type before running the commands. A command is built like a sentence: the command itself is a verb, something for the computer to do. The `ls` command lists directory contents. You can give the verb an object, a thing to act on. The `ls /` command lists the contents of the directory `/`. You can provide an adverb, a modifier that changes *how* the command acts. The `ls -p` command lists the contents of a directory, identifying which are files and which are directories. The shell interprets these parts of the command line: commands, options, and objects (or *operands*). There are other special commands that the shell interprets, which we'll discuss later. You can use them to join commands together.

A command can have two parts: the command name itself, and the *arguments*.

There *must* be a command name. It's the first word you type after the prompt. The command name is usually the name of the program you want to run. There may be a command name only; the pwd command is complete by itself.

After you type a command, press the Enter or Return key (depending on how it's labeled on your keyboard). From now on, I won't mention pressing Enter unless doing so is unusual in some way.

There are two types of command arguments:

- *operands:* The *objects* of the command.
- *options:* The *way* the command works.

OPERANDS

Operands are the *objects* of the command. They're what the command acts on. In the command cd .., the ".." is the operand. An operand is usually the name of a file or directory, because most commands operate on files or directories.

Some commands *always* require operands, some don't work if you give them operands, and some work with and without operands. Some commands can take more than one operand. It depends on the command.

■ FOR EXAMPLE:

- The command pwd never takes an operand. The command fails if you try to give it one.
- The command diff always requires two operands. (The diff command compares two files, so it needs the names of two files to compare.)
- The command ls always lists files and directories. The operand (or operands) to ls are the name of a file or a directory. The ls command then lists that file or the contents of that directory.
- If you don't provide an operand, ls lists the files in your current directory.
- If a command takes operands, they are the last items in the command.

OPTIONS

Options affect *how* a command does its job. The command ls lists files; the command ls -F lists files and indicates whether the files are directories, files, or special files. The -F option changes the format of the output and the information given. Try both ls and ls -F on your system now. Note that the *options* are different from the *operands*. The operands for ls are still file or directory names; the options change the information that ls displays about those operands.

Command options come after the command and always come before the operands. Options are *always* optional; that's why they're called options.

Options begin with a - (hyphen) character; an option is usually a single letter. However, there are exceptions to this rule.

Single-letter options can be grouped and usually placed in any order.

■ *FOR EXAMPLE:*

The command ls -a -F is the same as the commands ls -F -a, ls -aF, and ls -Fa. (The -a option causes ls to list hidden files and directories.)

Some options require their own arguments. The argument must come immediately after the option letter. Most commands require a space between the option letter and the argument; some require *no* space between the option letter and the argument. You can never group options that take arguments.

COMMAND SYNOPSES

Over the years, a standard short form has been developed for describing the options and operands for commands. This shorthand is used in each synopsis of a command. You see them in usage lines and in the on-line documentation (the manual pages).

A *usage line* is a command synopsis printed by the command itself. Most UNIX commands report what their options are. Usually the option -? displays this synopsis of the commands. Many programs display the usage line whenever you give the command a wrong option or operand. (Because this feature is up to the person who wrote the program, it isn't done in the same way on every system, or even in every program.)

The standard synopsis format is:

- Single-letter options are run together, just as they can be on the command line.
- An option that requires an argument is separate from the options that don't require arguments.
- *Italics* indicate that the word is a placeholder. It must be replaced by some appropriate value for your purposes. The most common one is *file*, which you should replace with the name of a file. Because most terminals can't display italics, a placeholder may be indicated in other ways, such as underlining, highlighting, or angle brackets, like this, <file>. (On some terminals, even underlining and highlighting won't show up.)
- [ ] around an argument indicates that the argument is optional. It isn't required to run the command. An operand or option may have optional parts; they're in brackets, too.
- . . . indicates that the previous argument can be repeated more than once.
- | indicates a conflicting pair of arguments: You can use the first one *or* the second one. (There can be more than two.) This is quite rare. The conflicting arguments may be placed in braces ({}).

■ *FOR EXAMPLE:*

The `grep` command finds patterns in a file or files. There are two forms of the `grep` command. The complicated form has the synopsis shown here. It is about as complex as synopses get.

```
grep [-E|-F] [-c|-l|-q] [-insvx] -e patterns ...
   [-f patternfile] ... [file ...]
```

In this form, the command must have an -e option; you must supply some kind of patterns after it. There can be more than one -e option. The following are optional arguments:

- Either the -E option or the -F option, but not both at once.
- Any one of -c option, -l option, or -q option, but not more than one.
- Any combination of the -i, -n, -s, -v, or -x options.

- One or more -f options, but each one must be followed by an argument. The placeholder is *patternfile*, to indicate it's a file containing *patterns*.
- Any number of files, indicated by *file*.

Usually the placeholders indicate somehow what the argument is.

■ FOR EXAMPLE:

You can figure out that a *patternfile* is a file that contains *patterns*.

The simple synopsis line for the grep command is:

```
grep [-c|-1|-q] [-insvx] pattern [file ...]
```

In this version, the *pattern* is a required operand.

LAB 2.1 EXERCISES

2.1.1 IDENTIFY THE PARTS OF A COMMAND

In the following command lines, identify the command name, the options (if any), and the operands (if any):

a) ls -aF ..

_____

_____

b) cat /etc/password

_____

_____

c) pwd

_____

_____

d) `ls -a`

_____

_____

e) `head -n 1 /etc/password /etc/groups`

_____

_____

f) `make -v -f makefile.new`

_____

_____

2.1.2 INTERPRET OPTIONS AND OPERANDS

a) How is an option different from an operand?

_____

_____

b) Do all commands have operands and options?

_____

_____

Enter the following commands:

```
ls
ls -F
```

c) How do they differ?

_____

_____

2.1.3 READ A USAGE LINE

The command `fold` has the following usage line:

```
fold [-bs] [-w width] [file ...]
```

Assume the file *letters* is in your working directory. For each of the following commands, tell whether or not it would be valid for the command `fold`?

a) `fold` _____

_____

b) `fold -w -s letters` _____

_____

c) `fold letters` _____

_____

d) `fold -b -q -w 60 letters vowels` _____

_____

e) `fold -q letters` _____

_____

LAB 2.1 EXERCISE ANSWERS

 This section gives you some suggested answers to the questions in Lab 2.1, with discussions related to those answers. Your answers may vary, but the most important thing is whether or not your answers work. Use these discussions to analyze differences between your answers and those presented here.

If you have alternative answers to the questions in these exercises, you are encouraged to post your answers and discuss them at the companion Web site for this book, located at:

```
http://www.phptr.com/phptrinteractive
```

You use English language equivalents to UNIX commands every day. The command itself is a verb.

Command options modify how the command behaves. Just as "backwards" modifies how you should walk, -1 modifies how ls should list files. A command option is the equivalent of an adverb.

Commands can have objects just like sentences do. The operand is the object. What should you kick? The can. What should the new working directory be? The directory /etc is the operand.

In UNIX commands, however, the options almost always come before the operands, which means that UNIX commands are the equivalent of the English "save in the box the results." It takes time to learn to organize your thoughts this way.

2.1.1 ANSWERS

In the following command lines, identify the command name, the options (if any), and the operands (if any):

a) ls -aF ..

Answer: Command Name: ls

Options: -aF

Operands: ..

The parts of the command are separated by spaces. At the beginning of the command is the command name, `ls`. Then come the arguments, separated by spaces. All arguments beginning with "-" are options, and the last argument or arguments are the operands.

It's built like an English sentence: List (`ls`) descriptively all (-aF) files in the parent directory (. .).

The command word almost always comes at the beginning of a UNIX command (there is an exception to this rule, but you're not likely to run across it). The command word is usually the name of a program somewhere on the system. (We'll discuss how your shell finds the program in a later chapter.) When you type `ls`, there is an `ls` program on the system.

> *Some commands don't need any more information: "duck" is complete by itself. (If you need to duck, you probably don't have time to hear the rest of the information.) The pwd command is complete by itself.*

b) `cat /etc/password`

Answer: Command Name: `cat`

Options: None

Operands: `/etc/password`

Consider this English sentence: "Kick the can." There is a command word, "kick," and the object, "can." The command `cat /etc/passwd` contains the command `cat` and an object, `/etc/passwd`.

c) `pwd`

Answer: Command Name: `pwd`

Options: None

Operands: None

This is a simple command with no options and no operands. In fact, the `pwd` command won't accept arguments.

d) `ls -a`

Answer: Command Name: `ls`

Options: `-a`

Operands: None

This command lists (ls) all files, including the hidden ones (-a). An English sentence equivalent might be "Walk backwards." How should you walk? Backwards. What files should you list? All of them.

   e) `head -n 1 /etc/password /etc/groups`

   Answer: Command Name: `head`

   Options: `-n 1`

   Operands: `/etc/password /etc/groups`

This one's trickier, because the option has its own object. The `head` command lists the first few lines (the "head") of a file. The `-n` option describes how many lines to list: in this case, one line.

   f) `make -vf makefile.new`

   Answer: This is a trick question. The command name is `make` *and the options are clearly* v *and* f, *but without knowing whether the* `-f` *option takes an argument, you cannot know if* `makefile.new` *is an operand, or an argument to the* `-f` *option.*

It's generally a bad idea to include an option that takes an argument in a grouping of options. You can get ambiguous results like this `make` command.

The only way to be sure if an option takes an argument is to check the documentation, or to see the usage line for the command. (You can usually get a usage line by running the command with the option `-?`, but this is not guaranteed.)

2.1.2 ANSWERS

   a) How is an option different from an operand?

   Answer: An option affects how the command operates. It begins with a hyphen character. An operand defines what the command acts on. It doesn't begin with a hyphen character.

Most commands can take more than one option and more than one operand.

Some options contradict each other. For example, an option to show no output contradicts an option to show lots of output. UNIX commands take one of these strategies.

- The *last* option on the command line is the one that takes effect.
- The *first* option on the command line is the one that takes effect.
- The program quits, complaining that you cannot use both options at once.

The strategy depends on the command; the command documentation should mention which option takes precedence.

b) Do all commands have operands and options?

Answer: No.

Some commands have operands but no options; other commands have options but no operands; and still other commands have neither.

c) How do they differ?

Answer: The ls *command lists the files; the* ls -F *command lists the files and indicates the type of the files (file, directory, and so on).*

Command options do follow rules about where they're placed and how you can use them.

USING OPTIONS IN COMMANDS

These are the rules for using options. There are exceptions, though, which are discussed in the next section.

- An option is a hyphen followed by a single character.
- Options can occur in any order, so long as the options occur before the operands.
- Single character options without arguments can be condensed into one long multicharacter option after a hyphen.
- If an option takes an argument, it requires the argument immediately after the option; the argument must be there. Otherwise, the program doesn't "know" which argument is supposed to go with the option.

■ *FOR EXAMPLE:*

The command sort   appointments sorts the file appointments and writes the results on the screen. The command sort -r appointments sorts the same file in *reverse* order and writes the results to the screen. The command sort -r -o results appointments sorts the same file in reverse order and writes the results into a file named results.

The command sort -or results appointments may work, but it will not work as you intended. On some systems (depending on exactly how sort was written by the programmer) it may interpret the line as "sort the files results and appointments and store the output in the file r."

EXCEPTIONS YOU WILL ENCOUNTER

There are exceptions. Most of the exceptions aren't standard UNIX programs, but you will eventually run into them:

- Programs written for the X Window System use words for options. Instead of -f *filename*, they use the option -file *filename*. You cannot group options to X programs.
- Programs distributed by the Free Software Foundation as part of their GNU project use both short (standard) options and long ones, but they introduce their long options with two hyphens. The "print usage information" option on most GNU programs is --help.

WHY SOME UNIX COMMANDS ARE INCONSISTENT

When UNIX was young and the commands were first being written, there was no standard way to take arguments. Programmers wrote the commands to work in whatever way they felt would be best. Some commands required a space between an option and its argument, while others didn't. Some commands had options that might or might not need an argument. Some other commands had so many options that they were broken down into subcommands that had their own options and operands.

When the POSIX.2 international standard for UNIX commands was being created, the committee tried to establish some rules for how options are used. Those rules are the ones given earlier, under "Using Options in Commands."

Despite the intentions of the standards makers, some commands are now too well entrenched to change. These commands are so common or so important that changing them would cost too much time and money. This is the case with the X programs. The GNU software accepts the standard style of options, but the authors feel that their way is better.

The Free Software Foundation believes software should be free. They do not mean "free of charge;" they mean that if you buy the program, you should also get the source code used to create the program, and you should be free to change it and modify it as you see fit. For years, they have been working on the GNU project, which is a free replacement for UNIX. (GNU stands for "GNU's Not UNIX.") GNU programs and utilities show up on most UNIX systems.

2.1.3 ANSWERS

The command `fold` has the following usage line:

```
fold [-bs] [-w width] [file ...]
```

The file *letters* is in your working directory. For each of the following commands, tell whether or not it would be valid for the command `fold`?

a) `fold`

Answer: Valid.

This command is the basic `fold` command, with all optional items omitted.

Given that some commands have more than 20 options (the version of `ls` on my machine has 24), it's difficult to remember what all of the options do. In fact, it's difficult to remember what all of the options *are*.

Part of this is the tool-oriented nature of the basic UNIX programs. The `ls` program tries to be the most versatile file-listing program around, so it provides 24 slightly different ways to list files. You can list files in one column or in several, you can sort the files by name or by time, and you can choose what information you want displayed about each file. There are hundreds of ways to mix the options to `ls`.

The standard synopsis format helps you get around this problem.

b) `fold -w -s letters`

Answer: Not valid: The `-w` *option is missing its argument.*

This is the kind of error that's difficult to discover by looking at the command you typed. You simply need to know whether an option takes an argument or not. The synopsis line tells you if it does.

> *The standard synopsis format has been around as long as UNIX commands have been documented. Learning to read these synopses is essential; they're used throughout the on-line documentation and in the usage lines programs print out.*

c) `fold letters`

Answer: Valid.

Options are, well, optional.

d) `fold -b -s -w 60 letters vowels`

Answer: Valid.

You don't have to group options behind a single hyphen.

e) `fold -q letters`

Answer: Invalid; there is no `-q` *option.*

Because there is no option by that name, it's a mistake to include one.

Some usage lines can get quite complicated, because some commands are complicated. Operands may have optional parts, so there may be `[]` brackets inside `[]` brackets. There may be optional parts that can be repeated (...).

■ *FOR EXAMPLE:*

The `cal` command displays a calendar. It has this usage line:

    cal [*month* [*year*]...]

There are three possible forms of the `cal` command.

1. By using all of the optional parts, you get this form:

        cal *month year*

In practice, you would replace both *month* and *year* with some other values. This displays the calendar for a particular month in a particular year. (If you try this, remember that the *year* has to be written with the century: "1998" is a different year than "98.")

2. By removing the innermost set of brackets, you get this form:

```
cal year
```

The *year* would be replaced by some year. Instead of displaying one month, the `cal` command displays all 12 months of that year.

3. By removing all of the optional items, you can see that the command `cal` alone will do something:

```
cal
```

Without any operands, `cal` displays the current month of the current year.

LAB 2.1 SELF-REVIEW QUESTIONS

To test your progress, you should be able to answer the following questions.

1) The first word in a command is always the command name.
   a) _____True
   b) _____False

2) Among the options of `ls` are the options −1, −C, and −F. The `ls` command can take −1 or −C, but not both; and it can always take −F. Which synopsis fragment correctly describes this?
   a) _____[−1FF]
   b) _____[−1F][−FF]
   c) _____[−1|F] [−F]
   d) _____[−F −1|F]

3) Suppose for `ls`, you enter all three options (as in **−1 −C −F**). What might the program do? (You may want to try this.)
   a) _____Print an error message and stop.
   b) _____Behave as though you had typed −1 −F.
   c) _____Behave as though you had typed −C −F.
   d) _____Any one of these; it depends on the command.

Quiz answers appear in Appendix A, Lab 2.1

L A B 2.2

FILE REDIRECTION AND PIPES

LAB OBJECTIVES

After this lab, you will be able to:

✓ Save Output in a File

✓ Use a File as Input

✓ Link Commands with Pipes

Many commands write their output to the screen. This is standard in UNIX, and is actually called the "standard output" file or "stdout." In the same way, the standard input (or "stdin") is the keyboard; the file operand is optional for many commands. There is also a third standard place for error messages, called "standard error" or "stderr." Standard error is normally the screen.

When using the keyboard as the input file, you need to indicate the end of a file. Press Control-D to end input.

The standard input and standard output are actually treated as files. Instead of letting the stream flow to the screen, you can redirect it into a file. If you do this, the command writes its output to a file instead of the screen, or takes its input from a file instead of the keyboard. This substitution of one file for another is called *file redirection*. You can redirect output to only one file at a time, and redirect input from only one file at a time, but you can redirect all input, output, and errors.

As mentioned in Chapter 1, the shell interprets all command lines. When interpreting a command line, the shell looks for special characters and "words" to make file redirection easier. These are:

> `>`   `>>`   `<`   `2>`   `|`

To redirect output into a file, use >.

> `command > filename`

If a file named `filename` already exists, it will be entirely overwritten by your new file. To append output to a file instead of overwriting it, use >>.

> `commandline >> filename`

To redirect input from a file instead of the keyboard, use <.

> `commandline < filename`

To save error messages into a file, use 2>.

> `commandline 2> filename`

To use one command's output as the second command's input, use |.

> `command1 | command2`

Commands that take input from standard input, change it, and then write it to standard output are often called *filter* programs.

■ FOR EXAMPLE:

- The command `ls / > rootlist` stores the output of the `ls /` in a file named `rootlist`.
- The command `more < rootlist` writes its input from the file `rootlist` to the screen one screenful at a time. Press <space> to see the next screenful, or press the Q key to quit.
- The command `ls / | more` sends its output directly to `more`.

A command that requires you to make use of file redirection is `cat`. `Cat` copies the information coming from its standard input to its standard output. Its command synopsis looks like this:

> `cat [-estuv] [file ...]`

You can create small text files using cat. *Type the command* cat > filename *and then type the text you want in the file. The* cat *command (and commands like it) do not prompt for input; just start typing. End input with Control-D.*

LAB 2.2 EXERCISES

2.2.1 SAVE OUTPUT IN A FILE

In your home directory, type the following command:

```
pwd > iamhere
```

a) What does this command do?

_____

_____

Use ls to prove that the file exists.

Display the contents of the file iamhere with the following command:

```
cat iamhere
```

Type the following commands:

```
cd ..
pwd > ~/iamhere
cd
```

b) What do these commands do?

_____

_____

Display the contents of the file iamhere with the following command:

```
cat iamhere
```

c) How did the contents of the file `iamhere` change?

_____

_____

2.2.2 USE A FILE AS INPUT

Type the following command:

```
cat < iamhere
```

a) What does this command do?

_____

_____

Type the following command:

```
cat < iamhere /etc/passwd /etc/groups
```

b) How does input file redirection differ from using file operands with `cat`?

_____

_____

2.2.3 COPY A FILE WITH FILE REDIRECTION

Type the following command:

```
cat < iamhere > here2
```

Next, type the following command:

```
cat > here3 < here2
```

a) What do these commands do? (Use `ls` to check)

_____

_____

Type the following command:

```
cat iamhere here2 here3 > allhere
```

b) What does this command do?

_____

_____

2.2.4 APPEND TO A FILE

Create a file called `more`, and then type the following command:

```
cat more >> allhere
```

a) What does this command do?

_____

_____

2.2.5 PIPE TO ANOTHER COMMAND

Type the following command:

```
ls -lR / | sort | more
```

a) Where is `ls` sending its output?

_____

_____

b) Do the error messages also go there?

_____

_____

c) Which command is acting as a filter?

_____

_____

2.2.6 ESCAPE FILE REDIRECTION CHARACTERS

Type the following command:

```
echo To redirect, use > filename
```

a) What happened?

_____

_____

Type the following command:

```
echo To redirect, use \> filename
```

b) What happened?

_____

_____

c) What does the \ character do?

_____

_____

LAB 2.2 EXERCISE ANSWERS

This section gives you some suggested answers to the questions in Lab 2.2, with discussions related to those answers. Your answers may vary, but the most important thing is whether or not your answers work. Use these discussions to analyze differences between your answers and those presented here.

If you have alternative answers to the questions in these exercises, you are encouraged to post your answers and discuss them at the companion Web site for this book, located at:

```
http://www.phptr.com/phptrinteractive
```

File redirection is an important concept in UNIX; it provides a way to link programs together so a set of small specialized programs can do the work of hundreds of larger programs. Command options provide a way to "fine tune" the small tools, and pipes and file redirection provide a way to join them.

2.2.1 ANSWERS

In your home directory, type the following command:

```
pwd > iamhere
```

a) What does this command do?

Answer: This command prints the working directory and saves it in the file iamhere.

This is *file redirection.* The output of the command pwd has been redirected; instead of going to the screen, it goes into the file iamhere.

The flow of data into or out of a command is often called a "stream." Like a stream, the information flows in a single direction: Once something has passed by, it's gone. File redirection is pointing the stream somewhere else.

The stream metaphor runs all through command terminology in UNIX. You redirect files and you build pipelines of commands and data. Some commands act as filters that may change the data as they flow through, while others act as "sinks" into which you pour data.

Pipes and file redirection are handled by the shell. When the shell reads and interprets your command line, it scans for certain special characters, as described in Chapter 1, "Your First Session." Some of the special characters are wildcard characters (which are described in Chapter 4), some are job control characters and some are file redirection characters. When the shell encounters a file redirection character (and certain other characters), it assumes that the command arguments are finished. You cannot place command arguments after a file redirection character.

To understand how file redirection works, realize that UNIX systems treat the keyboard and the screen as if they were files. (In fact, even devices attached to the system are just special kinds of files.)

For convenience, all programs on UNIX have access to three streams: one for input, one for output, and one for error messages. These three streams are named *standard input*, *standard output*, and *standard error*, or stdin, stdout, and stderr. Instead of the streams named "stdin" being on a disk somewhere in the computer, it's your keyboard. Stdout and stderr are your screen.

When you use a file redirection character, you're telling the shell to redirect what would be sent to the screen, to a different output.

Type the following commands:

```
cd ..
pwd > ~/iamhere
cd
```

b) What do these commands do?

Answer: In order, they change to the parent directory, save the working directory in the file iamhere *in your home directory, and then change back to your home directory.*

On the command line, you indicate file redirection with the > and input redirection with <:

```
command > filename
```

or

```
command < filename
```

The direction of the arrow indicates whether the information is going *to* the file (>) or *from* the file (<).

The file name doesn't have to be a file in the current directory; it can be anywhere on the system that you have permission to create a file.

You can display the contents of the file `iamhere` with the `cat` command:

```
$ cat iamhere
/usr/home/johnmc
```

The `cat` command copies its input to its output.

What does `cat` stand for? Some people say it's short for "concatenate," which means to link together. Others say it's short for "catenate," which means the same thing but is a more obscure word. Using a more obscure word pleases some people but bothers others.

Display the contents of the file `iamhere` with the following command:

```
cat iamhere
```

c)　How did the contents of the file `iamhere` change?

Answer: The contents of the file were replaced by the new file.

If the file you named to store the output already exists, its content is replaced. It's very easy to lose work this way: You save some information in a file temporarily, intending to work with it later; then you save some other information in the same file . . . and the original information is gone.

It's worse if you weren't saving that information temporarily. It can be very frustrating to redo a lot of work because you accidentally replaced the file.

In the Korn Shell, you can prevent this from happening by typing the following command:

```
set -o noclobber
```

After you type this command in a session, the Korn Shell prevents you from overwriting existing files using file redirection.

You can make this command run every time you log in to your UNIX account by putting it in your start-up file.

2.2.2 ANSWERS

Type the following command:

```
cat < iamhere
```

a) What does this command do?

Answer:This command displays the contents of iamhere *on the screen.*

If you don't specify an input file or files, cat takes its input from the keyboard. Unless you redirect its output, cat sends its output to the screen. To indicate the end of the interactive input, press Control-D. For example:

```
$ cat
"The difference between a computer and the human mind
   is the difference between a filing cabinet and a
   garden."
"The difference between a computer and the human mind
   is the difference between a filing cabinet and a
   garden."
(Arthur Black)
(Arthur Black)
Control-D
$
```

Each line of text appears twice: once when you type it, because the shell shows it to you, and once when cat prints it out. (This happens whenever you type input into a command that writes to standard output, and you don't redirect that output.) The cat command can take its input from a file you name or through file redirection:

```
$ cat iamhere
/usr/home/johnmc
$ cat < directory
/usr/home/iamhere
```

For cat, the difference is that you can redirect from only one file, but you can name many files on the command line.

Type the following command:

```
cat < iamhere /etc/passwd
```

b) How does input file redirection differ from using file operands with `cat`?

Answer: You can redirect from only a single file.

The commands `cat < iamhere` and `cat iamhere` have the same effect. The difference is that you can only redirect the input from one file, but you can use more than one file operand. That is, this command prints out the contents of all of the files listed:

```
cat contents toc manifest
```

But this command doesn't:

```
cat < contents toc manifest
```

The version of `cat` on my system prints the contents of *toc* and *manifest* but ignores *contents*.

 If you start a command and it does nothing, it may be waiting for you to type something. This often happens if you forget to name a file in the command. To quit, enter Control-D.

2.2.3 ANSWERS

Type the following command:

```
cat < iamhere > here2
```

Next, type the following command:

```
cat > here3 < here2
```

a) What do these commands do? (Use `ls` to check.)

Answer: Both commands copy their input files to their output files. The first copies iamhere *to* here2; *the second copies* here2 *to* here3.

You can redirect both standard input and standard output in the same command line.

Type the following command:

```
cat iamhere here2 here3 > allhere
```

b) What does this command do?

Answer: This command creates a file, `allhere`, which contains the contents of the three files `iamhere`, `here2`, and `here3`.

This is a useful way to join a set of text files.

2.2.4 ANSWERS

Create a file called `extra`, and then type the following command:

```
cat extra >> allhere
```

a) What does this command do?

Answer: This command adds the text in `extra` to the end of the file `allhere`.

Rather than overwrite the file, you can *append* to it, adding the new output to the end of the file. Use two > characters to append to a file instead of replacing it, like so:

```
command >> add_to_this_file
```

2.2.5 ANSWERS

Type the following command:

```
ls -lR / | sort | more
```

a) Where is `ls` sending its output?

Answer: The output of `ls` goes to the `sort` command.

A command pipe is a logical extension of the idea that input and output are both files. You can connect the output of one command directly to the input of another.

Programs that act as filters are programs that are meant to be used this way. Most utility programs discussed in this workbook are meant to be used as filters (that's why the file operands are optional). In a UNIX system, you can string together as many commands as you need to, up to the maximum length of a command. (The maximum length of a command is at least 1000 characters, and on most systems is 4000 or more. You'll never type a line that long, but you may create one with wildcards. Wildcards are discussed further in Chapter 4, "Files and Directories.") Some commands are sinks; most of the data disappears but some remains. The grep command searches for words or patterns, and is the most common example of a sink.

Today, almost 30 years after UNIX was created, some of the features of UNIX seem obvious or trivial. But some computer experts think that this idea—that you could connect stdin and stdout—is one of the most significant features UNIX introduced. It made UNIX a modular, tool-based system where users could solve their own problems with the parts at hand instead of asking a programmer to solve the problems.

But to use that power, you have to become familiar with the tools available. For now, remember that when a command produces more than a screen's worth of output, you can pipe it to more and read it at your leisure.

You can mix file redirection and pipes. Remember that pipes work with standard input and standard output. Suppose you wanted to save the error messages from each command in a pipeline. You might do it like this:

```
ls -1R 2> ls.err | sort 2> sort.err | lp 2> lp.err
```

Normally you don't do this, because you want to see the errors. I have used it occasionally when I've had commands with lots of errors and I need to save all of them to fix the problems.

This command pipeline saves the error messages from ls -1R (if there are any) in the file ls.err; it saves the error messages from sort in sort.err; and it saves the error messages from lp in lp.err. Even if there are no error messages, those files will still be created, although they won't contain any information.

b) Do the error messages also go there?

Answer: No. Error messages still go to the screen (standard error).

Even when you are storing the program's output in a file, the error messages are still written to the screen. The standard error file is still the screen, so the messages go there. You may someday need to save error messages in a file. To do this, use the following:

```
command 2> filename
```

The "2>" indicates that you are redirecting the information written to the standard error file instead of the standard output file.

In fact, standard input and standard output also have numbers; standard input is 0 and standard output is 1. The following commands:

```
command 1> filename
command 0< filename
```

Are identical to:

```
command > filename
command < filename
```

Because standard input and output are used so often, they are the defaults when no number is used.

You can also append standard error by using two > characters:

```
command 2>> filename
```

Because the numbers are used to refer to or describe files (the numbers are not the names of the actual files), they are called *file descriptors*.

Hint: You may someday want to redirect both standard error and standard output into the same file. Use the redirection symbol 2>&1. The numberx>&numbery *notation means "make the first file descriptor number,* numberx, *point to the same file as the second file descriptor number,* numbery." *In this case, make file descriptor 2 (stderr) point to the same file as file descriptor 1 (stdout) and then point them both to a file. The shell reads the command line from left-to-right, so if you want both streams to go to a file, you need to redirect standard output to a file first, then redirect standard error to standard output. The redirection > save 2>&1 sends standard error and standard output into save. The redirection 2>&1 > save sends standard output into save, but the second redirection of standard output "undoes" the redirection of standard error.*

c) Which command is acting as a filter?

Answer: The sort *command filters the output from* ls *before it goes into* more.

The sort command is a filter: all the data goes through it. The more command is a sink. The data gets to more, and stops. It stops in a useful way, but it does stop.

Whenever you have more than a screenful of output, run the command again but pipe the output to more. *Then you can read all of the output.*

2.2.6 ANSWERS

Type the following command:

```
echo To redirect, use > filename
```

a) What happened?

Answer: You created a file named filename, *which contained the words "To redirect, use ".*

The file redirection characters are an example of *shell metacharacters.* "Meta" is a prefix meaning "of a higher kind," so metacharacters are magic characters that have meanings beyond their obvious meanings.

Remember that the shell interprets each command line. After you press Enter, the shell scans the command line looking for these special characters. The shell finds the ">" in the command line and immediately treats it as a file redirection character. All of the file redirection characters in this lab are shell metacharacters.

Different shell metacharacters are discussed throughout this book.

Type the following command:

```
echo To redirect, use \> filename
```

b) What happened?

Answer: The echo *command printed:*

To redirect, use > filename

The backslash character, \, is another shell metacharacter.

c) What does the \ character do?

Answer: The \ character tells the shell to "turn off" the special behavior of >. It "escapes" the meaning.

Sometimes the shell reads through the command and "decides" that you're not finished typing it. (This can happen if you put a ' or a " character in a command.) In this case, the shell will display a secondary prompt character, usually ">", to indicate that it's still waiting for input.

To turn off the special meaning of a shell metacharacter, you put a backslash (\) in front of it. (This means that backslash is a metacharacter, too: its special meaning is "turn off the special meaning of the next character." If you really want a backslash, you have to put another backslash in front of it, like this: \\.)

You should try two other versions of the command:

```
echo To redirect, use '>' filename
```

and

```
echo To redirect, use ">" filename
```

Both types of quotation marks escape the meaning of shell metacharacters, but in slightly different ways. The single ' marks, escape all shell metacharacters, while the double quotation marks, ", escape the meanings of only some shell metacharacters.

■ FOR EXAMPLE:

Enter the commands

```
echo '$TERM'
```

and

```
echo "$TERM"
```

The first prints the word "$TERM" to the screen, but the second prints something different. The single quotation marks escape the special meaning of $, but the double quotation marks do not. This will become important later.

LAB 2.2 SELF-REVIEW QUESTIONS

To test your progress, you should be able to answer the following questions.

1) All UNIX programs have access to three files.
    a) _____True
    b) _____False

**LAB
2.2**

2) A filter command *must* change its input.
    a) _____True
    b) _____False

3) In the following table, match the special character with its meaning:

a) >   **i)** *Pipe* output of this command into the next command

b) | **ii)** Append output of this command into a file

c) >>   **iii)** Save standard error messages into a file

d) 2>   **iv)** Redirect input from this file instead of the keyboard

e) <   **v)** Save *output of this command into a file*

Quiz answers appear in Appendix A, Lab 2.2

C H A P T E R 2

TEST YOUR THINKING

 The projects in this section are meant to have you utilize all of the skills that you have acquired throughout this chapter. The answers to these projects can be found at the companion Web site to this book, located at:

http://www.phptr.com/phptrinteractive

Visit the Web site periodically to share and discuss your answers.

1) How would you use file redirection to store a command's output in a file named ">>2>|"? Would it be a good idea to create such a file?

2) Suggest a way to force a command to produce its usage line. Do all commands write usage lines?

3) Some commands are filters and some are not. In a long "pipeline" of commands, which can go at the beginning? Which at the end? Which in the middle?

4) Based on the information in this chapter, can you pipe a command's error messages (stderr)? If you wanted to transform the error messages using a filter program, how would you go about it?

5) The sed command is a filter. This command pipeline filters a file and mails it using the mailx command. Without knowing anything more about sed or mailx, can you think of a shorter way to write the following command line?

```
cat archivefile | sed -f script | mailx
```

ABOUT FILES AND DIRECTORIES

All information on the system is stored in files and directories. Programs are files, input and output are files, even directories are files. By understanding how the file system is organized, you can find the information you want, and you can organize your information better.

CHAPTER OBJECTIVES

In this chapter, you will learn about:

If you've used any kind of computer system before, you've encountered files. Files and directories on UNIX systems are like files and directories on a DOS or Windows system: In all cases, files hold information and directories hold files.

Any information you create and want to store on the system will be stored in files, and those files will be stored in directories. Before you can use these to your advantage, you need to know how the directory system is structured, what names are acceptable (and advisable) for files and directories, what information you can determine about a file, and how you determine that you're allowed to read or change a file.

L A B 3.1

THE DIRECTORY HIERARCHY

LAB OBJECTIVES

After this lab, you will be able to:

✓ Describe the Directory Hierarchy

✓ Interpret Absolute Path Names

✓ Interpret Relative Path Names

When we consider all of the files and directories on a UNIX system, we call it a *file tree*. It's an organized way of storing and referring to all files and directories. At the base of it all is the root directory, just like a regular tree. The root directory contains all other files and directories. Everything grows out of that directory, but for convenience we usually draw the tree upside down. The starting point is always the root directory. It contains files and other directories; those directories may contain files and other directories, and so on. (A directory is just a special kind of file.)

Imagine your closet. You can just hang your clothes in your closet, or you can organize it with, say, boxes. Items you wear every day are in the closet; items you need less often (or that you need separated) are in boxes in the closet. Inside those boxes may be other boxes. The file tree is much the same: the closet and the boxes are directories, and the clothes are files.

Every file has a name. We distinguish between a "path name" and "file name." A *path name* describes how to get to a particular file or directory, either from the root directory (in which case it is an *absolute path name*, sometimes called a *fully qualified path name*) or from the current working directory (in which case it is a *relative path name*). An absolute path name always starts with /, the name of the root directory.

The parts of the path name are separated by slash (/) characters, not backslash (\) characters (as on DOS and Windows).

Although two files may have the same name, no two files can have the same fully qualified name.

■ FOR EXAMPLE:

My home directory (/usr/john) contains the file ThingsToDo. Your home directory (/usr/you) also contains the file ThingsToDo. The path name of my file is /usr/john/ThingsToDo. The path name of your file is /usr/you/ThingsToDo. The fully qualified names of the files are different.

Drawing this as a tree diagram (but putting the root at the top), the paths look like the diagram in Figure 3.1.

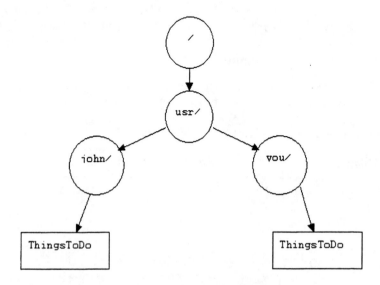

Figure 3.1 ■ A sample directory tree

You can see that usr is held in (or "under") /, and that both john and you are contained by usr.

Some terminology:

- A directory that contains a file or directory is its *parent*. The root directory in the diagram is the parent of the usr directory. The usr directory is the parent of the john and the you directories.
- As you might expect, a "contained" directories or file is called the *child* of the directory. The john and you directories are children of the usr directory. Sometimes a directory inside a directory is called a *subdirectory*. The john and you directories are also subdirectories of the usr directory.
- Directories or files in the same directory are called *siblings*. The directories john and you are siblings.
- If your current working directory is /usr/john, then you can refer to the directory you as /usr/you (the absolute path name) or you can refer to it as ../you (the relative path name).
- The .. directory is in every directory, and it means the parent of that directory. (The root directory's parent is the root directory, because you cannot go any higher.) The . directory is also in every directory, and it means the directory itself. The . directory is a useful shorthand for some commands. The . and .. directories can be used as any component of a path name.

Table 3.1 shows the absolute and the relative path names for all of the paths in the diagram if your current working directory is /usr/you.

Table 3.1 ■ Absolute and Relative Path Names

Absolute Path Name	Relative Path Name
/	../..
/usr	..
/usr/john	../john
/usr/john/ThingsToDo	../john/ThingsToDo
/usr/you	.
/usr/you/ThingsToDo	ThingsToDo

There are other short forms for path names; these are interpreted by your shell, so they won't work if you're using the Bourne Shell. These short forms only work if they're the first part of a path name:

- ~/ at the beginning of a path name (or a path name that is just ~) refers to your home directory.
- ~john/ at the beginning of a path name refers to the home directory of the user whose log-in name is john. This works with any user name. If the user doesn't exist or doesn't have a home directory, then the ~ has no special meaning.

LAB 3.1 EXERCISES

3.1.1 DESCRIBE THE DIRECTORY HIERARCHY

a) What is the root directory?

_____

_____

b) What is the root directory's path name?

_____

_____

c) How does a relative path name differ from an absolute path name?

_____

_____

d) What is the . . directory?

_____

_____

**LAB
3.1**

3.1.2 INTERPRET ABSOLUTE PATH NAMES

The path name /etc/passwd is interpreted as "the root directory contains the directory etc, which contains passwd".

Interpret the following path names:

a) /usr/john/../janet

_____

_____

b) ~/dictionary/

_____

_____

c) ~janet

_____

_____

3.1.3 INTERPRET RELATIVE PATH NAMES

Interpret the following relative path names:

a) books/recipes/../dramat

_____

_____

b) ./-ot

_____

_____

c) `./../...t`

LAB 3.1 EXERCISE ANSWERS

This section gives you some suggested answers to the questions in Lab 3.1, with discussions related to those answers. Your answers may vary, but the most important thing is whether or not your answers work. Use these discussions to analyze differences between your answers and those presented here.

If you have alternative answers to the questions in these exercises, you are encouraged to post your answers and discuss them at the companion Web site for this book, located at:

`http://www.phptr.com/phptrinteractive`

A *file system* is a method for organizing information. There can actually be several kinds of file systems on a UNIX system, but UNIX is organized so it all looks like one big system.

If you're a DOS or Windows user, remember that the path separator on UNIX systems is /, not \.

COMMON DIRECTORIES AND FILES

The directories in Table 3.2 usually exist on every system. Most of the names are traditional: UNIX doesn't enforce them, but nearly every system administrator follows them (in some form or another) and some programs rely on them. In some cases, several common names are shown.

Table 3.2 ■ Common UNIX Directories

Directory	Contents
/bin, /usr/bin	Programs and other executable files.
/dev	Device files (such as your terminal or hard drives).
/etc	Installation-specific files.
/home	An alternative location for user directories.
/lib, /usr/lib	Compiled C libraries. Only important for programmers.
/sbin	System programs.
/tmp, /usr/tmp	Directories for programs to store temporary files. On some systems, everything in temporary directories goes away when the system is shut down.
/usr, /home	User directories.
/usr/include	Header files for C programs. Only for programmers.
/usr/local	Local installation directories and files that correspond to the top-level directories. For example, /usr/local/bin contains executable files specific to your system.
/usr/sbin	System-administration files.
/usr/share	Platform-independent text files, such as manual pages.
/usr/src	Source files.
/usr/ucb	On some systems, this directory contains alternate versions of executable programs developed for the Berkeley versions of UNIX.
/var	Administrative files.
/var/adm, /usr/adm	System accounting information, diagnostic files, and other information needed by the system administrator.
/var/spool, /usr/spool	Spool files (temporary files awaiting processing). Spool files never go away when the system is shut down.

Sometimes there are two names because different names are used on different types of UNIX systems. However, sometimes both names exist on the same system, such as /bin, /usr/bin, and /usr/local/bin.

Sometimes this a convenience: the /usr/local/bin is normally used for programs that aren't part of the standard UNIX system, or programs that have been installed by the system administrator.

3.1.1 ANSWERS

a) What is the root directory?

Answer: The root directory is the directory that contains all other directories. It is the starting point for absolute path names.

On UNIX systems, there is only one root directory.

b) What is the root directory's path name?

Answer: The root directory's path name is always /.

On systems such as Windows or DOS, each file system has its own root directory and you must switch drives or "volumes." On those systems, every floppy disk drive or hard drive is a separate file system, with its own root directory.

You might think this makes DOS systems superior; after all, you can add file systems to a DOS system just by grafting on another disk drive with its own file system. You can do this in UNIX too, but the new file system is placed inside a directory on the old file system. The process of adding a new file system is called *mounting* the file system (because the system administrator does it with a command called mount).

c) How does a relative path name differ from an absolute path name?

Answer: An absolute path name is the path to a file from the root directory; a relative path name is the path to a file from the current working directory. An absolute path name starts with /.

Relative path names are a useful convenience. You don't want to type the entire path name every time you refer to a file.

d)   What is the . . directory?

Answer: The parent of the current directory.

The . and . . directories are a useful shorthand. If you're in the directory `/projects/plans/reports/approved` and you want to refer to the file `/project/plans/reports/unapproved/costs`, it's much easier to type `../unapproved/costs` than to type the entire path name.

3.1.2 ANSWERS

Interpret the following path names:

a)   `/usr/john/../janet`

Answer: The root directory contains the directory `usr`, which contains the directory `janet`. The sequence `john/..` points back to the usr directory.

The absolute path name `/accounting/receivable/pastdue/dead-beats` can be read as "In the root directory, the directory `accounting` contains the directory `receivable`, which contains the directory `past-due`, which contains the directory or file `deadbeats`."

You would certainly never use a path like the one in this example, but it is legitimate. Under some circumstances, you might see a path like this from an `ls` listing.

b)   `~/dictionary/`

Answer: Your home directory contains the directory `dictionary`.

A path name that *ends* in a slash indicates that the last component named is a directory.

■ *FOR EXAMPLE:*

The path name `/movies/northbynorthwest` might refer to a file or a directory. The path name `/movies/northbynorthwest/` indicates that `northbynorthwest` is a directory, not a file.

c) `~janet`

> *Answer:The home directory of the user with the log-in name* `janet`.

These short forms for path names (the ~ and *~name* forms) are interpreted by your shell. (They won't work if you're using the Bourne Shell.) These short forms only work if they're the first part of a path name.

3.1.3 ANSWERS

Interpret the following relative path names:

a) `books/recipes/../drama`

> *Answer:The current directory contains the directory* `books`, *which contains the directory* `drama`.

A relative path name is the path you take from your current working directory. The path name `postcards/images/` can be read as "The current directory contains the directory `postcards`, which contains the directory `images`."

b) `./-ot`

> *Answer:The current directory (.) contains a file named* `-o`.

A relative path name *always* starts at the current directory. A path name such as `./-o` is identical to the path name `-o`.

c) `./../...`

> *Answer:The file* ... *in the parent (..) of the current directory (.).*

Note that `...` is a valid file name, but `.` and `..` are reserved to mean the current directory and the parent of the current directory.

LAB 3.1 SELF-REVIEW QUESTIONS

To test your progress, you should be able to answer the following questions. You have the directories `/pubs/guides/user` and `/pubs/reference/manual`.

1) Which directories are siblings?
   a) _____*pubs* and *pubs*
   b) _____*guides* and *reference*
   c) _____*user* and *manual*

2) What is the parent of the `user` directory?
   a) _____*guides*
   b) _____*pubs*
   c) _____*reference*

3) What is the child of the reference directory?
   a) _____*pubs*
   b) _____*manual*

4) If your current directory is `/pubs/guides/user`, which of the following relative path names refers to `/pubs/reference`?
   a) _____*./././reference*
   b) _____*../../reference*
   c) _____*../../../reference*

Quiz answers appear in Appendix A, Lab 3.1

L A B   3.2

RULES FOR FILE NAMES

LAB OBJECTIVES

After this lab, you will be able to:

✓ List the Maximum Length for a File Name

✓ List the Characters Allowed in a File Name

✓ List Hidden Files

Every file on a UNIX system has a name. File names are case sensitive: Uppercase letters are considered different than lowercase letters,

A directory is considered a special kind of file. The rules that apply to file names also apply to directory names.

VALID FILE NAMES

On a UNIX system, there is only one character that is not allowed to be in a file name, the character /. This character is reserved for separating components (directories and file names) in path names.

If your files may be transferred to a different computer system, I recommend you stick to names that use the following characters:

```
ABCDEFGHIJKLMNOPQRSTUVXYZ
abcdefghijklmnopqrstuvxyz
1234567890.-_
```

**LAB
3.2**

This doesn't use any of the characters the shell interprets as special. Don't start file names with "-" because too many programs will confuse the file name with an option. Likewise, don't start file names with "." because then they are treated as hidden files.

File names that begin with a dot are treated as *hidden files* in UNIX. To list hidden files as well as the visible files, give the -a option to ls.

■ FOR EXAMPLE:

The command ls -a lists hidden files in the current directory:

```
$ ls -a
.                .mwmrc          phone
..               .sh_history     sample
.Xdefaults       memo            save
.login           newmemo         words
```

This directory contains the files memo, newmemo, sample, save, and words, and the hidden files .Xdefaults, .login, .mwmrc, and .sh_history.

Some file names are reserved. They already exist on the system and are used for specific functions or devices. For example, the directory names . (dot) and .. (dot-dot) are already in every directory. It contains files that are devices (just as your terminal is a device).

All modern UNIX systems have the getconf command, which lists system configuration parameters. You can use the command to find the maximum length of a file or directory name, and to find the maximum length of a complete path name.

■ FOR EXAMPLE:

The maximum size of a file name and a path name in my current directory is:

```
$ getconf NAME_MAX .
255
$ getconf PATH_MAX .
1024
```

On this file system, a file or directory name can be up to 255 characters long; an absolute path name can be over 1000 characters long.

Because different file systems (even remote file systems from other computers) can be mounted, the maximum name or path length might change when you change directories. These numbers are the maximum values on the hardware containing my home directory.

LAB 3.2 EXERCISES

3.2.1 LIST NAME AND PATH MAXIMUM LENGTHS

Type the following command:

```
getconf NAME_MAX .
```

a) What is the result?

_____

_____

b) What does it mean?

_____

_____

Type the following command:

```
getconf PATH_MAX /
```

c) What is the result?

_____

_____

d) What does it mean?

_____

_____

e) How many directories can be in a path name?

_____

_____

3.2.2 IDENTIFY VALID FILE NAMES

In the current directory, use file redirection to create files with the following names; record your results.

a) `supercalifragilisticexpialidocious`

_____

_____

b) `and/or`

_____

_____

c) `a\ file`

_____

_____

d) `/dev/null`

_____

_____

e) A

_____

_____

f) a

_____

_____

g) `.text.file`

_____

_____

3.2.3 LIST HIDDEN FILES

Use the commands `ls`, `ls -a`, and `ls -A` to view the contents of your home directory. (Your version of `ls` may not accept the `-A` option.)

a) What does the command `ls -a` do?

_____

_____

b) What does the command `ls -A` do?

_____

_____

c) How do you hide a file?

_____

_____

_____

LAB 3.2 EXERCISE ANSWERS

This section gives you some suggested answers to the questions in Lab 3.2, with discussions related to those answers. Your answers may vary, but the most important thing is whether or not your answers work. Use these discussions to analyze differences between your answers and those presented here.

If you have alternative answers to the questions in these exercises, you are encouraged to post your answers and discuss them at the companion Web site for this book, located at:

```
http://www.phptr.com/phptrinteractive
```

3.2.1 ANSWERS

Type the following command:

```
getconf NAME_MAX .
```

a)   What is the result?

Answer: Results will vary. On a Solaris system, version 2.0 or later, the result is 255.

This means that on a Solaris system, version 2.0 or later, the maximum length of a file name is 255 characters.

b)   What does it mean?

Answer: On most systems, the maximum length of a file name is 255 characters, although it may be as low as 14. That means that the longest name that can fit between two slashes is 255 characters.

On the original version of UNIX, the maximum length of a file name was 14 characters. Most versions of UNIX since then have increased that number to 255 characters.

Type the following command:

```
getconf PATH_MAX /
```

c) What is the result?

Answer: Results will vary. A Solaris system, version 2.0 or later, will print 1024.

This means that on a Solaris system, version 2.0 or later, the maximum length for a path name is 1024 characters. On some systems it's as high as 4096 characters.

d) What does it mean?

Answer: This is the maximum length for a fully qualified file name.

e) How many directories can be in a path name?

Answer: Results will vary for each system.

This depends on the length of each directory name; there's no absolute limit. If the maximum size of a path name is 1024 characters, you could have 512 single-character directories nested together: /a/b/c/d/e. If all the directory names are each 255 characters, then you can have only four of them.

HINTS FOR NAMING FILES

Naming files and directories is most of the work when you're organizing your files. Here are some hints for effective file naming.

- **Make the names long enough to be meaningful.** In six months, you won't remember what each file is, so the name will have to be clear. You probably have 255 characters to work with, so don't use cramped names. Will you really remember what "NES3q.98" means? Probably not. But you are likely to understand "NorthEastSales3rdQ.1998" more clearly.

- **If you're going to refer to a file often, keep the name easy to type.** You don't want to type a 255-charac-ter file name every time you want to look at your appointment schedule. Uppercase letters or characters like _ are often difficult to type.

- **Use directories to organize files.** When you discover you have a half dozen files all related to the same thing, make a directory and stick all the files together.
- **Be consistent.** Choose some naming habits and stick with them. They don't have to mean anything to anyone but you. Simple file extensions (such as .txt or .appt) can help you remember what a file is or help you find them. A former officemate always starts the names of temporary files with a comma. (If he needs the information over the long term, he renames the file.) Three months later, when he finds a file whose name begins with a comma, he knows he can delete it. It was just a temporary file.

Consistent naming behaviors help you find files; you'll see this more clearly in Lab 4.2 on wildcards.

You don't have to be obsessive about your naming practices. Some people are not by nature very consistent. That's fine. It's good enough if you're usually consistent. After all, the system is your servant, not your master.

3.2.2 ANSWERS

In the current directory, use file redirection to create files with the following names (it doesn't matter what's in the files); record your results.

a) `supercalifragilisticexpialidocious`

Answer: This works for most systems, unless your value for NAME_MAX *is less than 34 characters.*

Remember, on some systems, file names are limited to a maximum of 14 characters. However, it should work on most modern UNIX systems.

b) `and/or`

Answer: This fails. The / *character is not valid in a file name.*

The / character cannot be in a file name; otherwise, the system couldn't distinguish between the file *or* in the directory *and*, and the file with the name *and/or*.

c) `a\ file`

Answer: This works, but creates a file named "a file." The backslash "escapes" the space character. To create a file named "a\ file," you would have to type "a\\\ file."

This was discussed briefly in Chapter 2, "The Command Line." You could also create the file by typing 'a\ file.'

Remember that the shell interprets the command line before running the command. That includes changing the file name you've provided if it contains a shell metacharacter (a character that the shell treats specially). You could even have a file name that contains a control character (a non-printable character) or an end-of-line character. (These are guaranteed to give ls odd output.)

 Creating a file with space and metacharacters in the name is a bad idea. Every time you have to work with it, you would have to remember how many backslashes to use to escape the space and the backslash. It is not worth the trouble.

d) `/dev/null`

Answer: This file already exists. Using cat *to list its contents shows that it's empty.*

The /dev directory is reserved for device files. The /dev/null file is standard and is worth knowing: The /dev/null file is guaranteed to be empty, no matter how much you redirect into it. It's useful for ignoring error messages: you redirect stderr to /dev/null:

```
command 2> /dev/null
```

e) `A`

Answer: This works.

The letter "A" is a short but valid file name.

f) `a`

Answer: This works.

Because UNIX file names are case sensitive, you could even have the files A and a in the same directory.

LAB 3.2

g) `.text.file`

> *Answer: This works, but typing* `ls` *will not show the file. You must type* `ls  -a` *or* `ls  -A` *to show that this file exists.*

This file contains two dots in its name. That's perfectly fine on a UNIX system.

> *If you're a DOS or Windows 3.1 user, remember that files do not need to have a dot character in their names. They can have zero, one, or more dots. On DOS and Windows systems, executable programs must have names ending in* `.exe`, `.bat`, *or* `.com`. *On UNIX systems, executable programs can have any valid name, but they need to have execute permission. (See Lab 3.4.)*

3.2.3 ANSWERS

a) What does the command `ls -a` do?

> *Answer: The* `ls  -a` *command lists hidden files, including the directories dot (.) and dot-dot (. .).*

Any file name that begins with dot is hidden. The `ls` command doesn't normally list it, and the * wildcard (discussed in Lab 4.2) doesn't match it. This is a convenience; it's not a serious attempt to hide information.

b) What does the command `ls -A` do?

> *Answer: The* `ls  -A` *command lists hidden files, but does not list the directories dot (.) and dot-dot (. .).*

Not all versions of `ls` support the -A option. For example, the versions on Solaris and UnixWare don't.

c) How do you hide a file?

> *Answer: Give it a name that begins with a dot.*

You're likely to find the following hidden files in your directory: .xde-
faults, .login, .profile, and .sh_history. There may be others;
many programs use hidden files as their start-up files.

LAB 3.2 SELF-REVIEW QUESTIONS

I) Which of the following characters cannot be included in a file's name?
   a) _____space
   b) _____tab
   c) _____end-of-line
   d) _____\
   e) _____/

2) A file name beginning with dot (.) must not contain any other dots.
   a) _____True
   b) _____False

3) The maximum length of a file name is always 14 characters.
   a) _____True
   b) _____False

4) The getconf command returns information about system limits.
   a) _____True
   b) _____False

5) You can create a file named dot-dot (. .).
   a) _____True
   b) _____False

   Quiz answers appear in Appendix A, Lab 3.2

L A B   3.3

INFORMATION ABOUT FILES

LAB OBJECTIVES

After this lab, you will be able to:

✓ List File Information

✓ Recognize Types of Files

The system stores information about each file and directory. Most of this information is visible with the command `ls -l`:

- The *type* of the file (directory, regular file, or special file).
- The number of names the file has (each name is called a *link*).
- The *permissions* on the file.
- The *size* of the file, in bytes.
- The name of the file's *owner*.
- The name of the *group* the owner belongs to.
- The file's *timestamps* (the date and time when it was looked at or changed).
- The file's *name*.

■ *FOR EXAMPLE:*

Here's a sample output of the ls -1 command:

```
$ ls -l
Total 2
-rw-rw-r-- 1 johnmc pubs    219 Mar 25 18:12 archie
drwxr-xr-x 2 johnmc pubs    512 Mar 26  9:43 betty
lrwxrwxrwx 1 johnmc pubs     13 Mar 26  9:45 reggie -
> /tmp/examples
```

(You can ignore the "Total" line.)

Each line afterward is read as described in Table 3.3.

**LAB
3.3**

Table 3.3 ■ Sample Results of ls -1

–	The first character (–) is the type of the file. There are six possible values:
	A – indicates a normal file.
	A d indicates a directory. betty in the example is a directory.
	An L or an l indicates a symbolic link. reggie in the example is a symbolic link.
	A b indicates a "block special file."
	A c indicates a "character special file."
	An f indicates a pipe file (some systems display a p instead of an f).
rw-rw-r--	The next nine characters describe the permissions of the file for the file's owner, the members of the owner's group, and all others. Each user can have read permission, write permission, or execute permission. This set of permissions allows the owner and members of the owner's group to read and write the file, but not execute it. Other users may read the file but not write it or execute it. (Permissions are the topic of Lab 3.4.)
1	The next number is the number of links to the file. A link is a name; every file and directory has at least one name and may have more. This file has only one link.

Table 3.3 ■ Sample Results of `ls -l` (Continued)

johnmc	The owner's log-in name.
pubs	The owner's group.
219	The size of the file in bytes.
Mar 25	The date the file was last changed.
18:12	The time on that day that the file was changed.
archie	The file's name. If the file is a symbolic link, this will contain a pointer to the "real" file.

FILE TYPES

The first character of the `ls -l` output indicates the type of file. On UNIX systems, there are seven types of files, indicated by the characters listed in Table 3.4.

Table 3.4 ■ The Seven Types of UNIX Files

–	Ordinary file. Most files are ordinary files.
d	Directory. A file that contains other files.
l	Symbolic link, sometimes called a "soft link." A file (or directory) that "points to" another file (or directory).
b	Block special file. This is a device, such as a disk drive.
c	Character special file. This is also a device, such as a monitor.
p	FIFO special file. A pipe (as in command pipeline) is a kind of FIFO special file.
s	Socket special file. This is a file used so programs can communicate with each other. Sockets don't occur on Solaris systems, but do occur on BSD systems.

Although all of these may be on your system at any time, you will normally only see the first three. The others are special files and are primarily used by the system or by programs.

A symbolic link is a pointer to another file. When you use the symbolic link's name in a command, it's just as though you were referring to the original file. In the example from the preceding section, the file `reggie` is a symbolic link that points to the file `/tmp/examples`. Symbolic links have two advantages over regular file links:

- Symbolic links work across mounted file systems, while hard links do not.
- You can make a symbolic link to a directory, but you cannot create a hard link to a directory.

LAB 3.3 EXERCISES

3.3.1 LIST FILE INFORMATION

Use the following listing to answer the questions in this exercise.

```
-rw-rw-rw-  1 bob   acctg  1039 Mar 15   9:58 back
-r--r--r--  2 jan   acctg   959 Apr  1   1:02 keep
-r--r--r--  2 jan   acctg   959 Apr  1   1:02 save
-rwxrw----  1 bob   acctg   100 May  1  12:15 store
dr-xr-xr-x  2 root  wheel   512 Jun 12   1997 zip
```

a) What command was used to get this listing?

_____

_____

b) Which entry is a directory?

_____

_____

c) What user and group owns the file back?

_____

_____

d) When was the file keep last modified?

_____

_____

e) How many names (links) does the file keep have?

_____

_____

If more than one, which of the names is the file's other name?

_____

_____

f) Which has gone unchanged the longest?

_____

_____

3.3.2 RECOGNIZE TYPES OF FILES

a) In an ls -l listing, what character would indicate a directory?

_____

_____

b) What's the difference between a soft link and a hard link?

_____

_____

c) In an `ls -l` listing, what does the character "l" at the beginning of an entry mean?

_____

_____

LAB 3.3 EXERCISE ANSWERS

 This section gives you some suggested answers to the questions in Lab 3.3, with discussions related to those answers. Your answers may vary, but the most important thing is whether or not your answers work. Use these discussions to analyze differences between your answers and those presented here.

If you have alternative answers to the questions in these exercises, you are encouraged to post your answers and discuss them at the companion Web site for this book, located at:

`http://www.phptr.com/phptrinteractive`

In some documentation about UNIX, you'll see the declaration that "all files are text files." What does that mean? It means that UNIX systems don't impose any format on the files; any format is imposed by the application program that uses the file.

All files on UNIX systems are text files in this sense only. They have no fixed size and no fixed components so far as the UNIX operating system is concerned. (If it's a spreadsheet file, the spreadsheet may very well enforce rules about what's in the file, but that's not something the operating system cares about.)

In fact, most modern computer systems also treat files in this way, so it's no longer something to fuss over.

In a UNIX text file, lines end with a linefeed character. On DOS and Windows files, lines end with a carriage return character and a linefeed character. When looking at a DOS or Windows text file on UNIX, each line ends with a ^M character.

There are two types of links: hard links and soft (or symbolic) links. A link is a name for a file; any file can have more than one name. A regular use cannot create a hard link to a directory, but can create a symbolic link to a directory. A hard link is also limited to two files on the same file system, but a symbolic link is not. The file size is the size of the file in bytes.

**LAB
3.3**

The file time (or "time stamp") shown in the ls -l listing is the time when the file was last modified. Usually this means the file was changed or modified in some way. (For this reason, it's called the *modification time*.)

3.3.1 ANSWERS

Use the following listing to answer the questions in this exercise.

```
-rw-rw-rw- 1 bob   acctg   1039 Mar 15   9:58 back
-r--r--r-- 2 jan   acctg    959 Apr  1   1:02 keep
-r--r--r-- 2 jan   acctg    959 Apr  1   1:02 save
-rwxrw---- 1 bob   acctg    100 May  1 12:15 store
dr-xr-xr-x 2 root  wheel    512 Jun 12   1997 zip
```

a) What command was used to get this listing?

Answer: The command ls -l.

The -l stands for "long" because this is the long format for the output.

The size of the file is expressed in *bytes*. Traditionally, a *byte* is the amount of storage space required to store one letter or number. On some systems —such as those that use non-Western languages, such as Japanese Kanji— a character may take up more than one byte. A total of 1024 bytes make a kilobyte (Kb); 1024 Kb make a megabyte (M); and 1024 MB make a gigabyte (GB).

Some UNIX systems have a maximum file size built into them. If you're running the Korn Shell, you can check your maximum allowed file size with the ulimit command. The size is given in units of 512 bytes; divide by 2 to get the number of Kb. (On the C Shell, the command is limit.) If you do have limits on the resources you're allowed to use, only the system administrator can change them.

There may be other restrictions on the size of files you can create; your system administrator will tell you.

b) Which entry is a directory?

Answer: The directory is `zip`, as indicated by "d" at the beginning of the line.

Directories don't actually contain other files; they contain the information about where the other files are. When you see a file size for a directory, it is the size of this directory information, not the total size of all the files in the directory.

The other file types (block, character, and FIFO) are "special" files that are used internally by the system. A block special file handles information in "blocks"; this means it deals in large chunks of data—possibly thousands of characters' worth. Each disk drive is a block file, for example. A character special file is also a device, but it deals with data one character at a time. Your keyboard is a character special device; your monitor screen may be one. A FIFO is a special file used by one program to communicate with another program.

c) What user and group owns the file `back`?

Answer: The file `back` is owned by `bob` of the group `acctg`.

A file is associated with only one owner and one group. The user "bob" can read any file that belongs to group "acctg" and has read permission set for the group. Most users belong to only one group, but a user can belong to more than one.

d) When was the file `keep` last modified?

Answer: The file `keep` was last modified at 1:02 on April 1 of this year.

For each file, the system also records two other times:

- When the file was last accessed. This time is updated when someone looks at a file. You can see this time, the access time, by adding the -u option to `ls`.

- When information about the file was last changed. This time is updated when any of the other information is changed, such as its permissions or its name. You can see this time by adding the -c option to ls. The -c and -u options contradict each other; on my version of ls, the first one on the command line takes effect.

When you create a file, all three times are the same.

Normally, you're only concerned with the modification time, when a file last changed, and that's what ls -l shows you. The other two times are sometimes useful when you're trying to find a particular file.

e) How many names (links) does the file keep have?

Answer: The file keep has two links.

The number in the second field is 2, indicating two links.

If more than one, which of the names is the file's other name?

Answer: Based on this list, the other name is save.

Even though they look like two different files, only the name is different for a hard-linked file. All of the other information is the same in both listings. Both the files keep and save have two links, are the same size, have the same owner, and have the same modification times. It is probable that they're the same file.

f) Which has gone unchanged the longest?

Answer: The directory zip has gone unchanged since 1997; all of the others have been changed this year.

A file's modification time is shown with the month and day and the hour and minute using a 24-hour clock. If the file hasn't changed for six months or more, ls displays the year instead of the hour and minute.

3.3.2 ANSWERS

a) In an `ls -1` listing, what character would indicate a directory?

Answer: The character "d" at the beginning of the entry indicates a directory.

If all you want to do is distinguish between the files and directories, try listing the directory contents with `ls -F` or `ls -p` (though not all versions of `ls` accept the `-p` option). These options are discussed in Chapter 4.

b) What's the difference between a soft link and a hard link?

Answer: A soft link is a file that contains a pointer to another file; a hard link is an extra name for the file. A soft link can be made across file systems and to a directory.

As an example, the file named `/projects/plans/karnak/notes` may also have the name `/usr/home/johnmc/karnak/todo.list`. Changing the file `/projects/plans/karnak/notes` also changes `/usr/home/johnmc/karnak/todo.list`, because they're the same file.

Directories always have two or more links. Every subdirectory contains a `..` directory, which counts as a link to the parent directory. Files rarely have more than one link, although they can.

Hard links have limitations: You cannot create a hard link to a directory (although the system administrator can). (Directories are linked to `..` and `.`, but that's done by the system.) You cannot create a hard link to a file on another file system (that is, on a file system that's mounted onto yours).

c) In an `ls -1` listing, what does the character "1" at the beginning of an entry mean?

Answer: The "1" indicates a soft or symbolic link.

Symbolic links don't have the same limitations that hard links do. They have other drawbacks, however. We'll examine this more closely in the Chapter 4, when we discuss making and removing links.

LAB 3.3 SELF-REVIEW QUESTIONS

To test your progress, you should be able to answer the following questions.

1) Every user has only one group.
    a) _____True
    b) _____False

2) You cannot make a hard link to a directory.
    a) _____True
    b) _____False

3) The `ls` command can only show one time, the modification time.
    a) _____True
    b) _____False

4) In the following table, match the character from the `ls -l` listing with the file type:

a) Ordinary file	**i)** l
b) Symbolic link	**ii)** d
c) Directory	**iii)** –
d) Block special file	**iv)** b

Quiz answers appear in Appendix A, Lab 3.3

L A B   3.4

FILE AND DIRECTORY PERMISSIONS

LAB OBJECTIVES

After this lab, you will be able to:

✓ Describe File Permissions

✓ Change File Permissions

✓ Change Directory Permissions

✓ Understand Your Default Permissions

Among other information, the `ls -l` listing describes the permissions on a file. The permissions control who is allowed to use or change a file.

When you specify a directory name as the operand of `ls`, it normally shows you the *contents* of the directory. You can show the file information on the directory itself by specifying the `-d` option.

There are three sets of permissions, one set for the file's owner; one set for the group (normally the group to which the owner belongs), and a third set for all other users. The set of file permissions is sometimes called the file's *mode*.

Each of those three sets can have any or all of *read*, *write*, and *execute* permission.

You need read permission to see the contents of a file or a directory. You need write permission to change the contents of a file or directory, or to delete it. You need execute permission to run a file as a program or to cd into a directory.

The permissions can also be represented as numbers, shown in Table 3.5.

Table 3.5 ■ Permissions

Number	Permission meaning
0	No permissions
1	Execute permission only
2	Write permission only
3	Write and execute permissions
4	Read permission only
5	Read and execute permission only
6	Read and write permissions
7	Read, write, and execute permissions

When presented as numbers, the permissions on a file are sometimes referred to as its *mode*. There are three numbers, one for the user, one for the group, and one for all others. A file that is mode 777 can be read, changed, or written by anyone. For this reason, you shouldn't create files that are mode 777.

When you create a file with redirection, the file has mode 666. Anyone can read or write the file. (When you create a directory, it has mode 777. Execute permission is necessary for directories.)

On some systems, the system administrator does not want this behavior. There is a way to set a default permission for all files created by a user. This default permission is called the umask (or user mask). It "subtracts" some permissions from the files a user creates. The user mask is *subtracted* from 777, and what's left is the default permission for a file created by that user. For example, if your umask is 007, then when you create a file, your file will have mode 660. (The mode cannot go below zero.)

CHANGING PERMISSIONS

The command to change a file's permissions is chmod (for **change mode**). You can either change a file's mode numerically or symbolically. The symbolic form uses letters: a to indicate permissions for all users, u for the user who owns the file, g for the group, and o for the other users.

- To add a permission, use +
- To subtract a permission, use –
- To set a permission exactly, use =
- Indicate the permissions with r, w, and x.

■ *FOR EXAMPLE:*

The command chmod 666 ThingsToDo gives the file ThingsToDo the mode 666 (everyone can read and write the file).

The command chmod o-w ThingsToDo changes the permissions on ThingsToDo by subtracting write permission (-w) from the "other" users (o).

The command chmod u=rx,g+w sets the permissions for the user to read and execute, and it adds write permission for the group.

Normally, a file has the same permissions as the directory in which it is created. (When you move a file, it keeps its permissions.) If you create a file in a directory with mode 777, the file has mode 666. Execute permission is not turned on, unless you explicitly set it with chmod.

LAB 3.4 EXERCISES

3.4.1 READ FILE PERMISSIONS

Use the following listing to answer the questions in this Exercise.

```
-rw-rw-rw- 1 dana tech    9129 Mar 13 19:00 grab
-r--r--r-- 2 jim  pubs   19026 Apr 21 21:29 hold
-rwxrw---- 1 dana tech   87695 May 17  7:57 invest
dr-xr-xr-x 2 root wheel    512 Jun  1  1997 zip
```

a) If you are not `dana`, `jim`, or `root`, and you are not a member of the `tech`, `pubs`, or `wheel` groups, which file can you change?

_____

_____

b) Which file can you not read?

_____

_____

c) Can you make `zip` your current directory?

_____

_____

d) If you are not `root` or a member of the `wheel` group, can you create files in the `zip` directory?

_____

_____

e) Which files can user `jim` edit?

_____

_____

f) On which files can user `jim` change permissions?

_____

_____

3.4.2 UNDERSTAND YOUR DEFAULT PERMISSIONS

a) If you create a file in a directory with mode 664, what are the permissions on the file?

_____

_____

b) What does the `umask` command do?

_____

_____

3.4.3 CHANGE FILE PERMISSIONS

In your home directory, create the file `notebook.txt`.

Type the following command:

```
chmod 644 notebook.txt
```

a) What does `ls -l` show the permissions to be?

_____

_____

Type the following command:

```
chmod a-x notebook.txt
```

b) What does the command do?

_____

_____

Type the following command:

```
chmod u+x,g+x notebook.txt
```

c) What does the command do?

_____

_____

d) What command would change the permissions on the file to rw-rw-r-- (mode **664**)?

_____

_____

3.4.4 CHANGE DIRECTORY PERMISSIONS

In your home directory, type the following commands:

```
mkdir workbook.examples
chmod ag=rwx,o=r workbook.examples
```

a) What does `ls -ld` show the permissions to be?

_____

_____

Type the following commands:

```
chmod a-x workbook.examples
cd workbook.examples
```

b) What happens?

_____

_____

Why?

_____

_____

Type the following commands:

```
chmod u+x,g+x workbook.examples
cd workbook.examples
```

c) What does the command do?

_____

_____

LAB 3.4 EXERCISE ANSWERS

This section gives you some suggested answers to the questions in Lab 3.4, with discussions related to those answers. Your answers may vary, but the most important thing is whether or not your answers work. Use these discussions to analyze differences between your answers and those presented here.

If you have alternative answers to the questions in these exercises, you are encouraged to post your answers and discuss them at the companion Web site for this book, located at:

```
http://www.phptr.com/phptrinteractive
```

3.4.1 ANSWERS

Use the following listing to answer the questions in this Exercise.

```
-rw-rw-rw- 1 dana tech    9129 Mar 13 19:00 grab
-r--r--r-- 2 jim  pubs   19026 Apr 21 21:29 hold
-rwxrw---- 1 dana tech   87695 May 17  7:57 invest
dr-xr-xr-x 2 root wheel    512 Jun  1  1997 zip
```

a) If you are not dana, jim, or root, and you are not a member of the tech, pubs, or wheel groups, which file can you change?

Answer: You can change the file grab; it's the only one with write permission for "others."

You need write permission to change the contents of the file or directory. You need write permission to change or delete a file.

b) Which file can you not read?

Answer: You cannot read the file invest. It doesn't have read permission for "others."

User dana and any members of the tech group can read and write the file *invest*.

c) Can you make zip your current directory?

Answer: Yes. It has execute permission for "others."

Remember, you need execute permission on a directory to make it your current directory.

d) If you are not root or a member of the wheel group, can you create files in the zip directory?

Answer: No. The directory would need write permission for "others."

Every user on the system belongs to one or more groups. Groups are a security feature. With groups, you can share files with some users without sharing files with all users. Instead of dividing all users into "me" and "them," groups divide all the users on the system into "us" (people in your group) and "them" (the others). In this case, the root user and anyone in the wheel group can go into the zip directory.

You can belong to more than one group, but it's not common. One group will be your "primary" group. When you create a file, it will have permissions for your primary group.

There is a program that will change the group to which a file belongs; it's called chgrp (for **change group**). You can only make a file belong to a group that you belong to.

e) Which files can user jim edit?

Answer: Jim can edit the file grab; although he owns the file hold, he doesn't have write permission for it.

Of course, because he owns the file hold, he could change the permissions on it and give himself write permission.

f) On which files can user jim change permissions?

Answer: He can change permissions on hold, because he owns it.

The owner of a file is allowed to change the permissions on the file using the chmod program. The owner can also change who owns the file by using the chown program (for **change owner**). On some systems, for security reasons, only the system administrator can use it, to "give files away." If you are allowed to chown a file, you cannot "unchown" it. Once you've given the file away, you don't own it any more, and you cannot assign the file's ownership. (The system administrator can change the ownership on a file he or she doesn't own, however.)

The system administrator (user root) can chown and chmod all files, no matter who owns them.

3.4.2 ANSWERS

a) If you create a file in a directory with mode 664, what are the permissions on the file?

Answer: The file will have the permissions 666 minus the value of your umask.

The default permission on a file is 666, minus the value of your umask. The directory's permissions are important only because you need to have write permission in a directory in order to create a file.

b) What does the umask command do?

Answer: The umask command "masks out" certain permissions from your default file permissions.

Even if your umask is set, you can still create files with the "forbidden" permissions, but you need to set those permissions using chmod.

You should only need to think about your umask if you have created a file and it doesn't have all of the permissions you expect. First check the permissions on the directory. If that doesn't explain why the file's permissions are strange, check your user umask.

The command to set your user's mask is also called `umask`. Without any argument, the `umask` command shows your current user mask. The argument to `umask` is the permissions you want to subtract. The command `umask 022` means that files you create will not have write permission for the group or for others.

■ FOR EXAMPLE:

If you don't want "others" to be able to read, write, or execute your files, give the command `umask 007`. (The 00 isn't necessary, but it helps keep straight which permissions you're setting.) A common `umask` command is `umask 022`. This keeps others and members of your group from being able to change files you create.

3.4.3 ANSWERS

In your home directory, create the file `notebook.txt`.

a) What does `ls -l` show the permissions to be?

Answer: Mode 644 shows up as a permission string `rw-r--r--`.

Remember the numbers for permissions: read permission is 4, write permission is 2. The permission 6 is 4 + 2 (read + write). Some people find it easier to think about each permission having its own number, so user read permission is 400, while other read permission is 4. If that works better for you, think of it that way.

When you use a number as the file mode with `chmod`, the file mode is absolute: The file's permission becomes that number. *All* of the permissions are changed. If you accidentally type 77 instead of 777, the `chmod` command treats the file mode as 077. Suddenly you've removed your own read, write, and execute permission instead of assigning it. (As long as you own the file, you can fix the permission, though.)

Type the following command:

```
chmod a-x notebook.txt
```

b) What does the command do?

Answer: The command subtracts execute permission for all users. Because no one had execute permission, there's no change. The permission string is still rw-r--r-- *(mode 644).*

With symbolic modes, you add or subtract permissions. You specify the category of permissions (user, group, other, or all; if you don't specify a category, it defaults to all). Then you specify if you're adding or subtracting permissions and what permissions you're changing. If you try to take away a permission that isn't there, there's no effect.

Type the following command:

```
chmod u+x,g+x notebook.txt
```

**LAB
3.4**

c) What does the command do?

Answer: The command adds execute permission for the user and the group. The permission string is now rwxr-xr-- *(mode 754).*

You can join multiple categories with commas.

d) What command would change the permissions on the file to rw-rw-r-- (mode 664)?

Answer: Either of the commands chmod 664 notebook.txt *or* chmod u-x,g=rw notebook.txt *would change the permissions appropriately.*

You could also use the command chmod ug=rw,o=r. Remember that the = operator sets permissions exactly instead of adding or subtracting them.

3.4.4 ANSWERS

In your home directory, create the directory workbook.examples.

a) What does ls -ld show the permissions to be?

Answer: If you have no umask *set, the permissions are* rwxrwxrw-.

Remember that directories are created with mode 777, minus your umask.

Type the following commands:

```
chmod a-x workbook.examples
cd workbook.examples
```

b) What happens?

Answer: You cannot cd *into the directory; the system gives a "permission denied" message.*

Why?

Answer: You must have execute permission to enter a directory.

This is why directories have a different default permission than files: The execute permission is necessary on a directory, but not on a file. Execute permission is only necessary on files that are commands.

Type the following commands:

```
chmod u+x workbook.examples
cd workbook.examples
```

c) What does the command do?

Answer: The command adds execute permission for the directory's owner.

There is an option to chmod that affects a directory and all of the files inside it, -R. If you want to add group write permission to the directory workbook.examples and all of the files in that directory. You can use the following command:

```
chmod -R g+w workbook.examples.
```

**LAB
3.4**

LAB 3.4 SELF-REVIEW QUESTIONS

To test your progress, you should be able to answer the following questions.

1) You can create a directory you can cd into, but not list its contents.
    a) _____True
    b) _____False

2) When you change the permissions on a directory, you also change the permissions on every file in that directory.
    a) _____True
    b) _____False

3) You can chmod any file that belongs to your group.
    a) _____True
    b) _____False

**LAB
3.4**

4) A file is mode 777. After a chmod u=rw command, its file mode is which of the following?
    a) _____644
    b) _____766
    c) _____677
    d) _____600
    e) _____776

Quiz answers appear in Appendix A, Lab 3.4

CHAPTER 3

TEST YOUR THINKING

 The projects in this section are meant to have you utilize all of the skills that you have acquired throughout this chapter. The answers to these projects can be found at the companion Web site to this book, located at:

http://www.phptr.com/phptrinteractive

Visit the Web site periodically to share and discuss your answers.

1) On a system where the maximum size of a path name is 4096 characters and the maximum size of a file name is 255 characters:

   a) What's the largest number of directories in a path name?

   b) What's the smallest?

2) How might you find out whose home directory uses the most space on the system?

3) What are the security advantages of groups?

CHAPTER 4

FILES AND DIRECTORIES

 Most of the work you do on the system will involve files and directories. Files are how data is stored over the long term. Now that you know how files exist on the system, you need to be able to use them. You will use these commands every day.

CHAPTER OBJECTIVES

In this chapter, you will learn about:

There is a difference between understanding the file tree's structure and being able to work with files and directories. Many of the files you use will actually be created and modified by programs you use (such as your editor). There's more to working with files than just creating them. Creating directories, removing directories and files, and copying or moving files and directories are all housekeeping tasks you'll need to do.

The other important part of this chapter is specifying *which* files and directories you want to work with. All of the shells provide *shell wildcards* as a convenient shorthand way to specify more than one file at a time. If you've used DOS, you're familiar with wildcard expressions such as *.* and ?at.txt. UNIX system wildcards go further than the DOS wildcards. They make it possible to isolate only a few files in a directory of hundreds.

L A B 4.1

DISPLAYING THE CONTENTS OF A DIRECTORY

LAB OBJECTIVES

After this lab, you will be able to:

✓ Display Directory Contents

✓ Identify Directories and Files

✓ Sort Directory Contents

✓ Display Nonprintable File Names

As you learned in previous chapters, the `ls` command lists the contents of a directory. If you supply `ls` with the name of a file or files, it lists only those files; if you supply the name of a directory, it lists the *contents* of the directory. If you supply no operands at all, `ls` lists the contents of the current directory.

To list the contents of a directory, you need read permission on the directory. It's possible to be able to list the contents of a directory without being able to `cd` to the directory. It's also possible to be able to `cd` to the directory without being able to list the contents of the directory. However, usually when you set a directory's permissions, you'll specify both r and x permissions at the same time.

So far, the only way you have of telling whether a name indicates a file or directory is the long file listing. For a very full directory, the ls -1 listing is too much information. The -p option indicates directories by putting a / after the name. The -p option is not available on all systems. The -F option also indicates, using a letter code, which files are directories, but it also indicates all of the other file types as well, as shown in Table 4.1.

Table 4.1 ■ UNIX File Types

	Regular file (no character at all).
/	Directory.
@	Symbolic link.
*	Execute permissions are set (usually a program).

Some systems have other characters as well to indicate other special file types.

■ *FOR EXAMPLE:*

Listing the contents of the current directory with both ls -p and ls -F:

```
$ ls -p
Mail/       notes/      welcome.txt
backups/    projects/   xit
bin/        thingstodo
$ ls -F
Mail/       notes/      welcome.txt@
backups/    projects/   xit*
bin/        thingstodo
```

In the ls -F output, only thingstodo is a regular file. The file xit is some kind of program, and welcome.txt is a symbolic link. All the other entries are directories.

OUTPUT FORMATS

You've already seen some options that modify the output of ls. The -l option prints a long listing, and the -a option includes hidden files in the output. Other options change the format of the information that ls presents.

Normally, ls prints its output to the screen in columns, like this:

```
$ ls
Mail          notes         welcome.txt
backups       projects      xit
bin           thingstodo
```

The files are sorted in ASCII order down the first column, then the second column, and so on. The ls command tries to fit as many columns on a line as possible. The columns are all the same size, based on the size of the longest name in the directory.

ls behaves differently if you redirect the output. When you send the output to a command or a file, ls prints the files in one column. The -C option makes ls print its output in columns even if the output is being redirected.

As you learned in Chapter 3, the option -a makes ls display hidden files.

Several options deal with how files are sorted. The -r option reverses the order of sorting, so ls -r sorts the files in reverse alphabetical order. The -t option sorts the files by modification time, so the files changed most recently are listed first. This option, or ls -lt, can be useful when you want to find out which files have been changed recently in a directory. The -r option can also be used with -t.

Another useful option to ls is -q. It causes nonprinting characters to display as '?'.

■ *FOR EXAMPLE:*

The character Control-H is commonly used as a backspace character. On most UNIX systems, Control-H is a legal character in a filename, but not recommended.

```
$ ls
ac
$ ls ac
ls: file not found
$ ls -q
ab?c
```

The file name is actually "ab"-Control-H-"c". The Control-H causes the monitor to back up one character and write over the letter it just printed. The file name displays on screen as "ac" but when the system looks for a file named *ac*, it fails. The -q option causes ls to print the control character as ?, so it doesn't behave as a backspace.

LAB 4.1 EXERCISES

4.1.1 DISPLAY DIRECTORY CONTENTS

In a directory that contains visible files, type the following commands:

```
ls
ls | pg
```

a) Why is the output different?

_____

_____

b) What option could you give `ls` so the output of `ls | pg` would look like the output of `ls`?

_____

_____

c) Create the file `Supercalifragilisticexpialidocious`. Now list the directory contents. How has the formatting changed?

_____

_____

4.1.2 IDENTIFY DIRECTORIES AND FILES

a) What three options to `ls` allow you to distinguish directories from files?

_____

_____

b) Given the following output, which command was used: `ls -p` or `ls -F`?

```
Fruits/   Spices/   find*
```

_____

_____

c) What does the character @ mean after a file name in `ls -F` output?

_____

_____

d) What does the character * mean?

_____

_____

e) Can you make any file you own show up with an * character?

_____

_____

4.1.3 SORT DIRECTORY CONTENTS

a) Are files and directory names sorted across the rows or down the columns?

_____

_____

b) Which comes first in the sorting, lowercase letters, capital letters, or does it matter?

_____

_____

c) What options would you use to sort the newest file first?

_____

_____

d) What option would you use to sort the files in reverse order?

_____

_____

**LAB
4.1**

4.1.4 DISPLAY NONPRINTABLE CHARACTERS

a) What does the `ls -q` command do?

_____

_____

b) Why would you want to use this option?

_____

_____

LAB 4.1 EXERCISE ANSWERS

This section gives you some suggested answers to the questions in Lab 4.1, with discussions related to those answers. Your answers may vary, but the most important thing is whether or not your answers work. Use these discussions to analyze differences between your answers and those presented here.

If you have alternative answers to the questions in these exercises, you are encouraged to post your answers and discuss them at the companion Web site for this book, located at:

```
http://www.phptr.com/phptrinteractive
```

4.1.1 ANSWERS

In a directory that contains visible files, type the following commands:
```
ls
ls | pg
```

a) Why is the output different?

Answer: When `ls`' output is redirected, it changes formats to print one file to a line.

The `ls` command is used to list the contents of a directory or to print information about a specific file. One of the features of `ls` is that it changes formats when its output is redirected or piped.

You can use `ls` to see if a particular file exists (as in the `ls ac` example earlier). You can also use `ls` to see information about a file, as described in Chapter 3.

Some systems have a command, `lc`, that lists files by category. Other systems, such as Solaris and Unixware, accept `lc` as an alternative name for `ls`, but the `lc` command identical to the `ls` command. (On those systems, `lc` is a hard link to the `ls` command.)

The `pg` command is a "pager" program. It displays one screenful (or "page") of text at a time. To display a new page of text in `pg`, press Enter. To quit, press `q` and then Enter. The `more` command (mentioned in Chapter 2, "The Command Line") is also a pager. You can use both `pg` and `more` to display the contents of files as well as the results of commands.

b) What option could you give `ls` so the output of `ls | pg` would look like the output of `ls`?

Answer: The `-C` option forces the output to be in columns.

Sometimes you want the output in columns, even though it's being piped into another command. (I used the -C option to capture the output for these examples.)

c) Create the file `Supercalifragilisticexpialidocious`. Now list the directory contents. How has the formatting changed?

Answer: There will now be only one or two columns, depending on other files in the directory.

The `ls` command tries to create equally-sized columns based on the size of the largest name.

LAB 4.1

4.1.2 ANSWERS

a) What three options to `ls` will allow you to distinguish directories from files?

Answer: The options `-1`, `-F`, and `-p` all allow you to distinguish directories from files.

b) Given the following output, which command was used, `ls -p` or `ls -F`?

```
Fruits/   Spices/   find*
```

Answer: The `*` indicates that the command was probably `ls -F`.

The `-p` option to `ls` indicates only directories (with `/`), but `-F` uses `*` to indicate executable files. (It's possible that the file's name really was *find** with an asterisk as part of the name, but it's unlikely.)

c) What does the character @ mean after a file name in `ls -F` output?

Answer: The file is a symbolic link.

d) What does the character * mean?

Answer: The file's execute permissions are set.

If any execute permissions on the file are set, the * will show up whether you have execute permission or not. Another user could use `chmod u+x` so that only he or she could execute the file; you couldn't execute the file, but it would still show up with an * character when you run `ls -F`.

e) Can you make any file you own show up with an * character?

Answer: Yes. Simply do a `chmod a+x` on the file.

Remember, you can change permissions on any file you own.

4.1.3 ANSWERS

a) Are files and directory names sorted across the rows or down the columns?

Answer: Normally, the columnated output of `ls` is sorted down the columns.

You can make `ls` sort its output across the rows by giving the -x option.

b) Which comes first in the sorting, lowercase letters, capital letters, or does it matter?

Answer: Names starting with capital letters are displayed first.

This is called an ASCII sort. All information inside the computer is represented as numbers. The ASCII character set is a standard set of numbers for representing the letters, numbers, and punctuation. (The initials ASCII stand for American Standard Code for Information Interchange.) There are 128 characters in the basic character set, covering the characters A through Z, and a through z, the numbers 0 through 9, and assorted punctuation characters. For example, the letter "A" is actually stored in the computer as the number 65. It's followed by all of the uppercase letters (the code for "Z" is 90). The lowercase letters have higher code numbers (the code for "a" is 97).

When file names (or any words or letters in the computer) are sorted in ASCII order, it means that they are sorted according to the actual ASCII codes used for those letters. An "A" is encoded as 65, so it naturally comes before "a," which is encoded as 97. A "B" is encoded as 66, so it also comes before "a" and so on.

For your convenience, here is the order in which the printable ASCII characters sort, broken into groups for easier reading:

```
space character
!"#%^&'()*+,-./
0123456789
:;<->?@
ABCDEFGHIJKLMNOPQRSTUVWXZY
[\]^_
abcdefghijklmnopqrstuvwxyz
{|}~
```

So `ls` lists a file name that begins with ! before one that begins with #.

c) What options would you use to sort the newest file first?

Answer: The -t option sorts files by time.

You can confirm this by typing the command ls -lt. The newest files are at the beginning of the list. The time is the modification time, as you learned in Chapter 3. (Using -c plus -t causes ls to sort by the files' creation times, and using -n plus -t causes ls to sort by the files' access times. I cannot think of any reason you would have to use those options, but they are available.)

d) What option would you use to sort the files in reverse order?

Answer:The -r option sorts files in reverse order.

The -r option reverses the order of whatever sort you've specified. To sort the files with the oldest modification time first, use ls -rt. To sort in reverse ASCII order, use ls -r.

4.1.4 ANSWERS

a) What does the ls -q command do?

Answer: It displays nonprintable characters as question marks.

The nonprintable characters are called *control characters*. These are mostly the codes from 0 to 31. They don't print on the screen, as you can guess from the name. (The space character is considered a printable character, but the tab character is not.) Instead, control characters are used to send signals to the terminal and to the computer—to control it, in fact. For example, the code 8 is the code for backspace. The code 10 is the code to start a new line.

When you use the -q option to ls, each control character in a file's name is turned into a question mark character first. The terminal gets a question mark, not a control character, and question marks don't do anything special to a terminal.

b) Why would you want to use this option?

Answer:You would use this option to see if any file names contained nonprinting characters.

You might get control characters in file names because you can actually send control characters from your keyboard; that's why the Control key is there. For example, to send the code 7, you hold down the Control key and press the g key (because g is the seventh letter of the alphabet). (If you do this, your terminal will beep, because that's what the Control-G signal tells the terminal to do.)

LAB 4.1 SELF-REVIEW QUESTIONS

To test your progress, you should be able to answer the following questions.

1) In an ASCII sort, uppercase letters sort before lowercase letters.
    a) _____True
    b) _____False

2) Which command lists hidden files and sorts by time?
    a) _____`ls -aq`
    b) _____`ls -pq`
    c) _____`ls -Ftq`
    d) _____`ls -at`

3) Which command lists files in reverse order and indicates directories?
    a) _____`ls -rp`
    b) _____`ls -tr`
    c) _____`ls -qt`
    d) _____`ls -ar`

Quiz answers appear in Appendix A, Lab 4.1

L A B 4.2

SPECIFYING FILES USING WILDCARDS

LAB OBJECTIVES

After this lab, you will be able to:

✓ Specify All Files in a Directory

✓ Specify All Hidden Files

✓ Specify Files by Length of Name

✓ Exclude a Set of Files

A *wildcard pattern* is a shorthand way to specify file names. A wildcard character is a character that "stands for" other characters, just as a joker in a card hand may stand for other cards. For example, a ? character in a file name can stand for any single character.

Wildcards are yet another set of shell metacharacters. When the shell sees a file name containing a wildcard, it examines the list of files in the current directory and looks for any names that match.

- If *any* files match, the shell replaces the wildcard pattern with the list of file names that match, whether it's one or more files.
- If *no* files match, the shell doesn't change the wildcard pattern at all.

■ *FOR EXAMPLE:*

Your directory contains files named 1, 2, 3, and 10. The wildcard pattern "?" matches 1, 2, and 3, but not 10. The wildcard pattern "1?" matches 10.

You can use the wildcards listed in Table 4.2.

Table 4.2 ■ UNIX Wildcards

?	Matches any single character.
[abc]	Matches any one of the characters in the brackets (a or b or c in this example). To make] one of the characters that matches, place it first in the set, like this: []abc].
[a-c]	Matches any of the characters in the range given (a or b or c in this example). To make - one of the characters that matches, place it either first or last in the set, like this: [-abc]
[!ac]	Matches any single character *except* the characters in the brackets (any character except a or c)
*	Matches any (zero or more) characters

LAB 4.2 EXERCISES

4.2.1 SPECIFY ALL FILES IN A DIRECTORY

Create a directory named `wildcards` and change to that directory.

Type the following command:

```
echo *
```

a) What is the result?

_____

_____

Why?

_____

_____

Create files with the following names:

```
boat coat Goat goad color .hidden
```

Type the following command:

```
echo *
```

b) Which file is not listed?

_____

_____

Type the following command:

```
ls
```

c) How do the results differ?

_____

_____

4.2.2 SPECIFY SOME FILES IN A DIRECTORY

In the same directory, what wildcard pattern would match each of the following?

a) The names of hidden files?

_____

_____

b) All four-letter file names?

_____

_____

c) All four-letter file names ending in "oat"?

_____

_____

d) All four-letter file names with "oa" as the middle letters?

_____

_____

e) All file names beginning with "c" or "g"?

_____

_____

f) A file name beginning with an uppercase letter?

_____

_____

4.2.3 EXCLUDE SOME FILES

In the same directory, what wildcard pattern would specify each of the following?

a) List all nonhidden files that don't begin with G or g?

_____

_____

b) How would you also match hidden files?

_____

_____

LAB 4.2 EXERCISE ANSWERS

This section gives you some suggested answers to the questions in Lab 4.2, with discussions related to those answers. Your answers may vary, but the most important thing is whether or not your answers work. Use these discussions to analyze differences between your answers and those presented here.

If you have alternative answers to the questions in these exercises, you are encouraged to post your answers and discuss them at the companion Web site for this book, located at:

```
http://www.phptr.com/phptrinteractive
```

SPECIAL CASES FOR MATCHING

Because character classes use special characters, they have special cases.

What if you want to match a file name containing a "-" character as part of the range? Then you make it either the *first* character in the character class or the *last* character in the class. The pattern to match A-Z,], [, and - is [] [A-Z-].

To match hidden files with a wildcard pattern, you *must* start the pattern with a dot. A dot in the middle of a pattern does not match, even if the pattern begins with *.

To match a / character in a path name, you must explicitly mention the / in the pattern. Doing this is a quick way to search several directories.

■ *FOR EXAMPLE:*

From your home directory, to list all users whose home directories contain the file .profile, use the command:

```
ls ../*/.profile
```

The shell searches the file names for all path names beginning with "../" and ending with "/.profile", and that match * in between.

Both the Korn Shell and the C Shell provide other pattern-matching facilities, but the wildcards listed here are sufficient for any purpose except writing programs.

4.2.1 ANSWERS

Create a directory named wildcards and change to that directory.
Type the following command:

```
echo *
```

a) What is the result?

Answer: The result is "".*

Wildcard patterns are one of the most used notations in the entire UNIX toolbox.

The wildcard characters are interpreted by the shell, not by the command. (This is another area where UNIX is different from DOS; on DOS systems, each command interprets the wildcard characters.) When you type a wildcard pattern, the shell replaces it with the list of files that match that pattern.

If you use the C Shell, wildcard matching is referred to as shell globbing, *and ? and * are referred to as* glob characters.

Why?

Answer: When no files match the pattern, the shell passes the pattern itself to the command.

The echo command simply "repeats" what it's told—in this case, it was told *.

Create files with the following names:

    boat coat Goat goad color .hidden

Type the following command:

    echo *

b) Which file is not listed?

Answer: The file .hidden is not listed.

Now that there are files in the directory, * matches the names. When you type *, the shell turns that command into the names of the files in the directory. (Remember that the pattern * doesn't match any hidden files.)

Type the following command:

    ls

c) How do the results differ?

Answer: The files are organized into regularly spaced columns.

You can list the files in the current directory by using the command echo * as well as with the command ls. The ls command presents a more readable list, however.

The command ls is different from the command ls *, however. When you give the command ls, you're asking ls to list all of the files. The ls command checks for the first file in the current directory, and then the second, and so on until it has listed all of the files. This will always work, no matter how many files are in the current directory.

When you give the command ls *, it gets turned into the command ls followed by the list of all the file names in the directory. If there are *too many* files in the directory, the argument list to ls will become too long, and the command will fail. (On a Solaris system, the command line can be more than a million characters long; that's a lot of files!)

4.2.2 ANSWERS

In the same directory, what wildcard pattern would specify each of the following?

a) The names of hidden files?

Answer: The pattern .* *matches all hidden files.*

The pattern matches all file names that begin with a dot and have zero or more characters following that dot. Because all hidden files have names that begin with a dot, the pattern matches all hidden files.

Neither * nor ? will match the dot at the beginning of a name; only a dot at the beginning of the pattern will match it.

b) All four-letter file names?

Answer: The pattern ???? *matches all four-letter file names. Because there are no hidden files with four-letter names, it doesn't matter that* ???? *won't match hidden files.*

The ? wildcard stands for any single character, but there must be a character there to match. The pattern "ba?" matches ban but it also matches bad and bat.

c) All four-letter file names ending in "oat"?

Answer: The pattern ?oat *matches all four-letter file names ending in* "oat".

d) All four-letter file names with "oa" as the middle letters?

Answer: The pattern ?oa? *matches all four-letter file names with* "oa" *as the middle letters.*

e) All file names beginning with "c" or "g"?

Answer: The pattern [cg]* *matches all file names beginning with* "c" *or* "g".

Instead of matching *any* single character, you can reduce the number of matches by naming the characters you want to match using []. The pattern "ba[nt]" matches ban and bat, but it doesn't match bad, because the brackets don't contain a "d". The characters in the brackets are referred to as a *character class*.

**LAB
4.2**

f) A file name beginning with an uppercase letter?

Answer:The pattern [A-Z]* *matches all file names beginning with an uppercase letter.*

If you want to match any uppercase letter, you could go to the trouble of typing [ABCDEFGHIJKLMNOPQRSTUVWXYZ], but there is a short form. You can indicate a *range* of characters with a hyphen: the letters A to Z can be presented as [A-Z].

You can combine several smaller ranges. For example, the pattern to match any letter is [A-Za-z] (remember the ASCII sorting order).

If you're using the Korn Shell, there's an even shorter form, [:alpha:]. For instance, to match any name that begins with the digit 1 or a letter, you can use [1[:alpha:]]. The [:alpha:] goes inside another set of brackets. The [:alpha:] is an example of a *character class.*

4.2.3 ANSWERS

In the same directory, what wildcard pattern would specify each of the following?

a) List all nonhidden files that don't begin with G or g.

Answer:The pattern [!Gg]* .* *matches all file names that don't begin with "G" or "g".*

The ! at the beginning of the character set means that the set *excludes* characters instead of including them. (A ! anywhere else in the character set matches a ! character.)

 Older shells don't understand this [!abc] *format.You may not be able to use it on your system.*

All of these patterns still only match a single character. To match more than one character, use *. It is the broadest pattern: It matches zero or more characters.

The pattern * *doesn't* match a file name with / in it, and it doesn't match hidden files.

You can combine these patterns to match file names as precisely as you'd like.

b) How would you also match hidden files?

Answer:The pattern `[!Gg]* .*` *matches all hidden and visible file names. (Hidden file names start with ., so none of them start with "G" or "g".)*

You have to put the `.*` as a second pattern.

LAB 4.2 SELF-REVIEW QUESTIONS

To test your progress, you should be able to answer the following questions.

1) The wildcard pattern * matches the / character in file names.
   a) _____True
   b) _____False

2) Which files in the right column will match each of the patterns in the left column?

a) `A*`	**i)** `Andor`
b) `.???`	**ii)** `AM`
c) `*[!A-Z]*`	**iii)** `.env`
d) `*[a-z]`	**iv)** `Guide`
e) `.*????`	**v)** `.environ`
f) `*.*`	**vi)** `diatribe`

3) What pattern could you use with `ls` to list files with names starting with "-"?
   a) _____`-*`
   b) _____`?*`
   c) _____`./-*`
   d) _____`./?*`
   e) _____`[-]*`

Quiz answers appear in Appendix A, Lab 4.2

L A B 4.3

REMOVING FILES

LAB OBJECTIVES

After this lab, you will be able to:

✓ Remove Files

✓ Remove Files Interactively

✓ Remove Files with Names Starting with -

The command to remove files is `rm`, for remove. You must specify which file or files you want removed.

To remove a file, you need write permission on the parent directory. You may remove (or delete) any file you own.

Even if you don't have write permission on a file, you can remove it with `rm` if you have write permission on the directory the file is in.

If you don't have write permission on the file, the `rm` command asks you to confirm the deletion.

■ *FOR EXAMPLE:*

Assuming that you own the file `chain.letter`, but haven't got write permissions set on it, the following is what you would see:

```
$ rm chain.letter
```

```
rm: chail.letter: OVERRIDE protection 444 (yes/no)?
```

To remove it, type a response beginning with "y" or "Y." Any other response is taken as meaning "no."

Assuming you have permission, you can delete any kind of file with rm. Deleting a directory with rm is one of the topics of Lab 4.4.

LAB 4.3 EXERCISES

4.3.1 REMOVE FILES

Create the files a, b, and c in your directory.

Type the following command:

```
rm a b c
```

Create the files again and then type the following command:

```
rm -i a b c
```

a) How do the two commands differ? What does the -i option do?

_____

_____

4.3.2 REMOVE FILES INTERACTIVELY

Create files named a and b.

Type the following commands:

```
chmod a-w a b
rm a
rm -f b
```

a) What does the -f command do?

_____

_____

b) Although you don't have write permission on the files a and b, why are you allowed to delete them?

_____

_____

4.3.3 REMOVE FILES BEGINNING WITH -

Create a file named -X.

Type the following command:

```
rm -X
```

a) What happened?

_____

_____

Type the command:

```
rm ./-X
```

b) Why did the second command work even though the first one didn't?

_____

_____

LAB 4.3 EXERCISE ANSWERS

 This section gives you some suggested answers to the questions in Lab 4.3, with discussions related to those answers. Your answers may vary, but the most important thing is whether or not your answers work. Use these discussions to analyze differences between your answers and those presented here.

If you have alternative answers to the questions in these exercises, you are encouraged to post your answers and discuss them at the companion Web site for this book, located at:

`http://www.phptr.com/phptrinteractive`

4.3.1 ANSWERS

a) What does the `-i` option do?

Answer: The `-i` option makes `rm` *request confirmation for every file deletion.*

Because `rm` is a dangerous command, its default behavior is to do nothing. When you type `ls` without arguments, you get a list of the current directory; when you type `rm` without arguments, you get an error message. When you use the `rm -i` command, only responses beginning with "y" or "Y" are accepted as confirmation to remove the file; all other input means that the file is not removed.

 You should be cautious about using commands such as `rm -f *`*.*

Some people find that religious use of the `-i` option reduces the number of files they delete accidentally. Other people do not find `-i` helpful. (When I'm deleting many files at once, my fingers get into the habit of pressing the "y" key and I don't pay proper attention to the file names. I tend to delete as many files accidentally while using `-i` as while not using it.)

4.3.2 ANSWERS

a) What does the −f command do?

Answer:The −f option causes rm *to remove files "forcefully." Normally, you must confirm that you want to remove a file if you don't have write permission. With the −f option,* rm *does not ask for confirmation.*

To remove a file, you need write permission on the directory in which the file resides. If you cannot write to the directory, you cannot remove the file. If you have write permission in the directory, you are allowed to delete any file you have write permission on. You can also delete any file you own, whether you have write permission on the file or not (so long as you have permission on the directory). You're allowed to delete files you own because you could easily use chmod to make the file "deletable"; the rm command doesn't force you to do that work and then run rm again. The rm command does ask if you're sure you want to delete the file. The −f option prevents rm from making this inquiry.

You cannot remove a file if you don't have write permission in the *parent directory*. Without that permission, you will get a "permission denied" error, whether or not you have write permission on the file or if you own the file.

b) Although you don't have write permission on the files a and b, why are you allowed to delete them?

Answer:You are allowed to remove a file you own, whether you have write permission set on the file or not.

You may find it useful to remove write permission on any files you think are especially important. Obviously, it's inconvenient to do this on a file you have to change on a daily basis, but for files that are only changed once in a while, the prompt from rm can be a useful reminder, and can prevent an embarrassing accident.

You might want to try an rm command using both −i and −f at the same time. Different systems behave different ways: some systems take the last one on the command line, some systems let one option always take effect over the other, and other systems give an error message.

The rm command doesn't necessarily remove a file. It removes a *hard link* to a file; when all of the links are gone, the file is also gone. Most files have only one hard link (the ls -l output shows a 1 in the links column), so the rm command removes the file.

Once you have removed a file in UNIX, it's gone, probably forever. (If you want it back, your options are discussed in Chapter 6, "Emergency Recovery.") The rm command is dangerous, because it can eliminate hours or weeks or possibly years of effort from your system.

4.3.3 ANSWERS

Create a file named -X.
Type the following command:
```
rm -X
```

a) What happened?

Answer:*The command failed, with a message like the following:*

```
rm: illegal option -- X
```

When a file's name begins with a "–" character, most commands will try to treat the file name as an option. Whether there is an option by that name or not, the results will not be what you want.

Type the following command:

```
rm ./-X
```

b) Why did the second command work even though the first one didn't?

Answer: *In the first command, the file name* -X *was interpreted as an option because it began with a* – *character. By putting a* ./ *before the file name, it no longer began with a* – *character.*

You could also give the absolute path name. While rm might interpret the file name -X as an option, it will not interpret ./-X as an option. If you're deleting more than one file, you can also move the offending file name so it isn't the first file name in the list of operands: The command rm -X 02.txt doesn't work, but the command rm 02.txt -X works fine.

Another reason it might be difficult to remove a file is because the file's name might contain an nonprintable character, so you cannot actually give the file name to the `rm` command. The solution is to use `rm -i` and wildcards. By careful choice of a wildcard pattern, you should be able to reduce the number of file names passed to `rm` to one, two, or three.

LAB 4.3 SELF-REVIEW QUESTIONS

To test your progress, you should be able to answer the following questions. For these questions, assume your log-in name is "`jurgen`" and you belong to the group "`misc`".

```
$ ls -l
Total 2
-r--rw-r-- 1 jurgen misc   219 Mar 25 18:12 ankh
-r--r--rw- 1 claude misc   219 Mar 25 18:12 cross
-rw-rw-r-- 1 feodor r+d    219 Mar 25 18:12 star
```

1) The command `rm -if *` will prompt for confirmation before removing all files in the directory.
   a) _____True
   b) _____False

2) Which of the following files can you delete?

   i) ankh   **a)** i only

   ii) cross   **b)** i and ii only

   iii) star   **c)** i and iii only

                                  d) ii and iii only

                                  e) none of these

Quiz answers appear in Appendix A, Lab 4.3

L A B 4.4

CREATING AND REMOVING DIRECTORIES

LAB OBJECTIVES

After this lab, you will be able to:

✓ Create a Directory

✓ Remove a Directory

✓ Remove a Directory and Its Contents

The command to create a directory is `mkdir` (for **make dir**ectory). The command synopsis is:

```
mkdir [-p] [-m mode] dirname ...
```

The `dirname` is the name of the directory you want to create. It can be either a relative path name or an absolute path name. Normally, `mkdir` doesn't create intermediate directories. That is, if you want to create `work/sales`, the directory `work` must already exist. The `-m` option lets you specify the mode of the directory when you create it; using the `-m` option saves you from typing one `chmod` command.

■ FOR EXAMPLE:

If the directory work doesn't already exist, you can create them both with the same mkdir command, as follows:

```
$ mkdir work work/sales
```

The command mkdir -p work/sales has the same effect.

The command to remove a directory is rmdir (for **rem**ove **dir**ectory). Its synopsis is nearly identical to mkdir's:

```
rmdir [-p]  dirname ...
```

The rmdir command can only remove empty directories. Before you can remove a directory that contains files, you must remove all of the files and directories from the directory.

There is also a -p option to rmdir, which removes the intermediate components.

You can always remove a directory you own, the same as with files.

■ FOR EXAMPLE:

If you haven't put any files into the directories, you can remove both of them with the rmdir command, like so:

```
$ mkdir work/sales work
```

The command rmdir -p work/sales would have the same effect.

Another way to remove directories is by using the -r option to rm. The "r" stands for "recursive." When the rm command encounters a directory, it goes into the directory and removes all the files; if it finds another directory, it goes into that one, and so on.

For DOS and Windows users: On UNIX systems, the command md *is not a synonym for* mkdir. *The command* rd *is not a synonym for* rmdir.

The rm -r command removes files and directories. It's normally used to remove entire subdirectory trees with a single command.

 The rm -r *command is dangerous. It's too easy to accidentally remove directory trees and files you didn't want to remove. Check the directory tree you're removing twice before you use* rm -r.

LAB 4.4 EXERCISES

4.4.1 CREATE A DIRECTORY

Type the following command:

```
mkdir phone/calls phone
```

a) What happened?

_____

_____

b) Create the directories with a single command. List the two commands that would do this.

_____

_____

c) What are the permissions on phone?

_____

_____

On `phone/calls`?

_____

_____

On the directory containing `phone`?

_____

_____

4.4.2 REMOVE A DIRECTORY

You must have already created the directories `phone/calls`. **Create a file** named `phone/list`, and use `chmod` to give `phone/list` mode **466.**

Type the following command:

    rmdir phone phone/calls

a) What happened?

_____

_____

Type the following command:

    rmdir -p phone/calls

b) What happened and why?

_____

_____

4.4.3 REMOVE A DIRECTORY AND ITS CONTENTS

Type the following command:

```
rm -r phone
```

a) What happened and why?

_____

_____

The system administrator can remove any file or directory, no matter what the permissions on it are.

b) What would happen if the system administrator typed the following?

```
rm -rf / ?
```

_____

_____

LAB 4.4 EXERCISE ANSWERS

This section gives you some suggested answers to the questions in Lab 4.4, with discussions related to those answers. Your answers may vary, but the most important thing is whether or not your answers work. Use these discussions to analyze differences between your answers and those presented here.

If you have alternative answers to the questions in these exercises, you are encouraged to post your answers and discuss them at the companion Web site for this book, located at:

```
http://www.phptr.com/phptrinteractive
```

4.4.1 ANSWERS

Type the following command:

```
mkdir phone/calls phone
```

a) What happened?

Answer: The command failed.

The command tried to create the directory `phone/calls` before creating the directory `phone`. If the arguments were in the opposite order, the command would work.

Directories organize your files.

When a directory listing gets to be too large, it's difficult to find files. Although there are tricks to finding files (clever use of wildcards, for example), it's just easier to find files in a directory that doesn't have too many files. (How many is "too many" varies from person to person.) Creating directories is an easy way to keep your files conveniently grouped together.

The opposite problem is long, difficult path names to directories. Finding files among too many directories is rather like walking through a neighborhood where everything is too far apart: You can get everywhere, but it's tiring. (How many directories is "too many" also varies from person to person.)

b) Create the directories with a single command. List the two commands that would do this.

Answer: You could use either `mkdir phone phone/calls` *or* `mkdir -p phone/calls`.

As just mentioned, if the command creates the intermediate directories first, it works. It depends on the order of the arguments.

You can also use the -p option, which lets you create and prune long "branches" of a directory tree.

Unless you are setting up a large directory tree for people to share, you'll probably only use mkdir or rmdir on a single directory at a time. The fact that you can create more than one directory at a time is occasionally useful. For example, if you are reorganizing a large collection of files, you'll need to create and remove directories, and it's convenient to be able to create more than one at a time.

c) What are the permissions on phone? On phone/calls? On the directory containing phone?

Answer:The permissions on both files are the same as the permissions on the directory where you created phone.

Directories are created with mode 777 (read-write-execute permission for everyone), modified by your umask. No matter what your umask is, these intermediate directories are created so you can read and write them.

**LAB
4.4**

4.4.2 ANSWERS

Type the following command:

```
rmdir phone phone/calls
```

a) What happened?

Answer: The command failed because the directory phone *isn't empty: it contains both the subdirectory* calls *and the file* list.

The rmdir command requires the directory to be empty; this is a safety measure. It's easy to forget about an important file in a directory when you decide to delete it. The rmdir command does warn you when the directory is not empty. There's no -f option to rmdir because it doesn't ever ask for confirmation. If it can, the rmdir command removes an empty directory without comment.

Type the following command:

```
rmdir -p phone/calls
```

b) What happened and why?

Answer:The rmdir *command removed* calls *and then failed, because the directory* phone *isn't empty (it contains the file* list).

If you cannot delete a directory because it's not empty and you thought it was, check its contents with `ls -aq`. It's easy to overlook hidden files in a directory, or the occasional file named with a control character.

4.4.3 ANSWERS

Type the following command:

```
rm -r phone
```

a) What happened and why?

Answer: The `rm` *command prompts for confirmation that* `phone/list` *is to be deleted. Once you have entered "y" or "Y," the directory* `phone` *and all of its contents are removed.*

The `rm -r` command also warns you about directories you don't have permission to remove, just as it does for regular files. The `-f` option forces it to remove files and directories , so long as you have "w" permission in the parent directory. The `-r` option stands for "recursive." When the `rm` with `-r` option command finds a directory, it goes "into" the directory first, looking for files to delete. If it finds another directory, it enters that, and so on until it has reached the end of this particular branch of the directory tree. Then it begins to delete files and work its way back up. Several commands have "recursive" options, usually indicated by a `-r` or `-R` option. The `cp` command is one discussed later in this chapter.

b) What would happen if the system administrator typed `rm -rf /` ?

Answer: All files on the system would be deleted.

The warning about `rm` given in the previous lab is true here. With the `-r` option, you may not even know what files you're deleting. The command `rm -rf *` is particularly dangerous. If you type `rm -rf *`, the command won't delete files in directories where you don't have write permission. When system administrators log in as root, they have permission to delete *any* file. If a system administrator accidentally typed `rm -rf *` in the root directory, the entire file system would be deleted.

LAB 4.4 SELF-REVIEW QUESTIONS

To test your progress, you should be able to answer the following questions.

1) The "recursive" option to `rm` deletes directories and their contents.
   a) _____True
   b) _____False

2) Directories created with `mkdir` always have the same permissions as the parent directory.
   a) _____True
   b) _____False

3) You can remove more than one directory at a time with the `rmdir` command.
   a) _____True
   b) _____False

Quiz answers appear in Appendix A, Lab 4.4

**LAB
4.4**

L A B 4.5

COPYING AND LINKING FILES AND DIRECTORIES

+--+
| ### LAB OBJECTIVES |
| |
| After this lab, you will be able to: |
| ✓ Copy a File |
| ✓ Copy Files into a Directory |
| ✓ Copy a Directory |
| ✓ Hard Link a File |
| ✓ Soft Link a File |
+--+

File copies and file links are often confused. When you copy a file or directory, you're creating a duplicate file or directory. This copy is independent of the original. When you link a file, you're just creating another name. The fundamental difference between copying files and linking files is that when you copy a file, you're creating a new file. When you link a file, you're only creating a new name; there's still only one file.

COPYING FILES

You can use file redirection to copy a file, as shown in Chapter 2, "The Command Line," but it's not a convenient technique. The command for copying is cp; the synopsis is:

```
cp [-fR] original copy
```

The *original* file is copied to *copy*. (The *copy* argument is sometimes called the "target.")

To copy a file into a directory, use the directory's name as the target. You can copy more than one file into a directory, like so:

```
cp [-fR] original ... targetdirectory
```

The copies have the same file names as the originals, but are in the new directory.

■ *FOR EXAMPLE:*

Your current directory contains the file marilyn and the directory blondes.

```
$ cp marilyn madonna
$ cp marilyn madonna blondes
```

The first command creates a copy of marilyn with the file name madonna. In this form, you're specifying exactly what name the copy will have.

The second command creates copies of *both* files in the directory blondes. The files are named blondes/marilyn and blondes/ madonna.

COPYING DIRECTORIES

If you try to copy a directory, cp prints an error message. To copy a directory, you must use the -R option. (The "R" stands for **r**ecursive.) Some systems also support a -r option, which is similar to -R, but doesn't copy the special files, only regular files and directories.

LINKS

The command to link a file is `ln`. The synopsis is:

```
ln [-s] from to
```

By default, the `ln` command creates *hard links*, alternative names for files. The `-s` option causes it to create *soft links* (also called *symbolic links*).

A hard link is a new name for a file. Each name refers to the same file. A soft link is a new file that *points to* the original file.

LAB 4.5 EXERCISES

4.5.1 COPY A FILE

**LAB
4.5**

Create a file named groucho.

Type the following command:

```
cp groucho gummo
```

a) What does the command do?

_____

_____

Now type the following command:

```
cp groucho gummo harpo
```

b) What happens and why?

_____

_____

4.5.2 COPY FILES INTO A DIRECTORY

Create a directory named `marx`.

Type the following command:

```
cp groucho gummo marx
```

a) What happens?

_____

_____

b) What would the command `cp groucho marx/julius` do?

_____

_____

4.5.3 COPY DIRECTORIES

Type the following command:

```
cp marx ritz
```

a) What happens?

_____

_____

Type the following command:

```
cp -R marx ritz
```

b) What does the `-R` option do?

_____

_____

4.5.4 HARD LINK A FILE

Type the following commands:

```
ln groucho marx/julius
cat groucho
cat marx/julius
```

a) What does the `ln` command do?

_____

_____

Change the `groucho` file by typing the following command:

```
ls >> groucho
```

Type the following command:

```
cat marx/julius
```

b) Why are the file contents the same?

_____

_____

4.5.5 SYMBOLICALLY LINK A DIRECTORY

In your home directory, type the following command:

```
ln -s ~ sink
```

a) What does this command do?

_____

_____

Now, type the following commands:

```
cd sink
ls
pwd
cd sink
ls
pwd
```

b) What happens?

_____

_____

Now, type the following commands:

```
rm sink
pwd
cd ..
cd
```

c) What happened?

_____

_____

LAB 4.5 EXERCISE ANSWERS

 This section gives you some suggested answers to the questions in Lab 4.5, with discussions related to those answers. Your answers may vary, but the most important thing is whether or not your answers work. Use these discussions to analyze differences between your answers and those presented here.

If you have alternative answers to the questions in these exercises, you are encouraged to post your answers and discuss them at the companion Web site for this book, located at:

```
http://www.phptr.com/phptrinteractive
```

4.5.1 ANSWERS

Type the following command:

```
cp groucho gummo
```

a) What does the command do?

Answer: The command creates a copy of the file groucho *named* gummo.

When you copy a file, you're creating a duplicate of the file. You can copy any file you can read, so long as the copy is created in a directory where you can write. The contents of the file and its copy are identical, though the path names will be different.

The information *about* the file will probably be different. For one thing, you always own a copy you create. The permissions on a copy are your default file permissions, no matter what the permissions were on the original. The time of the copy's creation will be different than the original file's time stamp.

The cp command determines what the new name of a file is by looking at the last argument of the cp command line. If the last argument—the target—is a directory name, cp puts the copy in the directory. If the last argument doesn't exist or is the name of a file, then cp uses that name for the new file.

Now type the following command:

```
cp groucho gummo harpo
```

b) What happens and why?

Answer: The command fails. When you specify more than one file, the last argument must be a directory, and the directory must already exist before you can copy files into it.

If there are more than two file names in the command line, the program treats the *last* name as the name of a directory. All of the other files are copied into that directory. If the directory doesn't exist, the command fails.

4.5.2 ANSWERS

Type the following command:

```
cp groucho gummo marx
```

a) What happens?

Answers: The files groucho *and* gummo *are copied into the marx directory.*

When the last argument on the cp command line is the name of an existing directory, all of the other files named in the command are copied into that directory.

b) What would the command cp groucho marx/julius do?

Answer: The command would create a copy of the file groucho *named* julius *in the directory* marx.

In this case, the last argument is a file name, not a directory.

4.5.3 ANSWERS

a) What happens?

Answer: The command fails, because marx *is a directory.*

You cannot simply copy a directory, even an empty one. The cp command doesn't create a copy of a directory, unless you give the -R option.

LAB
4.5

b)   What does the −R option do?

Answer: The −r option causes the entire directory tree under marx *to be copied.*

To copy a directory, you need to specify the −R (recursive) option.

Different UNIX systems behave differently. One of these differences may show up in the cp program distributed with BSD-derived versions of UNIX.

Suppose you have a directory from that contains the file content, and the directory to that is empty. On most UNIX systems, you would expect the command cp −r from/ to to copy the from directory (and its contents) into to. After all, the / character simply confirms that from is a directory.

On some UNIX systems, though, this copies only the file content into to. You expect to create to/from/content, but instead you get to/content.

To copy the directory into b, you need to type the command as cp −r a b.

The difference is how the cp interprets the first directory name. If the first argument ends with a / character, cp. Instead of copying from, it copies the contents of from. It's equivalent to cp from/* to.

4.5.4 ANSWERS

a)   What does the ln command do?

Answer: The ln *command creates a hard link, a new name for the file* groucho.

Though you may not create them yourself, you will use links often, probably without realizing it.

A link lets a file be in two places at once, or have two names at once. Unlike copies, any changes you make to the linked file using one name show up immediately in the file when you look at it using the other name. Hard links are often used to give programs other names. For example, a UNIX program can "know" what its file name is, so the program's name may dictate its behavior. The commands vi and view are the same command, but they behave differently because they have different names. The program contains code that says, "If my name is `vi`, do this, but if my name is `view`, do something else."

The `ln` command has the same structure as the `cp` command when you're copying a single file, as follows:

```
ln original new
```

Change the groucho file by typing the following command:

```
ls >> groucho
```

Now, type the following command:

```
cat marx/julius
```

b) Why are the file contents the same?

Answer: Because `groucho` *and* `marx/julius` *are the same file.*

I have sometimes used a link to keep a copy of an e-mail associated with a project. The e-mail program requires the e-mail to be in a particular directory. I could copy the file, but then I would have to copy it again every time I get or send email related to this project. Instead, I create a hard link to the e-mail file in the project directory. That way, the mail file is handy while I'm working but I never have to worry about updating it. If the e-mail file is ~/Mail/sdk, I can create a link named `project.mail` in the current directory with the following command:

```
ln ~/Mail/sdk project.mail
```

When I add new mail to the file ~/Mail/sdk, it shows up in project.mail.

4.5.5 ANSWERS

In your home directory, type the following command:

```
ln -s ~ sink
```

a) What does this command do?

Answer: The command creates a symbolic link to your home directory; the link is named `sink`.

However, hard links only work on one file system. (In this case, I mean an actual file system device, such as a new hard drive, being added to the UNIX file system.) Suppose your system administrator has added a file system in the directory /network. You cannot hard link a file under the /network directory tree to any location outside of that directory tree. You could not, for example, link /network/examples/vi.5 to the name vi.5 in your home directory. You could hard link it to /network/private/vi.5, because they're both on the same (real) file system.

The other disadvantage of hard links is that you can only link regular files, not directories.

If you need to link across file systems or you need to link a directory, you can use a symbolic link. To create a symbolic link, use the -s option with the ln command. A symbolic link is a special file that points to another file or directory.

There is one peculiarity to the ln -s command: The path name given for the *original* file should be an absolute path name. If it isn't, there's a good chance that a link will be created, but it won't work.

Here's why: When ln -s creates the link file (new), it really creates a file that contains the name of original. If that name, original, is a relative path name, it is taken as relative for any program trying to use the symbolic link. The current directory of that program may not be your current directory when you created the link.

■ FOR EXAMPLE:

Suppose you want the file /projects/update to be a symbolic link to the file status in your home directory. You would type the following command:

```
ln -s status /projects/update
```

The ln command creates the link file /projects/update, and all seems well. But the /projects/update file points to a file named status. When a program tries to open /projects/update, the UNIX system looks inside, sees the name status, and looks for status in the current directory. The current directory of the user running the program might be anywhere on the system. The correct command in this case would be as follows:

```
ln -s /home/you/status /projects/update
```

By supplying an absolute path name, you're making sure that any program can use the link, no matter what its current directory is.

Now, type the following commands:

```
cd sink
ls
pwd
cd sink
ls
pwd
```

b) What happens?

Answer: *Each time you type* `cd sink`, *you add another* `sink` *to your current working directory. Because the* `sink` *link points back to itself, you can keep going into it.*

If symbolic links do things that hard links cannot, why not always use symbolic links? There are two reasons, discussed here and in the next answer.

First, because symbolic links can point to directories, it's very easy to get confused. The exercise showed this clearly: It's easy to set up a circular link. By creating a few symbolic links and moving a few directories, you could easily create entire directory trees as convoluted as pretzels.

Now type the following commands:

```
rm sink
pwd
cd ..
cd
```

c) What happened?

Answer: *The* `cd ..` *command fails, because the directory* `~/sink/sink` *doesn't exist anymore. The current working directory is gone.*

Remember: To remove a symbolic link, use `rm`. *Do not use* `rmdir`, *even if it's a link to a directory.*

The second problem with symbolic links is that they are files that aren't part of what they connect to. A symbolic link can work across file systems because it's just a pointer. It's a detour sign, sending programs to the file they actually want. When you remove the target file, nothing happens to the symbolic link. You can have links that point nowhere.

Imagine this: Because you hate typing the complete path name, you've created a symbolic link in your home directory to the directory where you do most of your real work. That way, instead of typing the complete path name to get to `/projects/xanadu/subproject/Alph/modules/khanate`, you can just type `cd ~/work`. Then the project supervisor, in a fit of zeal, rearranges all of the directories in the `/projects` hierarchy. Your working directory is now `/projects/r+d/coleridge/xanadu/Alpha/khanate`. What happens when you come in to work and type `cd work`?

Nothing, that's what. Suddenly your `work` directory points to nothing. On big systems, this can happen very easily. While reorganizing, the system administrator misses a couple of symbolic links, and suddenly you cannot find anything any more.

When you run across a dead-end symbolic link, let the system administrator know.

Old-time UNIX users refer to symbolic links as a necessary evil. They are useful (even essential) for some tasks, but easy to misuse.

LAB 4.5 SELF-REVIEW QUESTIONS

To test you progress, you should be able to answer the following questions.

1) A copied file has the same permissions as the original.
   a) _____True
   b) _____False

2) Some UNIX programs have more than one name.
   a) _____True
   b) _____False

3) If the last argument in a cp command is a file, there can be more than two file names in the command.
   a) _____True
   b) _____False

4) The contents of a copied file are identical to the original.
   a) _____True
   b) _____False

**LAB
4.5**

5) Which of the following does the command cp laurel hardy do, if both laurel and hardy are directories:
   a) _____It moves laurel into the directory hardy.
   b) _____It copies laurel into the directory hardy.
   c) _____It copies hardy into the directory laurel.
   d) _____It fails because laurel is a directory.

Quiz answers appear in Appendix A, Lab 4.5

L A B 4.6

MOVING AND RENAMING FILES AND DIRECTORIES

LAB OBJECTIVES

After this lab, you will be able to:

✓ Move Files

✓ Move Directories

✓ Rename a File or Directory

The command to move and rename files and directories is mv (for move). Unlike cp, there is only one copy of the file at any time. However, the syntax of the mv command is very similar to the cp command.

There are two forms of the mv command.

■ *FOR EXAMPLE:*

To move one file or directory to a new location, use the following command form:

```
mv originalname newname
```

To move one or more files into a directory that already exists, use this command form:

```
mv file ... directory
```

To rename a file or directory, use the first form of the mv command.

Finally, when moving a directory, you don't need to specify a recursive option, because you're only renaming the directory.

LAB 4.6 EXERCISES

4.6.1 MOVE FILES

Type the following command:

```
mv groucho marx/groucho
```

a) What does the command do?

_____

_____

b) What is the full path name of the file now?

_____

_____

c) What would have happened if the marx directory had not already existed?

_____

_____

4.6.2 MOVE DIRECTORIES

Type the following command:

```
mv marx ritz comics
```

a) What happened?

_____

_____

Create the directory `comics` and repeat the command.

b) What happened this time?

_____

_____

4.6.3 RENAME A FILE OR DIRECTORY

Type the following command:

```
mv comics teams
```

a) What does this command do?

_____

_____

b) Have the permissions on the directory `teams` changed?

_____

_____

LAB 4.6 EXERCISE ANSWERS

 This section gives you some suggested answers to the questions in Lab 4.6, with discussions related to those answers. Your answers may vary, but the most important thing is whether or not your answers work. Use these discussions to analyze differences between your answers and those presented here.

If you have alternative answers to the questions in these exercises, you are encouraged to post your answers and discuss them at the companion Web site for this book, located at:

```
http://www.phptr.com/phptrinteractive
```

4.6.1 ANSWERS

Type the following command:

```
mv groucho marx/groucho
```

a) What does the command do?

Answer: The command moves the file groucho *into the directory* marx, *with the name* groucho. *It replaces the* groucho *file that was already in the directory.*

The command to move a file is very much like the command to copy a file. The two forms of the mv command are the same as the two forms of cp, and some of the options are identical.

- There must be at least two operands, something to move *from* and something to move *to*.
- If there are three or more files or directories named in the command, the last one must be a directory.
- If the last operand is the name of a directory that already exists, all of the other files or directories will be moved into that directory.

If one of the targets of the move operation already exists and you don't have write permission for it, the mv command asks for confirmation (just like cp). And like cp, the mv command has a -f (force) option, which makes it move files without asking for confirmation.

Some versions of mv also have a -i option, which makes mv ask for confirmation before writing over *any* file, whether you have write permission on the target file or not.

b) What is the path name of the file now?

Answer: The path name (relative to the current directory) is marx/groucho.

On UNIX systems, moving a file and renaming a file are the same thing. When you move a file, you're renaming it. You're not actually moving the bits that make up the file, deep in the computer. Instead, you're changing how UNIX finds the file in the system. (This is a side effect of the fact that files can have more than one name.)

c) What would have happened if the marx directory had not already existed?

Answer: The command would have failed.

The mv command doesn't create intermediate directories.

The mv command doesn't necessarily overwrite or replace a file when you rename a file to an existing file name. What mv does instead is make a new link to the existing file and remove the old link (if the new link is in a different directory).

■ FOR EXAMPLE:

Suppose that thismonth and lastmonth are files. After you give the following command, the file thismonth replaces lastmonth.

```
$ mv thismonth lastmonth
```

Now suppose that lastmonth is only one of the names for that file; it's also named June1998. When you move the file thismonth to be lastmonth, the file June1998 doesn't go away, and the information in June1998 doesn't go away, even though the name lastmonth doesn't point to it any more. The information is still there, under the other name.

If you gave something else the name June1998, then the information would have no links pointing to it, and the operating system would get rid of it.

4.6.2 ANSWERS

Type the following command:

```
mv marx ritz comics
```

a) What happened?

Answer: The directories marx *and* ritz *were moved into the directory comics, creating* comics/marx *and* comics/ritz.

When you move a directory, the entire directory and its contents are moved. If the last argument on the command line exists, the directory or directories you're moving are made subdirectories of the target directory.

Create the directory comics and repeat the command.

b) What happened this time?

Answer: The directory comics *was moved into the existing directory* comics, *creating* comics/comics.

While you can rename a file to replace another file, you cannot replace an existing directory. If you really want to replace an existing directory by moving another directory "over top" of it, you have to delete the existing directory first.

4.6.3 ANSWERS

Type the following command:

```
mv comics teams
```

a) What does this command do?

Answer: The command renames the comics *directory to* teams.

In this case, you're really just renaming the directory comics to teams.

b) Have the permissions on the directory `teams` changed?

Answer: No, the permissions on a moved or renamed file do not change.

Like `cp`, you must have write permission on all directories involved to move a file. You don't need write permissions on the file you're moving. With `cp`, the new file has the default file permissions. Unlike `cp`, the permissions on a moved file do *not* change when you `mv` a file.

 You cannot move more than one file and change the names of the files in one command. On DOS, you can. It's possible to type the command `mv *.txt *.new` *and it renames all files with* `.txt` *file extensions to have* `.new` *extensions. This doesn't work on a UNIX system.*

LAB 4.6 SELF-REVIEW QUESTIONS

To test your progress, you should be able to answer the following questions.

1) A moved file gets your default file permissions.
    a) _____True
    b) _____False

2) When you move a file, you're only changing one of the file's links.
    a) _____True
    b) _____False

Quiz answers appear in Appendix A, Lab 4.6.

C H A P T E R   4

TEST YOUR THINKING

The projects in this section are meant to have you utilize all of the skills that you have acquired throughout this chapter. The answers to these projects can be found at the companion Web site to this book, located at:

`http://www.phptr.com/phptrinteractive`

Visit the Web site periodically to share and discuss your answers.

1) Type the command `ls > /dev/tty`. What is the format of the `ls` output? What did you expect to happen? Why?

2) The following listing describes a problem in creating a symbolic link:

```
$ pwd
/home/dana/test
$ ls -p
answers/
$ ln -s answers /tmp/storage
$ cd /tmp/storage
ksh: /tmp/storage: not found
$ ls -l /tmp/storage
lrwxrwxrwx  1 dana   user 4 Apr 18 16:53 /tmp/storage -
  > marx
```

a) What mistake was made in creating the symbolic link?

b) Can you explain what's wrong?

c) How would you fix it?

3) When you give the command mv *.txt *.new, how does the shell actually interpret this command in each of these cases:

a) There is one file that matches the pattern *.txt and no files that match the pattern *.new?

b) More than one file matches the pattern *.txt and no files match *.new?

c) One file matches *.txt and one file matches *.new?

d) Two files match *.txt and two files match *.new?

e) One file matches *.txt and one directory matches *.new?

C H A P T E R 5

FINDING HELP

 The good news is that nearly every UNIX system has on-line documentation. The bad news is that most of it is written by programmers for programmers.

CHAPTER OBJECTIVES

In this chapter, you will learn about:

The standard on-line documentation for UNIX systems is a set of manual pages describing commands, files, and other parts of the system. The pages are called "man pages" for short; you can read them on screen with the man command.

UNIX was one of the first operating systems to have on-line documentation as a standard feature. The man pages were intended as references. They were reminders to the programmers about program options or features that were not often used. Like most reference materials, many of the man pages assume you already know about UNIX and your system in particular. You go to them when you need a specific piece of information, such as "How does this command work?" or "What's the format of that file?"

If the man pages don't answer your question, there are still other sources of information about UNIX; there are books (such as this one), newsgroups, and World Wide Web pages. An easy and reliable way to get help is to ask another user. Visit the Web companion to this book at http://www.phptr.com/phptrinteractive for an on-line community dedicated to all things UNIX.

L A B   5.1

READING ON-LINE HELP WITH THE MAN COMMAND

LAB OBJECTIVES

After this lab, you will be able to:

✓ Read a Manual Page

✓ Specify a Section

✓ Search Other Directories for Man Pages

Asking someone else is a time-honored method of getting information. The obvious person to ask is the system administrator, but he or she is usually quite busy. It's better to search for the answer yourself before you ask for help; that way, you avoid wasting the administrator's time. You also avoid getting your administrator mad at you.

The man command displays subjects from the on-line manual pages. Normally, a subject is a command name, but some man pages are dedicated to other topics. You can only specify one subject at a time.

The man command displays the man pages using the more command. Any commands you can use in more you can also use while reading a manual page.

In the very early days of UNIX systems, there were also some documents intended to give you an overall view of the system. Those papers are not usually shipped any more, because they became obsolete as UNIX grew. Depending on the company selling your version of UNIX, there may be other documentation on your system. For example, UnixWare includes the "Help Desk" with its UNIX systems.

Other programmers have tried to improve on the man *command. One alternative is* xman, *which is supplied with the X Window System. Other alternatives include programs named* adam *(named for the first* man*) and* eve *(because it's an improvement on Adam). If these programs are on your system, you can try them and see if you prefer them. All of them will do at least as much as the* man *command does. You can also refer to Appendix B in this book, which contains references for all of the significant commands discussed in this book.*

The manual pages are stored in several places on the system. The standard location is the directory /usr/share/man. The pages are divided into subdirectories. The subdirectories are named for the reference manual sections—Section 1, Section 2, and so on—based on topic. Commands are in Section 1. If two subjects in different sections have the same name, the one from section 1 is displayed. You can force man to display a subject from a different section with the -s option.

When you specify a subject, the man command looks for a file by that name in the subdirectories of /usr/share/man. If you want the man command to look in a different directory, you can name the directory using the -M option.

■ FOR EXAMPLE:

Your system administrator may have set up a second, site-specific set of man pages in /usr/local/man. It has subdirectories just like the ones in /usr/share/man. To look in /usr/local/man for a man page on the subject *less*, use the following command:

```
man -M /usr/local/man less
```

LAB 5.1 EXERCISES

5.1.1 READ A MANUAL PAGE

Type the following command:

```
man man
```

a) What are the parts of a man page?

_____

_____

Press the Enter key while the man page is displayed.

b) What happens?

_____

_____

Press the Space bar while the man page is displayed.

c) What happens?

_____

_____

Type the following command:

```
/SEE ALSO
```

d) What happens?

_____

_____

Press the Q key while the man page is displayed.

e) What happens?

_____

_____

5.1.2 SPECIFY A SECTION

Type the following commands:

```
man intro
man -s 3 intro
man -s 1 intro
```

a) What does the -s option do? What if there is no -s option given?

_____

_____

b) Try the numbers 1 through 8 (man -s 1 intro, man -s 2 intro, and so on) Your system may not have all of these sections. Record what each section is for:

Section 1 _____

Section 2 _____

Section 3 _____

Section 4 _____

Section 5 _____

Section 6 _____

Section 7 _____

Section 8 _____

c) According to `ls -F`, what subdirectories are in `/usr/share/man`?

_____

_____

5.1.3 SEARCH OTHER DIRECTORIES FOR MAN PAGES

Type the following commands:

```
man -M /usr/X11/man xterm
man -M /usr/X11/man intro
```

a) What does the `-M` option do?

_____

_____

b) Why would you want to be able to search other directories for man pages?

_____

_____

c) What is displayed when you type the following command?

`echo $MANPATH`

_____

_____

LAB 5.1 EXERCISE ANSWERS

 This section gives you some suggested answers to the questions in Lab 5.1, with discussions related to those answers. Your answers may vary, but the most important thing is whether or not your answers work. Use these discussions to analyze differences between your answers and those presented here.

If you have alternative answers to the questions in these exercises, you are encouraged to post your answers and discuss them at the companion Web site for this book, located at:

```
http://www.phptr.com/phptrinteractive
```

5.1.1 ANSWERS

Type the following command:

```
man man
```

When you invoke the `man` command, it looks through the system for a man page by the name you've given. It looks in the subdirectories of `/usr/share/man`, and it may look in other directories.

a)   What are the parts of a man page?

Answer: A man page is composed of many parts, as outlined in Table 5.1.

The basic structure of a man page is shown in Table 5.1. Not all man pages have all sections, and sometimes new sections are invented as needed. (When that happens, it's usually obvious what the section is for.)

Table 5.1 ■ Basic Structure of a Man Page

Name	The name of the command, and a one-line description. Sometimes there is more than one command on a man page; this happens when the command can be called by different names, or when several closely related commands are being described.
Synopsis	The usage line or usage lines for the command. This is in the format described in Chapter 2, "The Command Line."
Description	A description of the command, what it does, and how it works. The description usually describes the options (though these may be in a separate OPTIONS section), and it describes any special requirements for the operands. If the program is particularly complex, or if it has its own commands, this may have subheadings and subsections. (Man pages for shells and editors are typical examples. You might want to look at `man ksh` or `man vi` to see examples of very long man pages.)
Options	If the options aren't described in the DESCRIPTION section, they will be in a separate OPTIONS section.
Return Code	When it finishes, every command gives the shell a number that indicates whether it ran successfully or had problems. That number is the return code. You will never see the return code unless you want to.
Diagnostics	A list of error messages. This section is often left out.
Examples	Examples of the command in use. This section is often left out.
Environment Variables	If the command takes advantage of any environment variables, they're described here. (See Lab 12.2, "Setting Environment Variables," although specific examples appear in this lab and in Chapter 6, "Emergency Recovery.")
Files	If the command uses any special files, these are mentioned here. Usually, they're also described, but the author of the man page may have felt the files were so well known that they didn't need to be documented. This section is left out if the program doesn't use any special files.

Table 5.1 ■ Basic Structure of a Man Page (Continued)

Bugs, Notes, or Notices	A list of problems or special characteristics of the program. You should only need to read this if you're having problems with the command. The BUGS listed here are rarely problems you will encounter; instead, they're design problems. A bug comment might be, "Program is too slow," or "Doesn't understand English very well." A heading other than BUGS is usually more accurate.
See Also or References	A list of man pages (or other documents) that are related to the topic of this one. These references are often useful if the man page you have is not the one you wanted; they are rarely useful if you want more information about the subject of the man page.
Authors	The name of the author, and possibly his or her e-mail address at the time the man page was written. This is often left out.

A man page is a manual entry for a single subject. A subject is usually a command, but it may be a programming item, a file description, or an abstract description of some part of the system. Not all commands have man pages. Even if it's more than a single page (such as the one describing the Korn Shell), it's still referred to as a single man page.

Press the Enter key while the man page is displayed.

b) What happens?

Answer: One more line of the file is displayed.

These answers assume that the system displays the man pages using the more command. Not all systems use more; some use a different pager. Commands to use while running more are listed later in this Lab.

Press the Space bar while the man page is displayed.

c) What happens?

Answer: One more screen of the file is displayed. The top three lines on the screen are the bottom three from the last screen displayed.

Again, this is specific to more. If you're running the pg pager, you can display the next screen of text by pressing Enter. You can display a help screen in pg by pressing h followed by Enter. (pg requires you to follow all commands with Enter.)

Type the following command:

```
/SEE ALSO
```

d) What happens?

Answer: The more *command searches the file for the words "SEE ALSO." If it finds the words, it moves forward in the file to display them.*

Some versions of more display the searched-for words on the top line of the screen, and others display them on the third line.

Press the q key while the man page is displayed.

e) What happens?

Answer: The more *command quits.*

These questions cover the basic commands when reading a file with more. Table 5.2 summarizes them.

Table 5.2 ■ Basic Commands Used with more

h	Display summary of commands
Space	Display next screenful of file
Enter	Display next line of file
q	Quit and return to command prompt
/string	Search for a word or a string of words

The oldest versions of more only let you go forward in a file. Newer versions let you go forward and backwards, so you can go back to the beginning of the man page.

If you have an old version of more on your system, you may want man to use a different command to display man pages. I recommend less, if it's on your system. It allows you to move forward and backward on your system. To get man to use less, you need to set the *PAGER* environment variable in your startup files; this is described in Chapter 12, "Commands and Job Control."

5.1.2 ANSWERS

Type the following commands:

```
man intro
man -s 3 intro
man -s 1 intro
```

a) What does the -s option do? What if there is no -s option given?

Answer: The -s option causes the man command to search a specific section of the reference manual. Without a -s option, man searches Section 1, then Section 2, and so on, until it finds a matching man page.

b) Try the numbers 1 through 8 (man -s 1 intro, man -s 2 intro, and so on). Record what each section is for:

Answer: Each manual section contains reference pages of a certain type, generally referred to by number, 1 through 9 (though some sections are identified by letters or by a number and letter).

The actual meanings of the section names depend on the version of UNIX you have. For Solaris, the sections are as shown in Table 5.3. You'll notice that on Solaris systems, there are no sections numbered 8 and 9.

Table 5.3 ■ Solaris Manual Sections

1	Commands and utilities
2	System calls
3	Programming library calls
4	File formats
5	Miscellaneous information
6	Games
7	Device descriptions

Some system administrators also add sections with letter names, such as l (for "local," meaning commands that have been installed on this system only), or n (for "network").

Unless you intend to become a programmer, you will probably only be concerned with sections 1 and 6. (Many systems no longer install games or the Section 6 manual pages.)

References to man pages are frequently followed by a number in parentheses, such as *man*(1), or *rogue*(6). The number is the manual section, rather like the chapter of the reference manual. The man page for man is in Section 1; the man page for rogue is in Section 6.

c) According to ls -F, what subdirectories are in /usr/share/man?

Answer: The answer depends on how your administrator has set up the system, but you should find:
```
cat1    cat2    cat3    cat4    cat5    cat7
```
You may also find cat6, *if the games are installed, or* cat8, *if you have a system modeled after BSD UNIX.*

These directories contain the formatted man pages displayed by man. After you type man man, the man command runs the command more / usr/share/man/cat1/man.1. (Again, some systems might use a different command than more, but they will use a pager command to display the man page.)

The man command requires the cat? subdirectories. It won't work if they aren't there.

The files in the subdirectories usually have the same extension as the section: cat1 contains files with the extension .1; cat5 contains files with the extension .5. Again, there are exceptions: On some systems, all formatted man pages have the extension .0.

There may also be a set of directories named man1 through man7. These are the files used to create the formatted man pages; you will probably never refer to them directly, and they are often not installed.

You might be able to view man pages directly from the cat? subdirectories. However, you might not. To save space, some vendors ship their documentation in a compressed format, and the man command unpacks it from this format.

5.1.3 ANSWERS

Type the following commands:

```
man -M /usr/X11/man xterm
man -M /usr/X11/man intro
```

a) What does the -M option do?

Answer: The -M option tells man to search in the directory /usr/X11/man *for man pages instead of in the directory* /usr/share/man.

The exact behavior of the -M option differs between systems. On most systems, the -M option tells man to search the specified directory *first*, before looking in /usr/share/man. If this is the case on your system, the command man -M /usr/X11/man man displayed the man page for man.

On other systems, the -M option tells man to look *only* in the specified directory. If this is the case on your system, the command man -M /usr/X11/man man displayed an error message.

Some systems have it both ways: They have a -M and a -m option. The -M causes man to look *only* in the specified directory, while the -m causes man to look in the specified directory *first*.

b) Why would you want to be able to search other directories for man pages?

Answer: Different software packages may install their man pages in directories other than /usr/share/man.

For example, the X Window System man pages are installed in /usr/X11/man. You might want to write and install your own man pages in a directory you own; with the -M option, you can display them as you would any other man page.

c) What is displayed when you type the following command?

```
echo $MANPATH
```

Answer: The actual answer depends on your system.

Like the -M option to man, the *MANPATH* environment variable lists directories that man should search for man pages. The man command always searches these directories; you don't need to supply an option.

You may not have the *MANPATH* environment variable set. If you don't, then man searches the directory /usr/share/man. If you do have it set, it's a list of directories separated by colons, like this:

```
/usr/share/man:/usr/local/man:/usr/X11/man
```

In this example, the man command looks for a man page first in the sub-directories of /usr/share/man, then in the subdirectories of /usr/local/man, and last in the subdirectories of /usr/X11/man.

If you give the -M option *and* you have the *MANPATH* environment variable set, the -M option is followed.

LAB 5.1 SELF-REVIEW QUESTIONS

To test your progress, you should be able to answer the following questions.

1) The man command displays man pages with the more command.
  a) _____True
  b) _____False

2) When reading a man page, there is no way to quit except by pressing the Space bar until you get to the end.
  a) _____True
  b) _____False

3) The operand for the man command is always a command name.
  a) _____True
  b) _____False

4) If you don't specify a section number, the man command only searches Section 1.
  a) _____True
  b) _____False

5) The first section of a man page lists the subject and a one-line description.
  a) _____True
  b) _____False

Quiz answers appear in Appendix A, Lab 5.1.

L A B   5.2

FINDING THE RIGHT MAN PAGE

LAB OBJECTIVES

After this lab, you will be able to:

✓ Find Related Commands

✓ Describe a Command

There are hundreds of man pages on a UNIX system. Finding the right man page can be difficult.

UNIX systems provide two ways for you to search through the man pages. Both make use of the one-line descriptions under the "NAME" heading.

The first searches through the one-line descriptions for a word or phrase. The second displays the one-line description for a command.

To search for a word or phrase, use the -k option to the man command. On some systems, the command is known as apropros; if the man -k command doesn't work, try apropros.

To see the one-line description for a specific subject, use the -f option to the man command. On the same systems that use apropros, the command is known as whatis. If the man -f command doesn't work, try whatis.

LAB 5.2 EXERCISES

5.2.1 FIND RELATED COMMANDS

Type the following command:

```
man -k intro | more
```

a) Looking at the results, what do the lines have in common?

_____

_____

b) Why pipe the results through more?

_____

_____

5.2.2 DESCRIBE A COMMAND

Type the following command:

```
man -f man
```

a) Compare that output with the man man output. What does the man -f option do?

_____

_____

LAB 5.2 EXERCISE ANSWERS

This section gives you some suggested answers to the questions in Lab 5.2, with discussions related to those answers. Your answers may vary, but the most important thing is whether or not your answers work. Use these discussions to analyze differences between your answers and those presented here.

If you have alternative answers to the questions in these exercises, you are encouraged to post your answers and discuss them at the companion Web site for this book, located at:

```
http://www.phptr.com/phptrinteractive
```

5.2.1 ANSWERS

Type the following command:

```
man -k intro | more
```

The `man -k` *keyword* command searches the one-line summaries of the system man pages for a specific *keyword*. It prints all of the one-line descriptions to the screen.

(In fact, the `man` command doesn't even search the man pages; the one-line summaries have already been stored in a file named `/usr/share/man/whatis`. There should be a `whatis` file in every directory tree searched by `man`.)

a) Looking at the results, what do the lines have in common?

Answer: All of the lines contain the string "intro" whether it's a separate word or part of a word.

When you specify a keyword, `man` searches not only for that word, but any word that *contains* that word. The command `man -k man` displays any man page that has the word "man" in its description, and it displays any page that has the letters "man," including the words "command," "mandatory," "manageable," and—if there's a description containing it—"mandolin."

Some versions of man allow the keyword to be a regular expression, which gives you more control. (Regular expressions are the topic of Chapter 8.) If your version of man allows this, you will have much more flexibility in using man -k.

The limitation of man -k is that it searches *only* the one-line descriptions. Even if you provide a keyword that correctly describes what you want, man -k only displays it if that keyword is in the one-line description.

b)   Why pipe the results through more?

Answer: Depending on the keyword, there could be dozens or hundreds of lines displayed. The more *command "captures" this output and displays it to you one screen at a time.*

For example, the command man -k a will easily overflow your screen, because many of the descriptions contain the letter "a."

The key to using man -k is to be selective in your choice of keywords, and to use the results to track down the command you want.

5.2.2 ANSWERS

Type the following command:

```
man -f man
```

a)   Compare that output with the man man **output. What does the** man -f **option do?**

Answer: It displays the one-line description for the man *command.*

The command man -f man is useful if you want a reminder of what a particular command does.

The man -f command also searches the whatis file. If there is no whatis file in the directory being searched (either in /usr/share/man, or the directories specified with -M or *MANPATH*), the man -f and man -k commands won't find anything.

■ *FOR EXAMPLE:*

You may need to poke around before you find exactly what you want. Suppose you want a command to show the current time. Using man -k yields the following (this list is shortened from the actual results):

```
$ man -k time
at, batch (1) - execute a command at a specified time
clock (3) - report CPU time used
crontab (5) - table of times to run periodic jobs
profil (2) - execution time profile
time (1) - time a command
time (3) - get date and time
times (3) - get process times
touch (1) - update file's access/modification times
uptime (1) - show how long the system has been up
```

Trying the time command doesn't work; it prints a usage message. The time(3) man page doesn't list a user command (Section 3 is functions for programmers), but the SEE ALSO section may list commands that use the function for getting a date and time.

You type:

```
$ man -s 3 time
/SEE ALSO
```

The SEE ALSO section contains these references:

```
date(1), ctime(3), tzone(5)
```

The date command is a user command (it's in Section 1). By reading the date man page, you can learn that while it will set a date and time, it also shows the current date and time:

```
$ man -f date
date (1) - print and set the date
$ date
Sat Apr 25 1998 19:25:33 EST
```

The `man -k time` command doesn't find the `date` command because the word "time" isn't in the description; it's in the rest of the man page.

LAB 5.2 SELF-REVIEW QUESTIONS

To test your progress, you should be able to answer the following questions.

1) The `man -k` command searches all of the man pages on the system.
   a) _____True
   b) _____False

2) The `man -k` and `man -f` commands can only show you the information from the one-line descriptions.
   a) _____True
   b) _____False

Quiz answers appear in Appendix A, Lab 5.2.

LAB 5.3

XMAN FOR THE X WINDOWS SYSTEM

LAB OBJECTIVES

After this lab, you will be able to:

✓ Start Xman

✓ Browse the Man Pages

✓ Read a Man Page

Many people find the X Windows xman program to be an easier way to find and read man pages than the man command.

To run this lab, you must be at a terminal running the X Window System. The X Window System is the topic of Chapter 13.

LAB 5.3 EXERCISES

5.3.1 START XMAN

Type the following command:

```
xman   &
```

Click on the Manual Page button.

a) What happens?

_____

_____

5.3.2 BROWSE THE MAN PAGES

Position the pointer over the Options button and hold down the left mouse button.

Move the pointer down to Display Directory and release the button.

a) What happens?

_____

_____

Click on the scroll bar.

b) What happens?

_____

_____

Click on a subject.

    c) What happens?

_____

_____

5.3.3 READ A MAN PAGE

With a man page displayed, press the Space bar.

    a) What happens?

_____

_____

Press the b key.

    b) What happens?

_____

_____

Position the pointer over the Options button and hold down the left mouse button.

Move the pointer down to Quit and release the button.

    c) What happens?

_____

_____

LAB 5.3 EXERCISE ANSWERS

This section gives you some suggested answers to the questions in Lab 5.3, with discussions related to those answers. Your answers may vary, but the most important thing is whether or not your answers work. Use these discussions to analyze differences between your answers and those presented here.

If you have alternative answers to the questions in these exercises, you are encouraged to post your answers and discuss them at the companion Web site for this book, located at:

`http://www.phptr.com/phptrinteractive`

The xman command provides a graphical way to list all of the available man pages in a section. This is one of its biggest advantages.

5.3.1 ANSWERS

Type the following command:

    xman &

The & character causes the command xman to run in the background: Even though the xman command has not finished, the command prompt appears in your xterm window. Without the & character, you could not enter other commands in the xterm window until you quit using xman. It's good practice to run most X Window System commands in the background.

The starting point for the xman command is the three-button box shown in Figure 5.1.

Click on the Manual Page button.

a)   What happens?
   Answer: Clicking on the Manual Page button causes xman *to display a man page.*

The default starting man page is the help file for xman itself, shown in Figure 5.2. (This is the help file for xman, not the man page for xman.)

Figure 5.1 ■ Xman starting box

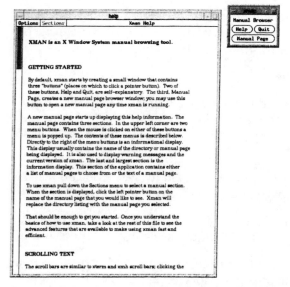

Figure 5.2 ■ Xman default help screen

Just like man, the xman command searches all of the directories mentioned in the *MANPATH* environment variable. If the *MANPATH* variable
isn't set, the xman command searches /usr/share/man.

5.3.2 ANSWERS

Position the pointer over the Options button and hold down the left mouse button.

The xman command offers the options listed in Table 5.4.

Table 5.4 ■ Xman **Command Options**

Display Directory	Displays the list of man pages in this manual section.
Display Manual Page	Changes the window to display the manual page selected in the directory window. If no manual page is selected, xman shows the xman help file.
Help	Displays the xman help file.
Show Both Screens	Splits the window so the top half shows the directory and the bottom half shows the man page. You can use the mouse to move the dividing line, making one larger and the other smaller.
Search	Displays a window with a field for text. You can search for a man page or do a keyword search.
Remove This Man Page	Clears away the current man page window. If there is only one man page window, selecting this quits xman.
Open New Man Page	Opens another man page window. This feature lets you have two man pages displayed at once, which isn't possible with man.
Show Version	Displays the version number of the program.
Quit	Quits xman.

Move the pointer down to Display Directory and release the button.

a) What happens?

Answer: Selecting the Display Directory menu item causes xman *to show the list of man pages in Section 1.*

Click on the scroll bar.

b) What happens?

Answer: Clicking on the scroll bar with the left mouse button scrolls down through the directory window. Clicking on the scroll bar with the right mouse button scrolls up through the directory window.

Clicking and holding on the gray bar with the middle mouse button (if your mouse has one) lets you move the gray bar either forward or backward through the directory window.

Click on a subject.

c) What happens?

Answer: The directory window is replaced by the man page.

5.3.3 ANSWERS

With a man page displayed, press the Space bar.

a) What happens?

Answer: The Space bar displays the next screenful of text, just as in the man *command.*

Press the b key.

b) What happens?

Answer: The b *key moves backward through the file: It displays the previous screenful of text.*

You can also use the scroll bar, just as with the directory window, but the Space bar and the b key don't work for the directory window.

Position the pointer over the Options button and hold down the left mouse button.
Move the pointer button down to Quit and release the button.

c) What happens?

Answer: Selecting Quit exits the xman *program.*

You can also exit by clicking on the Quit button in the original three-button box.

LAB 5.3 SELF-REVIEW QUESTIONS

To test your progress, you should be able to answer the following questions.

1) The xman uses the *MANPATH* environment variable, just like the man command.
    a) _____True
    b) _____False

2) The xman command can be used on any UNIX system.
    a) _____True
    b) _____False

3) You can quit an xman session by pressing the Q key while reading a man page.
    a) _____True
    b) _____False

4) The xman command allows you to display all of the Section 1 man pages from several directories.
    a) _____True
    b) _____False

Quiz answers appear in Appendix A, Lab 5.3.

C H A P T E R   5

TEST YOUR THINKING

The projects in this section are meant to have you utilize all of the skills that you have acquired throughout this chapter. The answers to these projects can be found at the companion Web site to this book, located at:

`http://www.phptr.com/phptrinteractive`

Visit the Web site periodically to share and discuss your answers.

1) Write your own version of the man man page. (You may need to use an editor first. The vi text editor are discussed in Chapter 9.) Remember that one of the goals is to have the information easy to find. Remember also that it has to be accurate as well, so test your claims against the actual program. While writing it, consider the following:

   a) What sections will you include? For example, do you need to describe environment variables? Will you create new sections?

   b) What sections will you exclude?

   c) Would it be worthwhile to abandon the traditional format altogether? Why or why not?

2) What is the best way to install it on the system? Consider the following:

   a) Which section should it be in?

   b) Which directory should it be installed in?

   c) What will the file name be?

3) How will you view it? How will you allow others to view it?

CHAPTER 6

EMERGENCY RECOVERY

This chapter is about problems and how to fix them. Although sometimes the computer may seem to be out to get you, it isn't. Really.

A computer and its operating system are complicated things. Even if you know all parts of the system, it might still behave in ways you cannot predict. Sometimes the cause of a problem is simple, such as a mistyped line. Sometimes the problem is quirky, such as a missing prompt. And sometimes a command doesn't work the way you expect. But if you understand a problem, you're halfway to fixing it. This chapter is all about helping you understand problems and getting yourself out of "sticky situations."

L A B 6.1

GETTING BACK TO THE COMMAND PROMPT

LAB OBJECTIVES

After this lab, you will be able to:

✓ Restore Prompt with End-Of-File

✓ Restore Prompt by Closing a Quotation

Sometimes the command prompt disappears or changes, and you don't know how to get back to the prompt. There are four common reasons, in roughly this frequency:

- **The command hasn't finished running yet.** The solution is to wait.
- **The command is expecting input from standard input.** The solution is to provide input from the keyboard. If you intended to redirect input but didn't, you can send the end-of-file indicator and rerun the command correctly.
- **The shell isn't ready yet to interpret the command.** This usually occurs because the Enter at the end of the command line is escaped somehow. The solution is to end the command so it can be interpreted.
- **There is a problem with the program or the system.** The solution is to send an interrupt signal and try again.

How long should you wait before trying one of these approaches? It depends on the command and how busy the system is.

If it's a command you've never run before, or it's a sorting or printing command, be patient. You don't know how long a new command should take to run, and sorting and printing commands are often slow.

If all of your commands are running slowly (for instance, `ls` takes several seconds to display the directory contents), then the system is slow, and you should be patient.

If the system is not slow, and you know the command should be quick—or you look at the command line on the screen and see that you've forgotten to name the file or to close a quotation—then end it using one of these techniques.

LAB 6.1 EXERCISES

6.1.1 RESTORE PROMPT WITH END-OF-FILE

Type the following command:

```
cat > output
```

a) What does the command prompt look like?

_____

_____

Press Control-D.

b) What happens?

_____

_____

c) What does the output file contain?

_____

_____

6.1.2 RESTORE PROMPT BY CLOSING A QUOTATION

Type the following command:

```
echo Don't ever use a single apostrophe
```

a) What does the prompt look like?

_____

_____

Type an ′ and press Enter.

b) What happens?

_____

_____

Type the following command:

```
echo Don\'t ever use a single apostrophe.
```

c) What happens?

_____

_____

LAB 6.1 EXERCISE ANSWERS

 This section gives you some suggested answers to the questions in Lab 6.1, with discussions related to those answers. Your answers may vary, but the most important thing is whether or not your answers work. Use these discussions to analyze differences between your answers and those presented here.

If you have alternative answers to the questions in these exercises, you are encouraged to post your answers and discuss them at the companion Web site for this book, located at:

```
http://www.phptr.com/phptrinteractive
```

6.1.1 ANSWERS

Type the following command:

```
cat > output
```

a)   What does the command prompt look like?

Answer: There is no prompt.

This is typical of a command waiting for input. You can identify this mistake by looking at the command line and checking for the file operand. If the file was forgotten, the command is probably waiting for input from the keyboard.

Press Control-D.

b)   What happens?

Answer: The command prompt appears.

The Control-D character causes or marks the end of interactive input for commands such as cat. Once the file has ended, the cat command is finished reading standard input, it exits, and the command is finished.

Like many other commands, `cat` can take file names as arguments. The files contain the program's input. When the file names are left out of the command, the input comes from the keyboard (the standard input).

It's possible, though unlikely, that Control-D is not your end of file indicator. This is mentioned in Lab 6.5.

c) **What does the `output` file contain?**

Answer:The `output` file contains nothing, because the first input after starting the command was an interactive end of file.

If you had typed any other text or commands before the Control-D, those would be recorded in the file.

Entering Control-D is the quickest and most convenient way to end a program waiting for standard input. It doesn't interfere with a properly running program, and it ends a program waiting for standard input with a minimum of fuss.

6.1.2 ANSWERS

Type the following command:

```
echo Don't ever use a single apostrophe
```

a) **What does the prompt look like?**

Answer:The prompt has changed from a "$" or "%'"sign to a ">" character.

This secondary prompt is the shell's way of telling you that the previous command was not finished.

Type an ` ` ` and press Enter.

b) **What happens?**

Answer:The command prints the following:

```
$ echo Don't ever use a single apostrophe
> '
Don't ever use a single apostrophe

$
```

Pressing Enter is normally the cue for the shell to read a command, interpret it, and run it. The apostrophe mark escapes the special meaning of pressing Enter. (This is called "quoting" and is one way to escape shell metacharacters.) Instead, the new line becomes part of the command. By typing another apostrophe mark, you end the quotation. The next time you press Enter, the shell interprets it correctly, and runs the command.

The `echo` command repeats its arguments, and in this case, the new line is one of the arguments.

Type the following command:

```
echo Don\'t ever use a single apostrophe.
```

c) What happens?

Answer:The command prints out the following:

```
$ echo Don\'t ever use a single apostrophe.
Don't ever use a single apostrophe.
$
```

In this case, the special meaning of the apostrophe is turned off by the \ character.

Double quotation marks (") are slightly different; they're "weaker" than apostrophes. Inside apostrophes, *all* shell metacharacters are escaped, but inside double quotation marks, only *some* are escaped.

■ *FOR EXAMPLE:*

The \ character, apostrophes, and double quotation marks all escape shell metacharacters, but in slightly different ways. The word $TERM\ contains two metacharacters, $ and \.

```
$ echo $TERM\

xterm
```

The shell treats both as special: The $ tells it to print the value of TERM, and the \ escapes the new line.

```
$ echo \$TERM\\
$TERM\
```

The backslash turns off (or escapes) the special meanings of both $ and \.

```
$ echo '$TERM\'
$TERM\
```

Inside the apostrophes, the special meanings of $ and \ are ignored.

```
$ echo "$TERM\"
> "
xterm"
```

Inside the double quotations, the special meaning of the new line is ignored, but the special meanings of $ and \ are not. The \ before " turns off the special meaning of the closing quotation mark, so another quotation mark must be typed.

LAB 6.1 SELF-REVIEW QUESTIONS

To test your progress, you should be able to answer the following questions.

1) The characters ' and " are shell metacharacters.
    a) _____True
    b) _____False

2) The shell uses a different prompt to indicate a command that continues onto a new line.
    a) _____True
    b) _____False

3) Which of the following reasons for a missing command prompt is false?
    a) _____The command takes a long time to execute.
    b) _____The command is expecting input from the keyboard.
    c) _____The command ended with a single backslash character.
    d) _____The entire command line was surrounded by apostrophes.

Quiz answers appear in Appendix A, Lab 6.1.

L A B   6.2

WHICH COMMAND ARE YOU RUNNING?

LAB OBJECTIVES

After this lab, you will be able to:

✓ Display your PATH

✓ Use command to Find a Program

✓ Use type to Find a Program

Sometimes you run a command and the results are not what you expect. Perhaps the command doesn't work at all, and prints a usage line that utterly disagrees with the usage line in the man page. Or perhaps the command works but not correctly.

You may get results you don't expect because you're not running the program you think you're running. This is especially common on systems that have both System V and BSD versions of commands, and on systems where the administrator likes to install customized versions of standard commands. It can also happen when someone else "fixes" your environment so you can use a particular program; that kind of fix can have side effects.

To understand why a command isn't working correctly, you have to make sure you're running the correct command.

When you type a command name, you don't have to type the complete path name (though you can if you want). The shell keeps three lists of commands:

1. The first is a list of customized commands you have set up, called aliases and functions.
2. The second list consists of commands that are actually part of the shell; the shell can just run these commands without looking for another program. These commands are called *built-ins*.
3. The third list is a list of directories, called the *PATH*. When you type a command, if a command is not an alias or a built-in the shell searches through those directories, looking for the command. It runs the first program it finds that has the same name as the command. In your *PATH*, the directory names are separated by colon characters (:), not by spaces.

You can display your *PATH* with the command

```
echo $PATH
```

Commands are normally in the directories:

```
/bin
/usr/bin
/usr/local/bin
/usr/ucb
/usr/X11/bin
```

You should check into commands that are located in other directories. A command in a user's home directory is particularly suspicious.

A command to determine which program a command actually runs is so useful that it's been invented more than once. Depending on your system, you may have one, two, three, or all four of these commands:

- The command command runs a command; If there is a function with the same name as a program, command makes sure that the program is run, not the function. The -v option displays how the shell interprets the command name.
- The type command is built into the Bourne and Korn Shells and tells you how the shell interprets a command

name. If the command name is interpreted as a program name, it displays the path of the program.

- The whence command is part of the Korn Shell, and displays the full path name of a command, or tells you if it's a function, an alias, or a built-in command of the shell.
- The which command is found on systems that have BSD UNIX programs. Like whence, it displays the full path name of a command. There are two important differences between which and type or whence. The which command only finds programs; it doesn't tell you if the command is also a shell function or alias. If which fails, it lists the directories it searched, but type and whence do not.

LAB 6.2 EXERCISES

6.2.1 DISPLAY YOUR PATH

Type the following command:

```
echo $PATH
```

a) What directories are listed?

_____

_____

Suppose your *PATH* were as follows:

```
/usr/local/bin:/bin:/usr/ucb
```

Next, you type the command ls.

b) Which of the following would get run:

_____

_____

```
/usr/local/bin/ls,
```

or

```
/bin/ls
```

6.2.2 USE COMMAND TO FIND A PROGRAM

The command command is not on all systems.

Type the following commands:

```
command -v vi
command -v noprogrambythisname
```

a) If the command worked, what is the path of the vi command?

_____

_____

b) What happens when the command doesn't exist?

_____

_____

6.2.3 USE TYPE TO FIND A PROGRAM

The type command is part of the Bourne and Korn shells, and can only be used if you are using one of those shells. (If you are not using those shells, use which instead.)

Type the following commands:

```
type vi
type noprogrambythisname
```

a) What happens when the command doesn't exist?

_____

_____

LAB 6.2 EXERCISE ANSWERS

 This section gives you some suggested answers to the questions in Lab 6.2, with discussions related to those answers. Your answers may vary, but the most important thing is whether or not your answers work. Use these discussions to analyze differences between your answers and those presented here.

If you have alternative answers to the questions in these exercises, you are encouraged to post your answers and discuss them at the companion Web site for this book, located at:

`http://www.phptr.com/phptrinteractive`

6.2.1 ANSWERS

Type the following command:

    echo $PATH

a) What directories are listed?

Answer:The answers vary with each system, but a typical PATH *might be:*

    /usr/local/bin:/bin:/usr/bin:/usr/ucb:/usr/X11/bin

When the shell looks for a program, it looks first in the directory /usr/local/bin, then in /bin, then in /usr/bin, then in /usr/ucb, and last in /usr/X11/bin.

Remember that the directory /usr/local/bin is often used for commands that are unique to your system. They are not standard, or they are nonstandard versions of programs. If a command is not behaving in the way you expect, you might be running a nonstandard version instead of the regular version.

The *PATH* may end with a colon. That indicates the shell should last look in your current directory, whatever it is.

Some UNIX experts feel it's bad to automatically search your current directory; others think it's only bad to search your current directory first. The problem is if you're in a directory containing a program or script, you might end up running a version of a program you didn't expect. On the other hand, this could happen if you mistype a command. My recommendation is that you not include the current directory in your *PATH*.

The only time it is an advantage or a problem is if you're going into directories where someone keeps programs or scripts. In that case, you don't want to be surprised by running a program you didn't expect. If you do need to run a program in the current directory, you can do it by starting the program name with ./.

Suppose your *PATH* were as follows:

```
/usr/local/bin:/bin:/usr/ucb
```

Next, you type the command ls.

b) Which of the following would get run:

```
/usr/local/bin/ls,
```

or

```
/bin/ls
```

Answer:The shell searches the directories in the PATH *from left to right; the version of* ls *in* /usr/local/bin *would get run, not the version in* /bin. *The only way to run the version in* /bin *would be to give the absolute path name:* /bin/ls.

6.2.2 ANSWERS

Type the following commands:

```
command -v vi
command -v noprogrambythisname
```

a)   If the command worked, what is the path of the `vi` command?

Answer: The `vi` *command is probably* `/usr/bin/vi`.

The `vi` command might be installed in a different directory.

b)   What happens when the command doesn't exist?

Answer: The `command` *command doesn't display any other error information when the command doesn't exist.*

The `which` command displays the list of directories it searched, but the `command` command doesn't provide that information. For example:

```
$ which noprogrambythisname
no noprogrambythisname in /bin /usr/bin /usr/X11/bin
    /usr/contrib/bin /usr/games /usr/local/bin
```

6.2.3 ANSWERS

Type the following commands:

```
type vi
type noprogrambythisname
```

a)   What happens when the command doesn't exist?

Answer: The `type` *command doesn't display any other error information when the command doesn't exist.*

The `type` command, like `command`, doesn't provide a lot of extra information.

LAB 6.2 SELF-REVIEW QUESTIONS

To test your progress, you should be able to answer the following questions.

1) To find a command, the shell looks first through the directories listed in your *PATH*.

    a) _____True

    b) _____False

2) Not everyone has the same *PATH*.

    a) _____True

    b) _____False

3) Some commands, such as `type`, are built into the shell.

    a) _____True

    b) _____False

4) If you have two commands with the same name, and one is a shell built-in and the other is a program that can be found along your *PATH*, which one gets run?

    a) _____The built-in

    b) _____The program

5) How can you run a program in your current directory, if your current directory is not listed in your *PATH*?

    a) _____Give the absolute path name of the program.

    b) _____Precede the command name with . /.

    c) _____Add a : to the end of your *PATH* to include the current directory.

    d) _____Add the full path name of your current directory to include it in your *PATH*.

    e) _____All of the above.

Quiz answers appear in Appendix A, Lab 6.2.

L A B   6.3

INTERRUPT A RUNAWAY PROGRAM

LAB OBJECTIVES

After this lab, you will be able to:

✓ Interrupt with a Signal

✓ List Your Processes

✓ Kill a Process

You can interrupt a program by sending an interrupt character. This is usually Control-C, but some systems used the Delete key; you can set the key-combination using `stty`. The interrupt character sends an "interrupt" signal to the program. (A running program is referred to as a *process*.)

The interrupt signal ends a program abruptly. Normally, a command "cleans up" after itself when it quits. An interrupted program may not do this. It's common for your terminal to behave oddly after interrupting a program that asks for keyboard input, such as a mail program or an editor.

The interrupt signal only ends the current process. Remember, you can run more than one program at a time; the interrupt signal has no effect on other programs running "in the background," or in another `xterm` window.

To interrupt a background process, use the `kill` command. A background process is one that isn't using the terminal. You start it and while it runs, you can still use the terminal to run other programs. To make a program a background process, add "&" after the command. (Background processes are discussed in more detail in Chapter 12, "Commands and Job Control.")

Because the process isn't visible at the terminal (that's why it's a background process), the interrupt character won't work. It only sends a signal to the command that's running at the terminal.

You need two things: A way to send the signal (the `kill` command), and a way to identify the process you want to kill. The command name isn't enough to identify the process, because you could be running the same command more than once at the same time (maybe in different windows).

Every process has an ID number, called the process ID or the PID. Use the `kill` command to send the signal, and use the `ps` command (for "process status") to identify the program.

■ FOR EXAMPLE:

The `ps` command lists information about the programs you are currently running.

```
$ ps
   PID   TTY       TIME CMD
   8321  pts000    0:00 ps
   8078  pts000    0:00 ksh
```

The first column, PID, is the process ID. The last column, CMD, is the actual command being run. If there had been arguments to the commands, they would have been shown too. The TTY field is the name of the terminal the program is running at. (Some processes aren't running on terminals and have "?" in that field.) The TIME is the length of time the program has been running. In this case, neither program has been running for even a second.

To terminate a program, type `kill` *pid*.

The `kill` command can send other signals. The option `-9` sends a much more urgent "die" signal to a process. You may need to use `kill -9` *pid* if the basic `kill` command fails.

LAB 6.3 EXERCISES

6.3.1 INTERRUPT WITH A SIGNAL

The `sleep` command does nothing except wait for as many seconds as you specify.

Type the following command:

```
sleep 100
```

Next, type Control-C.

a) What happens?

_____

_____

b) Can you imagine any side effects to interrupting a program?

_____

_____

6.3.2 LIST YOUR PROCESSES

Type the following commands:

```
sleep 120 &
ps
```

(If you don't see the `ps` command, use `ps -a` instead.)

a) What is a PID?

_____

_____

b) Why use a number instead of the program name?

_____

_____

c) What is the process ID of the `sleep` command? What about the `ps` command?

_____

_____

Type the following command:

```
ps -el | grep yourloginname
```

(If `ps -el` doesn't work on your system, try `ps -ax` instead.)

d) Are the same commands displayed, or more, or fewer?

_____

_____

e) What is the PID of the `ps` command this time?

_____

_____

6.3.3 KILL A PROCESS

Type the following command:

```
sleep 100 &
```

Use ps to get the PID of the sleep command.

Type the following command:

```
kill -1 pid
```

a) What happens?

_____

_____

Press the Enter key.

b) What is displayed?

_____

_____

LAB 6.3 EXERCISE ANSWERS

This section gives you some suggested answers to the questions in Lab 6.3, with discussions related to those answers. Your answers may vary, but the most important thing is whether or not your answers work. Use these discussions to analyze differences between your answers and those presented here.

If you have alternative answers to the questions in these exercises, you are encouraged to post your answers and discuss them at the companion Web site for this book, located at:

```
http://www.phptr.com/phptrinteractive
```

6.3.1 ANSWERS

Type the following command:

```
sleep 100
```

Type Control-C.

a) What happens?

Answer: The command prompt returns. The Control-C key combination sends the "interrupt" signal to the process; the process is interrupted and stops.

Actually, the Control-C key combination sends the "interrupt" character, which is turned into an interrupt signal. The distinction is important because not all programs can be stopped with a Control-C. Whether a program can be stopped by the interrupt key combination depends on the terminal mode. The terminal mode determines how the system interprets control characters.

A UNIX program can let the terminal handle key combinations such as Control-C. The terminal turns Control-C into the interrupt signal. (Some UNIX documentation refers to this as "cooked" mode, because the keys you type are being treated before getting passed to the program; other documentation calls it "canonical" mode.)

However, a UNIX program can also ask the terminal to pass all key combinations without changing them. (This mode is called "raw" mode, or "noncanonical" mode.) Editor programs often do this; Control-C may mean "close a window" instead of "interrupt this program." In this case, it's the program's responsibility to handle any key combinations.

To interrupt a program in raw mode, you need to use the built-in interrupt command (if the program has one) or you need to use the `kill` command.

6.3.2 ANSWERS

Type the following commands:

```
sleep 120 &
ps
```

a) What is a PID?

Answer: To identify a running program, you need to know its process identification number, or PID. Every program has a unique PID. The PID is the first or second column of ps *output (depending on the version of* ps *you're using).*

On some systems, you need to use the -a ("all processes") flag to include the ps command in the output.

■ *FOR EXAMPLE:*

```
$ ps
   PID  TTY       TIME CMD
  8812  pts000    0:00 ps
  8078  pts000    0:00 ksh
```

In this output, the PID is the left-most column. The ps process has the process ID of 8812. The Korn shell process has the process ID of 8078.

b) What is the process ID of the sleep command? What about the ps command?

Answer: The actual value changes each time you run the command. There are only so many process ID numbers to go around (although there are far more than can run at any one time). When the highest number has been used, it starts back again at the lower numbers. The lowest process ID numbers are reserved. Process 0, for instance, is always the first process, the one that starts the operating system.

The information that ps displays is only a snapshot of the system. As soon as ps stops running, the information becomes slightly out of date. Still, the information it presents is usually good enough.

The ps command (without options) only shows you commands associated with your terminal window. If you were to log into another terminal at the same time, a ps command in one terminal would not show you information about the programs running in the other terminal window.

Type the following command:

```
ps -el | grep yourloginname
```

(If ps -el doesn't work on your system, try ps -ax instead.)

c) Are the same commands displayed, or more, or fewer?

Answer: This command usually displays more commands than a simple ps *command.*

Without extra options, ps displays only some of the commands you're running. It displays only commands started from your current log-in shell. However, there are more programs running on the system.

The -el options cause ps to print every process on the system (-e) in a long format (-1). This is a lot of output; to sift through it, this command line pipes it through grep. The grep command searches through all of the output and prints only the lines that mention your log-in name. (The grep command is discussed in Chapter 7, "Finding Files.")

On some systems, the options are different: -a (for "all") and -x (for "extended information").

d) What is the PID of the ps command?

Answer: Some of the commands (such as your shell) will be the same. Others will be new. For example, this time you're running ps -el *instead of just* ps.

You may have commands running that only show up with ps -el output. These may be processes running in a different terminal or processes that run without a terminal. (A process without a terminal will have "?" in the tty field.) You may have a program that checks your e-mail for you (for example) or performs some other service, or maybe you're running another xterm window on the same system.

Others are "zombies"—processes that are neither alive nor dead. (Technically, a zombie is a process that has recently exited, but its parent—the process that started it, often your shell—hasn't acknowledged its death yet.) Every process becomes a zombie for a little while when it's quitting; this is the time when it cleans up and puts all its system resources back. Normally, the zombie state lasts only a fraction of a second. Sometimes, though, things get messed up (often because of an interrupt signal). When they do, the process may not finish dying; its zombie will hang around. One of the columns in the ps -el output shows the process's status. If that column shows a Z, the process is a zombie. You cannot kill a zombie process.

6.3.3 ANSWERS

Type the following command:

```
sleep 100 &
```

Use ps to get the PID of the sleep command.
Type the following command

```
kill -1 pid
```

a) What happens?

Answer:The process is ended, or killed.

The kill command sends a signal to a program. It's called kill because that's normally what it is used for, although it can send other signals.

You can only kill a process that you own. You cannot use kill to end someone else's process. (The exception, of course, is the superuser, the system administrator. The superuser can kill anyone's process.)

b) b) What is displayed?

Answer:The results are as follows:

```
$ sleep 100 &
[1]      8889
$ ps
   PID   TTY       TIME CMD
  8890   pts000    0:00 ps
  8877   pts000    0:00 ksh
  8889   pts000    0:00 sleep
$ kill 8889
$ ps
   PID   TTY       TIME CMD
  8877   pts000    0:00 ksh
  8891   pts000    0:00 ps
[1] + Terminated                    sleep 100 &
$
```

The basic kill command sends a terminate signal. You can also provide numbers, from -1 to -9. The numbers are approximately in order of severity. The -1 is a mild signal called HUP, for "hang up" (remember that UNIX was first developed by the phone company). The most severe signal is sent with the -9 option. Use kill -9 only if the basic kill command has already failed you. (Before you use `kill -9`, make sure it's your process you're trying to kill! It's very easy to mistype a number in the process ID.)

If `kill -9` fails, then you cannot kill the process. Let the system administrator know. This is almost never necessary.

LAB 6.3 SELF-REVIEW QUESTIONS

To test your progress, you should be able to answer the following questions.

1) Control-C interrupts programs running at the terminal.
    a) _____True
    b) _____False

2) Control-C interrupts programs running in the background.
    a) _____True
    b) _____False

3) Which of the following statements is false?
    a) _____A process is a program while it's running.
    b) _____There is only ever one process running the same program at a time.
    c) _____Every process has a number, its PID.
    d) _____No two processes have the same number at the same time.

4) Not all systems use Control-C to interrupt programs; identify the other common key used:
    a) _____Backspace
    b) _____Control-D
    c) _____Delete
    d) _____Control-H
    e) _____Control-?

5) Which technique would you use to kill the program started with this command line:

```
ls -1R / > ~/fullindex &
```

    a) _____Control-C
    b) _____`ps`, then `kill`

Quiz answers appear in Appendix A, Lab 6.3.

L A B 6.4

CLEARING YOUR DISPLAY

LAB OBJECTIVES

After this lab, you will be able to:

✓ Redraw the Screen

✓ Restore Your Screen Attributes

For each type of terminal, the UNIX system keeps a list of control codes. For many reasons, the wrong control code may be sent. For example, perhaps a program sends the control code to change the color of the text, but the program is killed before the program changes the color back. Or perhaps the connection is over a noisy telephone line. Sometimes the program sends the wrong information for your terminal type.

One of the control codes (Control-L) is often used to redraw the screen. It works for editors and for pager programs (such as more); it may work for some other programs. (A program may use the Control-L command for some other purpose.) The shell usually does not accept Control-L to refresh the screen.

Because there are so many different codes, the BSD programmers invented a special argument to stty, the word "sane." The command stty sane resets the terminal to a "reasonable" value.

Sometimes `stty sane` does not fix the problem. In that case, you'll have to log out and log in again.

Before doing Exercise 6.4.2, you may want to read the `stty` *man page to see if it accepts "sane" as an argument.*

LAB 6.4 EXERCISES

6.4.1 REDRAW THE SCREEN

Type the following commands:

```
(sleep 10; ls >&2 ) &
more /etc/passwd
```

Wait 10 seconds.

a) What happens?

_____

_____

Type the following character:

```
Control-L
```

b) What happens?

_____

_____

6.4.2 RESTORE YOUR SCREEN ATTRIBUTES

Not all systems have the command `stty sane`.

First, make your terminal behave poorly by typing the following commands:

```
stty -opost
ls
```

a) What do these commands do?

_____

_____

Type the following commands:

```
stty sane
ls
```

b) What happens?

_____

_____

Type the following command:

```
stty -a
```

c) Is the terminal set to "opost" or "-opost"?

_____

_____

LAB 6.4 EXERCISE ANSWERS

 This section gives you some suggested answers to the questions in Lab 6.4, with discussions related to those answers. Your answers may vary, but the most important thing is whether or not your answers work. Use these discussions to analyze differences between your answers and those presented here.

If you have alternative answers to the questions in these exercises, you are encouraged to post your answers and discuss them at the companion Web site for this book, located at:

http://www.phptr.com/phptrinteractive

6.4.1 ANSWERS

Type the following commands:

```
(sleep 10; ls >&2 ) &
more /etc/passwd
```

Wait 10 seconds.

a) What happens?

Answer: Ten seconds after you type the sleep *command, the output of* ls *appears on the screen, in the middle of the text displayed by* more.

The semicolon (;) allows you to put more than one command on a line. The parentheses group the two commands together so that the & character at the end applies to *both* of them, instead of just to the last command on the line. This sort of command line is discussed further in Chapter 12, "Commands and Job Control." For now, you might want to note the fact that the following characters are all shell metacharacters:

```
( ) ; &
```

If you need to use an actual parenthesis or semicolon or ampersand in a command, it must be escaped, either with a backslash (\) character or by putting it in apostrophes or double quotes.

Type the following character:

```
Control-L
```

b) What happens?

Answer: The Control-L signal tells the computer to draw everything on the screen again.

Using Control-L does not work for all programs. Some programs use Control-L for their own purposes. Those programs "grab" the Control-L character and takes it as a cue to do something else. What they do depends on the program.

6.4.2 ANSWERS

First, make your terminal behave poorly by typing the following commands:

```
stty -opost
ls
```

a) What do these commands do?

Answer: On almost all terminals, this messes up the display.

Type the following commands:

```
stty sane
ls
```

b) What happens?

Answer: The display is corrected; the command prompt begins at the left-hand side of the screen with every new line.

On most terminals, the stty -opost command messes up the display. It prevents new lines of text from starting at the left side of the screen, like this:

```
$ stty -opost
$ ls
apple    banana   corn
                $
```

The command prompt is not at the left side of the screen. This should be similar to what you saw with "-opost."

Type the command:

```
stty -a
```

c) Is the terminal set to "opost" or "-opost"?

Answer: The `stty sane` *command resets the value of the "opost" characteristic from "-opost" back to "opost." This is much easier than trying to learn all of the values for your terminal and correcting them.*

The –a option causes `stty` to list all of your current settings. To see the setting of "opost" or "-opost," you must use the –a option.

**LAB
6.4**

■ FOR EXAMPLE:

Here's sample output for a `stty -a` command. The "opost" setting is near the bottom.

```
$ stty -a
speed 9600 baud;
rows = 24; columns = 80; ypixels = 0; xpixels = 0;
intr = DEL; quit = ^|; erase = ^h; kill = ^u;
eof = ^d; eol = <undef>; eol2 = <undef>; swtch = <undef>;
start = ^q; stop = ^s; susp = ^z; dsusp = <undef>;
rprnt = ^r; flush = ^o; werase = ^w; lnext = ^v;
parenb -parodd cs7 -cstopb hupcl cread -clocal -loblk -
   parext
-ignbrk brkint ignpar -parmrk -inpck istrip -inlcr -igncr
   icrnl -iuclc
ixon -ixany -ixoff -imaxbel
isig icanon -xcase echo -echoe echok -echonl -noflsh
-tostop -echoctl -echoprt -echoke -defecho -flusho -pen-
   din -iexten
opost -olcuc onlcr -ocrnl -onocr -onlret -ofill -ofdel
```

If your system does not support `stty sane`, you should log out and log back in.

The Control-L command is a quick solution to a messy terminal screen. The `stty sane` command fixes a confused terminal description. It's like the difference between using the windshield wipers on your car and replacing the windshield. Control-L wipes the windshield clear, which doesn't help much if the problem is a crack. The `stty sane` command replaces the windshield, which doesn't help if you're driving in the rain.

Some systems also have a command called `reset` which resets the terminal display, just as `stty sane` does.

THE LAYERS OF COMMAND EXECUTION

Both the `stty` command and the quoting problems from Lab 6.1 demonstrate an important principle in figuring out UNIX problems. Any command passes through different "layers" on its way to being run. The results of the command may pass through layers as well. Figuring out a problem may depend on identifying the layer where the problem is happening.

LAB 6.4

For example, you type `ls *`. Here's what happens, more or less:

1. The keystrokes are examined by a program called the `tty` driver; the `stty` command is a way of adjusting the `tty` driver. If one of the keystrokes is a control character, the `tty` driver handles it, doing what's required. In this case, there are no control characters. The `tty` driver passes the keystrokes ("ls *") to the shell.

2. The shell checks for shell metacharacters and replaces the `*` with the list of files in the current directory. For demonstration purposes, there are only two files: *diary* and *journal*. Then, the shell looks for the `ls` command. It searches each directory in your *PATH* until it finds `ls`. Once both are found, the shell puts them together in one command (`/bin/ls diary journal`) and gives that to the operating system.

3. The operating system runs the command `/bin/ls diary journal`.

4. The `ls` command sends its output to standard output. The operating system "knows" that's the screen, so it gives the output to the `tty` driver, which is the component of the operating system in charge of placing characters on your terminal screen.

5. The `tty` driver converts the output into the right format for your terminal screen. If one of the file names had contained a control character, it might have caused the `tty` driver to do something unexpected.

You don't need to apply this level of analysis to every problem you have, but if your first fix to a problem doesn't work, maybe you're trying to fix the wrong layer. No amount of fiddling with the `tty` driver using `stty` is going to help if the problem is really a bad argument to `ls`.

LAB 6.4 SELF-REVIEW QUESTIONS

To test your progress, you should be able to answer the following questions.

1) The Control-L command always redraws the screen.
   a) _____True
   b) _____False

2) The `stty sane` command redraws the screen also.
   a) _____True
   b) _____False

3) The `stty` command sets and displays the characteristics of your terminal.
   a) _____True
   b) _____False

4) If your command prompt is drifting across the screen with each new command rather than being at the left side, which of these will correct the problem?
   a) _____Control-L
   b) _____Log out and log back in
   c) _____`stty sane`
   d) _____(a) and (b)
   e) _____(a) and (c)
   f) _____(b) and (c)
   g) _____(a), (b), and (c)

Quiz answers appear in Appendix A, Lab 6.4.

LAB 6.5

SETTING YOUR CONTROL CHARACTERS

LAB OBJECTIVES

After this lab, you will be able to:

✓ Display Your Control Keys

✓ Set the Erase Key

✓ Set the Interrupt Key

✓ Set the Kill-Line Key

The stty command is also used to set some of the control key-combinations that have already been discussed, such as the following:

- The interrupt character (abbreviated "intr"), normally Control-C.
- The end-of-file character ("eof"), normally Control-D.
- The erase character, sometimes set to the Delete key instead of Backspace.
- The clear-line character ("kill"), which is sometimes set to the @ key.

Without arguments, the `stty` command lists some of your current terminal settings. The -a option causes `stty` to list all of your current settings. To see your control keys, you must use the -a option.

■ FOR EXAMPLE:

If you go back to the previous example of `stty -a` output, the control character settings are the important lines; the third, fourth, and fifth lines of output, reproduced here:

```
intr = DEL; quit = ^|; erase = ^h; kill = ^u;
eof = ^d; eol = <undef>; eol2 = <undef>; swtch =
   <undef>;
start = ^q; stop = ^s; susp = ^z; dsusp = <undef>;
rprnt = ^r; flush = ^o; werase = ^w; lnext = ^v;
```

In this case, the interrupt ("intr") character is sent by the Delete key, the backspace ("erase") character is sent by Control-H (the ^ character indicates a control-key combination). The backspace key also sends Control-H.

**LAB
6.5**

LAB 6.5 EXERCISES

6.5.1 DISPLAY YOUR CONTROL KEYS

Type the following command:

```
stty -a
```

a) What happens?

_____

_____

b) What are the definitions for the following control keys on your system?

eof _____

_____

erase _____

_____

intr _____

_____

kill _____

_____

6.5.2 SET THE ERASE KEY

**LAB
6.5**

Type the following command:

```
stty erase +
```

Now, type the following:

```
mistake+++++++
```

a) What happens?

_____

_____

Press the backspace key.

b) What happens?

_____

_____

6.5.3 SET THE INTERRUPT KEY

Type the following command:

```
stty intr ^h
```

a) What does this command do?

_____

_____

Type the following command:

```
sleep 20
```

Press the backspace key.

b) What happens?

_____

_____

6.5.4 SET THE KILL-LINE KEY

Type the following command:

```
stty kill @
```

a) What does this command do?

_____

_____

Type the following command:

```
sleep 20 @
```

b) What happens?

_____

_____

LAB 6.5 EXERCISE ANSWERS

This section gives you some suggested answers to the questions in Lab 6.5, with discussions related to those answers. Your answers may vary, but the most important thing is whether or not your answers work. Use these discussions to analyze differences between your answers and those presented here.

If you have alternative answers to the questions in these exercises, you are encouraged to post your answers and discuss them at the companion Web site for this book, located at:

```
http://www.phptr.com/phptrinteractive
```

At the end of the exercises, you should restore your settings with `stty sane`.

6.5.1 ANSWERS

Type the following command:

```
stty -a
```

a) What happens?

Answer: The command prints all of your terminal settings.

The -a option causes stty to print all of your terminal settings. This can be a long list, so you might need to pipe it through a pager, such as more.

b) What are the definitions for the following control keys on your system?

eof

erase

intr

kill

Answer: Although your system may be different, the default values are as follows:

eof	^d (Control-D)	
erase	^h (Control-H)	On some systems, this may be the Delete key instead, which is identified as either ^? or as DEL, depending on the system.
intr	^c (Control-C)	
kill	^u (Control-U)	On older systems, this may be the @ key.

Not all programs can be stopped with the interrupt character. Some programs, such as editors, change how control characters are interpreted. In the EMACS editor, for instance, Control-H is the command to bring up the help window, not the command to backspace over text.

It's also possible to turn off the interpretation of the control characters using the stty command, although you shouldn't do it. When the terminal is interpreting control characters, the terminal is said to be in *canonical mode* (on BSD systems, this is called *cooked mode*). When the terminal driver is *not* interpreting control characters, the terminal is said to be in *noncanonical mode* (or *raw mode*). In fact, that's what editors do—they change the mode of the terminal to noncanonical mode, so the control characters aren't interpreted. (Some man pages, such as the stty man page, refer to these modes.) Normally you want your terminal in canonical mode.

6.5.2 ANSWERS

Type the following command:

```
stty erase +
```

Now, type the following:

```
mistake+++++++
```

a) What happens?

Answer: The + character is now the erase character. Each time you press +, you back-space over a character.

Press the backspace key.

b) What happens?

Answer: Instead of erasing characters, the backspace key causes "^H" to be displayed on the screen.

Because you changed the erase character, the character sent by the back-space key is now treated as an ordinary character. It's displayed as "^H".

6.5.3 ANSWERS

Type the following command:

```
stty intr ^h
```

a) What does this command do?

Answer: This command sets the interrupt character to Control-H.

You can set the key with either a ^ and an h character, or by pressing the backspace key, or by pressing Control-H.

Type the following command:

```
sleep 20
```

Press the backspace key.

b) What happens?

Answer: The `sleep` *command quits and the command prompt appears.*

The interrupt character is turned into the interrupt signal; the signal interrupts the running program. With this setting, you can interrupt a running program by pressing Backspace.

6.5.4 ANSWERS

Type the following command:

```
stty kill @
```

a) What does this command do?

Answer: *This command sets the kill character to @.*

The default for the kill signal used to be the @ key; on most systems, it is now the Control-U key combination. (When the kill signal is @, it's impossible to type email addresses, which are usually in the form *login@machine-address.*)

Type the following command:

```
sleep 20 @
```

b) What happens?

Answer: *Normally, the clear-line (or kill) character (now the @ key) erases the command line.*

Whether it's @ or Control-U, the kill character may not work for you. Just as with the interrupt character, some programs will "catch" the kill character and interpret it differently. This might happen in other programs, such as terminal programs or `telnet`, but not usually in the shell itself.

There are other control characters; for example, `werase` erases words. You may want to learn about them, but just as the kill command may be intercepted by the terminal program, these other signals may be caught as well.

> *After finishing this lab, you should probably use the* `stty sane` *command to reset your control keys.*

LAB 6.5 SELF-REVIEW QUESTIONS

To test your progress, you should be able to answer the following questions.

1) Interrupt or kill or other control characters can be assigned to any key or key-combination.
    a) _____True
    b) _____False

2) The control character to backspace over text is called "delete."
    a) _____True
    b) _____False

3) The signal such as interrupt works when the program has set the terminal in cooked or canonical mode.
    a) _____True
    b) _____False

4) Control-C is used by some programs as a command, not as an interrupt signal.
    a) _____True
    b) _____False

5) Which command sets the control character to clear the line?
    a) _____stty -a
    b) _____stty werase ^U
    c) _____stty kill ^U
    d) _____stty intr ^U
    e) _____stty erase ^U

Quiz answers appear in Appendix A, Lab 6.5.

L A B   6.6

RESTORING A FILE

LAB OBJECTIVES

After this lab, you will be able to:

✓ Check for Backup Files

✓ Ask the Administrator to Restore Files

✓ Describe the Trashcan Strategy

As mentioned in Chapter 4, "Files and Directories," there is no way to "undelete" a file on a UNIX system. The reasons are hidden in the technical details of file storage.

This doesn't mean that you cannot get the file back. Almost all administrators run regular backups, storing important files on some removable storage device such as a tape. An administrator will usually be glad to restore a file from the backup tape.

Only files that were backed up can be restored. At a large site, the administrator may only back up certain file systems, typically the ones related to work. The directory /tmp is often *not* backed up because it contains only temporary files.

Remember: When you restore a file from backup, you lose any changes that were made to the file between when it was backed up and when you deleted it.

If you are extremely concerned about this, you can adopt the "trashcan strategy." In this method of working, you don't really delete anything immediately. You use a different command (perhaps Rm) to move all files to a temporary directory (a trashcan). When you want to get a file out of the trashcan, you might use the command undelete. The undelete command would move a file out of the trashcan directory to the current directory.

Although programs to do this are available, they are not standard. You must ask your system administrator to get them and install them.

LAB 6.6 EXERCISES

6.6.1 CHECK FOR BACKUP FILES

a) Can you get back a file you've deleted, without help?

_____

_____

b) How are file backups made?

_____

_____

c) If your machine had a floppy disk drive, how would you implement a backup schedule for your work?

_____

_____

6.6.2 ASK THE ADMINISTRATOR TO RESTORE FILES

a) What files can be restored?

_____

_____

b) Are there any files that cannot be restored?

_____

_____

c) How are files restored?

_____

_____

6.6.3 DESCRIBE THE TRASHCAN STRATEGY

LAB 6.6

a) What is the "trashcan strategy"?

_____

_____

b) What would an `undelete` command do?

_____

_____

LAB 6.6 EXERCISE ANSWERS

 This section gives you some suggested answers to the questions in Lab 6.6, with discussions related to those answers. Your answers may vary, but the most important thing is whether or not your answers work. Use these discussions to analyze differences between your answers and those presented here.

If you have alternative answers to the questions in these exercises, you are encouraged to post your answers and discuss them at the companion Web site for this book, located at:

`http://www.phptr.com/phptrinteractive`

6.6.1 ANSWERS

a) Can you get back a file you've deleted, without help?

Answer: No. When a file backup is used to restore a file, the system administrator has made a copy of the file and is putting that copy back where the original was.

You can get the file back if you implement the "trashcan" strategy mentioned earlier, or if you are the system administrator.

You can also make your own backups, but they won't be as reliable as the system administrator's backups. When you make a backup, you're restricted to whatever medium you have available, usually a floppy disk (on some desktop systems) or another part of the filesystem.

b) How are file backups made?

Answer: On a regular basis, the system administrator copies files onto some removable medium, usually magnetic tape. This can be either a full backup, where all of the files are copied onto tape, or a partial (or incremental) backup, where the only files backed up are those that have changed since the last backup.

Backups are usually done late at night, because the process of doing a backup is time consuming and takes up system resources. By running the backups when no one is using the computer, the backup runs as swiftly as it can and no one else's work is hampered.

c) If your machine had a floppy disk drive, how would you implement a backup schedule for your work?

Answer: In three steps: Identify the files that have changed, copy them to the floppy drive, and label them.

This is the basic philosophy of file backups. The *first* time you do a backup, you must save all of the files you want backed up. Because floppy disks don't have a lot of space, you'll have to decide which of your directories should be backed up. Even if you have enough floppy disks to save all of your files, floppy disk drives are slow, and you might not want to spend your entire night popping floppy disks in and out of the computer.

Identifying the files that have changed is actually the easy part. One of the features of the find program (which is discussed in Chapter 7, "Finding Files") is that it can find files that have been changed in the last 24 hours.

It's also very important to label your backups. There's no use saving information if you cannot find it later.

6.6.2 ANSWERS

**LAB
6.6**

a) What files can be restored?

Answer: Any file that's been backed up can be restored. Any changes made after the last backup are lost.

For one project, I kept three sets of personal backups on different directories in the system: One set was an hour old, one set was four hours old, and one was from the previous day. The four-hours-old backup protected me against problems I hadn't caught in the last four hours. The day-old backup was extra insurance that I would not lose more than a day redoing work. Those were exceptional circumstances, however.

b) Are there any files that cannot be restored?

Answer: Only files that have been backed up can be restored.

You cannot restore files that haven't been backed up. This may be files that have been created since the last backup (the file you created five minutes ago, for instance), or it may be files that aren't backed up on a regular basis (such as your personal phone list).

Which files get backed up and when? That's a policy decision, and it is different from one place to another.

There's no reason you cannot back up files yourself. For an important project where the files change hourly, the system administrator's backups may not be enough.

You'll have to check with your system administrator about policy at your site.

c) How are files restored?

Answer: The system administrator restores files on request. The files may be copied back to replace the deleted files, or the administrator may also decide to restore the entire directory somewhere else. Then you can copy the restored files to their rightful places.

**LAB
6.6**

■ *FOR EXAMPLE:*

You have just deleted the file `/product/process/configuration.list`. Fortunately, it hasn't changed since the last backup. You ask the system administrator to restore the file. Instead of restoring just the one file, the administrator decides to restore all of `/product/process`, and tells you it's in `/tmp/restore`:

```
$ ls -F /tmp/restore
process/
$ cp process/configuration.list /product/process
$
```

To restore the file, you copy it from the restore directory to its original location. If there were other files in `/product/process` that you had accidentally deleted, you could copy them, too.

At some point, the administrator will ask you if you're finished with /tmp/restore; if you are, the directory will be deleted. If you're not, the administrator will probably suggest you move the necessary files out of /tmp. (Because the directory /tmp is for temporary files, you should not rely on its contents for longer than a day.)

6.6.3 ANSWERS

a) What is the "trashcan strategy"?

Answer: In the trashcan strategy, a file is not really deleted. When you remove a file, you really just move it into a storage area, a trashcan. Then you have a grace period in which to retrieve the command.

Remember that you must empty the trashcan every once in a while. Otherwise, you will run out of disk space.

b) What would an undelete command do?

Answer: An undelete command in this strategy moves a file out of the trashcan back to its original location.

This strategy has its advantages and disadvantages.

In favor of it, you can retrieve files you deleted. This is a big advantage.

Against it are:

- You still have to empty the trashcan. At some point, the decision to remove the files must be made, because you don't have enough disk space to store every file.
- You must learn a different set of commands that are not on every system. Some people think this makes you vulnerable when you move to a system without the commands: you'll merrily delete files, forgetting that you cannot get them back. These people think it's better to learn to think twice and delete once first.
- You'll probably have to get the system administrator to install the special software, although there are personal solutions you can set up yourself.

A freely available set of programs for implementing just this strategy were posted to the Usenet newsgroup comp.sources.unix. The package is the Project Athena commands containing `delete, undelete, purge,` and `expunge.`

In my experience, having to remember to empty the trashcan is more trouble than remembering not to delete files in the first place. Instead of using the trashcan strategy, I make important files read-only whenever possible. The `rm` command prompts you before removing a read-only file, so you have a second chance if you accidentally try to remove the file.

LAB 6.6 SELF-REVIEW QUESTIONS

To test your progress, you should be able to answer the following questions.

1) The backups will contain all files on the system.
   a) _____True
   b) _____False

2) You must ask the system administrator to help you restore a backed up file.
   a) _____True
   b) _____False

3) One disadvantage of the trashcan strategy is that you won't be able to "undelete" files if you move to a different UNIX system.
   a) _____True
   b) _____False

4) Which of the following is *not* a consideration when doing system back-ups?
   a) _____Decide which directories should be backed up.
   b) _____Backup at a time when the system isn't very busy.
   c) _____Label the backup medium.
   d) _____Identify the files that have changed.
   e) _____All of these are important.

Quiz answers appear in Appendix A, Lab 6.6.

CHAPTER 6

TEST YOUR THINKING

The projects in this section are meant to have you utilize all of the skills that you have acquired throughout this chapter. The answers to these projects can be found at the companion Web site to this book, located at:

`http://www.phptr.com/phptrinteractive`

Visit the Web site periodically to share and discuss your answers.

1) Explain the output in this listing:

```
$ echo Don't use Sergei's program
Dont use Sergeis program
```

2) What is the command trying to do? How would you rewrite it?

3) Some systems have two versions of the echo command. How would you discover which you were using? How would you specify the other for one command?

4) One of the versions of echo is built into the shell program. Could you kill it with kill? What would happen?

C H A P T E R 7

FINDING FILES

 No matter how organized you are, sooner or later you'll need to find a particular file.

The large number of files on a UNIX system makes it likely you'll misplace one. The system provides tools to find a particular file, either by searching for a particular word in the file or for some information about the file.

The two most common commands are grep and find. The grep command searches files and prints the lines in the files that match a word or phrase. The find command searches a directory for files with specific attributes. There are other commands you can use as well, such as the ls -R command. You will learn all about these commands in this chapter.

L A B   7.1

SEARCHING FILES BY CONTENT

LAB OBJECTIVES

After this lab, you will be able to:

✓ Find a File That Contains a Word

✓ Ignore Case in a Search

✓ List File Names, Not Context

The grep command searches files (or standard input) for a word or phrase. This is the command to use when you remember something about the file's content but not the name of the file itself. You may be searching for that apple rhubarb crumble recipe or e-mail from someone in Peoria. Using the grep command, you can find all of the files that contain a particular word or phrase.

Before starting these exercises, create three files, blue, mary, and peep. You can either use cat to create them (remember to end input with Control-D), or you can use an editor. (The first lab in Chapter 9, "The vi Editor," provides enough information to create these files.) In the first file, blue, write:

```
Little boy blue
Come blow your horn
The sheep's in the meadow
The cow's in the corn
```

In the second file, mary, write:

```
Mary had a little lamb
Its fleece was white as snow
And everywhere that Mary went
The lamb was sure to go
```

In the third file, peep, write:

```
Little Bo Peep has lost her sheep
And doesn't know where to find them
Leave them alone
And they'll come home
Wagging their tails behind them
```

LAB 7.1 EXERCISES

7.1.1 FIND A WORD IN A FILE

Type the following command:

```
grep Little blue
```

a) What does the output look like?

_____

_____

Type the following command:

```
grep Little blue mary peep
```

b) What does the output look like?

_____

_____

Type the following command:

```
grep in blue mary peep
```

c) What does the output look like?

_____

_____

7.1.2 IGNORE CASE IN A SEARCH

Type the following command:

```
grep -i Little blue mary peep
```

a) What happens?

_____

_____

b) What does the -i option do?

_____

_____

7.1.3 LIST FILE NAMES, NOT CONTEXT

Type the following command:

```
grep -il little blue mary peep
```

a) What does the output look like?

_____

_____

b) What does the -l option do?

_____

_____

c) Can you imagine a reason for listing the files only?

_____

_____

LAB 7.1 EXERCISE ANSWERS

This section gives you some suggested answers to the questions in Lab 7.1, with discussions related to those answers. Your answers may vary, but the most important thing is whether or not your answers work. Use these discussions to analyze differences between your answers and those presented here.

If you have alternative answers to the questions in these exercises, you are encouraged to post your answers and discuss them at the companion Web site for this book, located at:

```
http://www.phptr.com/phptrinteractive
```

7.1.1 ANSWERS

Type the following command:

```
grep Little blue
```

a) What does the output look like?

Answer: The output would be as follows:

```
$ grep Little blue
Little boy blue come blow your horn
```

The grep command prints out the line that contains the pattern. If more than one line had contained the word "Little," grep would have printed out each line.

The structure of the grep command is:

```
grep options pattern [file ...]
```

The *pattern* is the word or phrase you're searching for. You don't need an option letter to introduce the pattern (the grep command is older than standardized option formats). You can make the pattern one of the options, if you want:

```
grep -e pattern [file ...]
```

If you introduce the option with -e, you can search for patterns that begin with "-".

The pattern is called a pattern because it's really a "regular expression pattern"; these are discussed in the next chapter. A word or phrase is one kind of regular expression pattern.

There are actually three grep commands: grep, egrep, and fgrep. The grep command searches for regular expressions. The egrep command searches for a different kind of regular expression (called an "extended" regular expression; that's where the "e" comes from). The fgrep command searches for strings (phrases and words) only, not regular expressions. (You can substitute fgrep for any of the grep commands in this lab.)

On most systems, there are options to make `grep` behave like either of the other two commands: `grep -E` forces `grep` to search for extended regular expressions (`egrep`), and `grep -F` forces `grep` to search for strings (`fgrep`). (On Solaris, these options are not available in the standard version of `grep`, but *are* available in an alternate version, `/usr/xpg4/bin/grep`.)

Type the following command:

```
grep Little blue mary peep
```

b) What does the output look like?

Answer: The output would be as follows:

```
$ grep Little blue mary peep
blue:Little boy blue come blow your horn
peep:Little Bo Peep has lost her sheep
```

When you name more than one file as arguments to `grep`, each line of output is identified with the name of the file. The file `mary` doesn't contain the word "Little" so there's no output for it.

Type the following command:

```
grep in blue mary peep
```

c) What does the output look like?

Answer: The output would be as follows:

```
$ grep in blue mary peep
blue:The sheep's in the meadow
blue:The cow's in the corn
peep:And doesn't know where to find them
peep:Wagging their tails behind them
```

The output contains the two lines from `blue` that contain the word "in" and it contains two lines from `peep` that contain the letters "in". The `grep` command doesn't distinguish between words and parts of words.

Why call it "grep"? The standard text editor on UNIX, ed, has a command to print all of the lines in the file that contained a particular regular expression. The command is g/re/p, which stood for "global/regular expression/print." The grep command does the same thing outside an editor, so it got the same name.

When you put more than one pattern on the line, any one of the patterns matches.

■ FOR EXAMPLE:

Suppose you wanted to find only the line that contains both "in" and "And." The first thing you might try is two patterns:

```
$ grep -e in -e And peep
And doesn't know where to find them
Wagging their tails behind them.
```

This finds lines that contain "in" *or* that contain "And." It doesn't find the line that has both "in" and "and."

To apply both criteria, you can apply them in sequence using a pipe:

```
$ grep in peep | grep And
And doesn't know where to find them
```

The first grep finds both lines that contain "in"; the second grep weeds out any lines that don't contain "And."

7.1.2 ANSWERS

Type the following command:

```
grep -i Little blue mary peep
```

a) What happens?

Answer: The following output results:

```
$ grep -i Little blue mary peep
blue:Little boy blue come blow your horn
mary:Mary had a little lamb
peep:Little Bo Peep has lost her sheep
```

b) What does the -i option do?

Answer: The -i *option to* grep *causes it to ignore the case when searching. This option is a great time-saver; you don't need to worry about whether the word you're searching for is capitalized, uppercase, or lowercase. If it's a common word, you may not want to use this option; it can produce too many results.*

7.1.3 ANSWERS

Type the following command:

```
grep -il little blue mary peep
```

a) What does the output look like?

Answer: The output is:

```
$ grep -i little blue mary peep
blue
mary
peep
```

b) What does the -l option do?

Answer: The -l *option to* grep *causes it to list only the file names and not the actual lines. In a directory full of files that contain many instances of the word you're searching for, this option can be a bit faster than a straight* grep *command.*

c) Can you imagine a reason for listing the files only?

Answer: The reason must be that you only need the names and not the context. Usually, this is because you're going to process those files in some way. Chapter 12, "Commands and Job Control," discusses a way to use the results of a command as the arguments to another command. Using grep -l, *you can, for example, write a single command to edit all files in the directory that contain a particular word.*

You can also use the -l option for reasons of speed. If you're certain you'll recognize the file name when you see it, the -l option can be slightly faster than grep command without -1. (There are other versions of grep that may be faster yet. On some systems, the egrep command is the fastest of the three, because the programmers have put the most effort into making it fast.)

LAB 7.1 SELF-REVIEW QUESTIONS

To test your progress, you should be able to answer the following questions.

1) The grep command searches files or standard input.
   a) _____True
   b) _____False

2) The grep command cannot search for patterns that begin with '-', because the command will interpret the pattern as an option.
   a) _____True
   b) _____False

3) The fgrep command searches for words instead of patterns.
   a) _____True
   b) _____False

4) When you specify two patterns in a grep command, grep displays only the lines that have both of those patterns.
   a) _____True
   b) _____False

Quiz answers appear in Appendix A, Lab 7.1.

L A B   7.2

SEARCHING FILES BY ATTRIBUTE

LAB OBJECTIVES

After this lab, you will be able to:

- ✓ List All Files
- ✓ Find a File by Name
- ✓ Use a Wildcard in the Name
- ✓ Find the File, Ignoring Case
- ✓ Find a File by Type
- ✓ Find a File by Age
- ✓ Use Multiple Attributes to Find Files

The `find` command starts in a directory and checks all of the directory's contents. It applies a series of tests against each file or directory; if one of the tests is false, then `find` moves on to the next. If the directory contains a subdirectory, `find` also checks the contents of the subdirectory, and so on. If you start at `/`, `find` will eventually check every file on the system.

The syntax for the `find` command is this:

```
find [options] starting-directory test ...
```

You need to specify a *starting directory*, where the search will begin, and you need to specify the tests. (If you don't specify a test, `find` prints the name of every file it finds.)

Some of the tests are described on the `find` man page as being "always true." It's easier to think of these as commands: things for `find` to do when it has a file that passes all the other tests.

LAB 7.2 EXERCISES

7.2.1 LIST ALL FILES

From your home directory, type the following command:

```
find . -print
```

From your home directory, type the following command:

```
ls -R .
```

a) What does the `-R` option to `ls` do?

_____

_____

7.2.2 FIND A FILE BY NAME

In the same directory as the files from the previous lab, create the file `Blue`. The content doesn't matter. You can create an empty file with the following command:

```
>Blue
```

Type the following command:

```
find . -name blue -print
```

a) What does the output look like?

_____

_____

7.2.3 USE A WILDCARD IN THE NAME

Type the following command:

```
find . -name ?lue -print
```

a) What are the results?

_____

_____

Type the following command:

```
find . -name \?lue -print
```

b) What are the results?

_____

_____

7.2.4 FIND THE FILE, IGNORING CASE

Type the following command:

```
find -i . -name blue -print
```

a) What is the output?

_____

_____

Not all systems have the -i *option for* find, *so this command may not work on your system.*

Enter the following command:

```
find . -name [Bb]lue -print
```

b) What happens? Can you explain why?

_____

_____

7.2.5 FIND A FILE BY TYPE

Type the following command:

```
find . -type f -print
```

a) What kind of files are listed?

_____

_____

Type the following command:

```
find . -type d -print
```

b) What kind of files are listed?

_____

_____

Type the following command:

```
find . -print -type d
```

c) Why are the results different than in Question b?

_____

_____

7.2.6 FIND A FILE BY AGE

Type the following command:

```
find . -mtime 2 -print
```

Use ls -l to check the times on the files listed.

a) If find selected files, how old are they?

_____

_____

Type the following command:

```
find . -mtime -2 -print
```

Use ls -l again.

b) If find selected files, how old are they?

_____

_____

Type the following command:

```
find . -mtime +2 -print
```

Use ls -l again.

c) Again, if find selected files, how old are they?

_____

_____

7.2.7 USE MULTIPLE ATTRIBUTES TO FIND FILES

You can include more than one test. Normally, *all* the tests have to apply to the file for it to match, but you can include an "or" (match this test or that test) with –o. A file passes if the first test is true or if the second test is true. Multiple tests joined by –o must be in parentheses.

Type the following command:

```
find . ( -name blue -o -type f ) -print
```

a) What happened and why?

_____

_____

b) How can you fix this?

_____

_____

LAB 7.2 EXERCISE ANSWERS

This section gives you some suggested answers to the questions in Lab 7.2, with discussions related to those answers. Your answers may vary, but the most important thing is whether or not your answers work. Use these discussions to analyze differences between your answers and those presented here.

If you have alternative answers to the questions in these exercises, you are encouraged to post your answers and discuss them at the companion Web site for this book, located at:

http://www.phptr.com/phptrinteractive

7.2.1 ANSWERS

From your home directory, type the following command:

```
find . -print
```

The actual results depend on what's in your directory. However, here are the results from my home directory:

```
$ find . -print
.
./.login
./.profile
./.vtlrc
./.UpgradeVer2.1
./.dtfclass-old
./.Xdefaults
./.wastebasket
./.wastebasket/.Wastebasket
./Mailbox~

./Mailbox~/Mail
./.sh_history
./Blue
./wildcards
./wildcards/boat
./wildcards/coat
./wildcards/goat
./wildcards/coal
./wildcards/color
./wildcards/.hidden
./blue
./mary
./muffet
```

The find command starts in the current directory and matches each file and directory it finds against the test -print. Because the file matches (-print is true for all files), find prints the name and goes on to the next. The starting point can be any directory, but the more subdirectories and files there are under the starting point, the longer find takes to search. The longest search starts in the root directory, because that includes all files on the system.

From your home directory, type the following command:

```
ls -R .
```

The actual results depend on what's in your directory. However, here are the results from my home directory:

```
$ ls -R
Blue
Mailbox~
blue
mary
muffet
wildcards

./Mailbox~:
Mail

./wildcards:
boat
coal
coat
color
goat
```

Although the results are nearly the same, there are two differences: First, the find command listed the hidden files, and ls did not (although it would if you added the -a option). Second, the format is different. The output of find is a relative path name for each file, whereas the output for ls -R is arranged in chunks, one chunk for each directory.

a)   What does the -R option to ls do?

Answer: The -R option is the "recursive" option (just as cp has a recursive option). With the -R option, ls lists the contents of each directory as it comes to it.

7.2.2 ANSWERS

Type the following command:

```
find . -name blue -print
```

a) What does the output look like?

Answer: The output is as follows:

```
$ find . -name blue -print
./blue
```

This `find` command searches beneath the starting directory. For each file and directory, it checks the tests: Is the file named "blue"? If it isn't, `find` goes on to the next file or directory. If it is named "blue," then `find` tries the next test, -print. Is it true? It's always true and `find` prints out the path name of *blue* relative to the starting directory.

Even though there's only one file named "blue," the `find` command still checks all of the files. You can see that a search that started in the directory / would take a long time, because all of the files would be checked.

THE LOCATE COMMAND

Some older BSD systems had an alternate version of `find`. When you gave it only one argument, the name of the file, it listed all the files on the system that had that name as part of their path names.

This command is still on BSD systems, but the name has been changed to `locate`, to avoid confusion.

```
$ locate blue
/usr/mitch/blue
/usr/tara/bluedog/bagels
/usr/tara/bluedog/phone
/usr/tara/bluedog/prices
```

The names that `locate` finds actually come from a list. Every night, a command stored the names of all files on the system in this list. The `locate` command is just the same as a `grep` command on the list.

This is much faster than a regular `find` command, but it's also less secure. Normally, `find` only finds files in directories you can read. This nightly list of files is almost always several hours out of date, and the command that makes the list has permission to read all directories.

For example, suppose you had a private directory named `private`. Anyone who wanted a list of the file names in that directory can get it with the command `locate private`.

7.2.3 ANSWERS

Type the following command:

```
find . -name ?lue -print
```

a) What are the results?

Answer: The command fails:

```
$ find . -name ?lue -print
find: No such option
```

Remember that the shell expands wildcards *before* the command is run. The `find` command actually gets the command `find . -name Blue blue -print`. There's no operator before "blue," so `find` treats it as an option. There is no option "blue" for `find`.

Type the following command:

```
find . -name \?lue -print
```

b) What are the results?

Answer: The results are as follows:

```
$ find . -name \?lue -print
./Blue
./blue
```

Once the shell metacharacter ? is escaped with a backslash, the command works as you expect. You could also have surrounded the "?lue" with double quotation marks or single quotes instead of using the backslash.

7.2.4 ANSWERS

Type the following command:

```
find -i . -name blue -print
```

Note that the option goes before the path name.

a) What is the output?

Answer:The output is as follows:

```
$ find -i . -name blue -print
./Blue
./blue
```

The -i option makes the search case insensitive.

Enter the following command:

```
find . -name [Bb]lue -print
```

b) What happens? Can you explain why??

Answer:The command prints an error message, because the [wildcard is not escaped.

To match either *Blue* or *blue*, use the command:

```
find . -name \[Bb]lue -print
```

(Only the opening bracket needs to be escaped. This is because only [is a metacharacter, although it's a metacharacter that expects a] later on. The] by itself isn't special at all.)

If you wanted a true case-insensitive search that would match (for example) *blue*, *blUe*, or *bLuE*, you would have to specify uppercase and lowercase letters for each character in the name:

```
find . -name "[Bb][Ll][Uu][Ee]" -print
```

In this case, quotation marks are easier to type than four backslashes.

7.2.5 ANSWERS

Type the following command:

```
find . -type f -print
```

Again, the results depend on the content of your directory, but in my home directory, they are:

```
$ find . -type f -print
./.login
./.profile
./.vtlrc
./.UpgradeVer2.1
./.dtfclass-old
./.Xdefaults
./.wastebasket/.Wastebasket
./.sh_history
./Blue
./wildcards/boat
./wildcards/coat
./wildcards/goat
./wildcards/coal
./wildcards/color
./wildcards/.hidden
./blue
./mary
./muffet
```

a) What kind of files are listed?

Answer: All of the files listed are files. The -type *f test is only true for files.*

Type the following command:

```
find . -type d -print
```

The results for my home directory are:

```
$ find . -type d -print
.
./.wastebasket
./Mailbox~
./wildcards
```

b) What kind of files are listed?

Answer: All of these are directories. The -type *d test is only true for directories.*

For each file type, there is an argument to the -type test. The arguments are listed in Table 7.1. It shouldn't be difficult to remember these arguments; they are the same as the file types displayed by ls -l.

Table 7.1 ■ Arguments to the `find -type` test

File type	-type **argument**
Block special file	b
Character special file	c
Directory	d
Fifo or pipe	p
Regular file	f
Socket	s
Symbolic link	l

Type the following command:

```
find . -print -type d
```

This command prints all of the files and directories. In my directory, again:

```
$ find . -print
.
./.login
./.profile
./.vtlrc
./.UpgradeVer2.1
./.dtfclass-old
./.Xdefaults
./.wastebasket
./.wastebasket/.Wastebasket
./Mailbox~

./Mailbox~/Mail
./.sh_history
./Blue
./wildcards
./wildcards/boat
./wildcards/coat
./wildcards/goat
./wildcards/coal
./wildcards/color
./wildcards/.hidden
./blue
./mary
./muffet
```

c) Why are the results different than in Question b?

Answer: The order of the tests is important: the tests that restrict or eliminate files should come first. Command tests (such as `-print`*) should be last.*

When the `find` command looks at a file, it tries each test. If one test fails, then `find` goes on to the next file. But remember that the tests that are commands are "always true." When the test is evaluated, they execute their commands. (The `find` man page refers to these commands as being "side effects.") So when the command `find . -print -type d` gets a file (suppose the file `peep`), it tries the tests in this order:

1. First, it checks the `-print` test. That's always true, so `find` prints the name.
2. Second, it checks the `-type d` test. That's false, so it goes on to the next file.

But it has already printed the name! That's not the result you want. The `-print` test must go after the `-type d` test.

You'll find the `find` command runs faster if you put the tests that eliminate files first and always put the tests with "side effects" last on the command line. (The `-print` test is not the only one.)

7.2.6 ANSWERS

Because you may not have files that match, you should know that the `-mtime` test is the "modification time" for the file: the time when it was last modified. Remember that each file has three times associated with it (modification time, change time, and access time). There are `find` tests for each time: They are `-mtime`, `-ctime`, and `-atime`, respectively.

Type the following command:

```
find . -mtime 2 -print
```

You may or may not have files that match in your directory. Following is the result in my directory:

```
$ find . -mtime 2 -print
./.login
```

a) If `find` selected files, how old are they?

Answer:The `-mtime` test checks the age of files by days. A file more than 24 hours old and less than 48 hours old is two days old. In my directory, the `.login` file had been modified 30 hours earlier.

Type the following command:

```
find . -mtime -2 -print
```

b) If find selected files, how old are they?

Answer: You may or may not have files that match. The −mtime −2 *test matches any file that was modified less than two days ago. In my directory, the results are as follows:*

```
$ find . -mtime -2 -print
.
./.sh_history
./Blue
./blue
./mary
./muffet
```

Type the following command:

```
find . -mtime +2 -print
```

c) Again, if find selected files, how old are they?

Answer: The −mtime +2 *test matches any file that was last modified more than two days ago. In my directory, the results are as follows:*

```
$ find . -mtime +2 -print
./.profile
./.vtlrc
./.UpgradeVer2.1
./.dtfclass-old
./.Xdefaults
./.wastebasket
./.wastebasket/.Wastebasket
./Mailbox~

./Mailbox~/Mail
./wildcards
./wildcards/boat
./wildcards/coat
./wildcards/goat
./wildcards/coal
./wildcards/color
./wildcards/.hidden
```

7.2.7 ANSWERS

Type the following command:

```
find . ( -name blue -o -type f ) -print
```

a) What happened and why?

Answer: The parentheses characters, (and), are shell metacharacters. The shell treats them specially before the command is run.

b) How can you fix this?

Answer: To group tests using parentheses, you need to escape or quote the parentheses. This command works:

```
find . \( -name blue -o -type f \) -print
```

Both (and) are shell metacharacters, and need to be escaped or the `find` command will never see them.

You should read the `find` man page to look at some of the tests that can be performed.

THE COST OF `FIND`

The `find` command can be very useful. It can also be very slow. It takes up a lot of system resources. When the system is already slow, don't start a `find` command that searches many directories; you'll get the system administrator (and everyone else) mad. Try and confine your searches to the smallest directory tree possible.

You may also discover that error messages from `find` are distracting: It's difficult to spot the file names you're interested in between the error messages about directories you don't have permission to read.

■ FOR EXAMPLE:

Here's the beginning of a `find` command to list all of the files on the system:

LAB 7.2

```
$ find / -print
find: cannot read dir /lost+found: Permission denied
find: cannot read dir /usr/lost+found: Permission denied
/
/usr
/usr/share
/usr/share/release_info
```

Those two directories (/lost+found and /usr/lost+found) are directories where I don't have execute permission. To eliminate those messages, I can redirect the error messages to /dev/null:

```
$ find / -print 2> /dev/null
/
/usr
/usr/share
/usr/share/release_info
```

LAB 7.2 SELF-REVIEW QUESTIONS

To test your progress, you should be able to answer the following questions.

1) The find command performs all of its tests and then prints the file name if all of the tests are true.
   a) _____True
   b) _____False

2) The ls -R command does a recursive directory listing.
   a) _____True
   b) _____False

3) You only need parentheses to group find tests if there are choices (either this test is true or that test is true).
   a) _____True
   b) _____False

4) You could look for all files that haven't been modified in 6 months with the command find . -mtime +180 -print.
   a) _____True
   b) _____False

Quiz answers appear in Appendix A, Lab 7.2.

C H A P T E R 7

TEST YOUR THINKING

 The projects in this section are meant to have you utilize all of the skills that you have acquired throughout this chapter. The answers to these projects can be found at the companion Web site to this book, located at:

`http://www.phptr.com/phptrinteractive`

Visit the Web site periodically to share and discuss your answers.

1) Suppose you're trying to back up some important files. How would you find all of the files in `/projects` that have changed today?

2) Is it enough to check only the files that have been modified today? Would there be a reason to check for files using `-ctime` or `-atime`?

3) Knowing what you now know, how would you find all of the files in the `/projects` directory and its subdirectories that contain the word "avocado"? Can you do it? If not, why not?

C H A P T E R   8

REGULAR EXPRESSIONS

A regular expression is a compact way to describe a string of characters. Regular expressions are incredibly useful when searching text.

CHAPTER OBJECTIVES

In this chapter, you will learn about:

Regular expressions are used whenever you search text in UNIX. They take some effort to master, but once you know them, you'll want to use them everywhere.

A *regular expression* is a shorthand way to describe a string. (A *string* is any sequence of characters.) The regular expression itself is often called a *pattern*. When a sequence of characters can be described by a particular expression, we say that it "matches" the expression. For example, "cat" is a pattern that matches only the letters "cat."

Besides the characters that match themselves, there are some characters that have a variable meaning. They're called *metacharacters*, just as the shell wildcards are metacharacters. In fact, some of the regular expression metacharacters are the same as shell wildcard metacharacters: The characters " [" and "*" are also regular expression metacharacters.

L A B 8.1

BASIC REGULAR EXPRESSIONS

LAB OBJECTIVES

After this lab, you will be able to:

✓ Match a String

✓ Match the Beginning or End of a Line

✓ Match a Single Character

✓ Match One Character in a Set

✓ Match Repeated Characters

✓ Group Expressions

✓ Match Metacharacters

REGULAR EXPRESSIONS ARE NOT WILDCARDS

The easiest way to approach regular expressions is to think of them as shell wildcards that can do more. With them, you can be more specific about the pattern you want to match.

When you're describing a file name with a shell wildcard, you really have three choices: specify a character; specify what a character is not; or say "anything" using the * wildcard. Regular expressions offer you more choices. You can, for example, specify any line that has the any three characters repeated twice in a row.

It's important to remember that regular expressions are not wildcards. They do some things in different ways. Three differences are particularly important:

1. Where wildcards use "?" to mean any single character, regular expressions use " . " (the dot character).
2. Both wildcards and regular expressions use "*" in similar, but not identical, ways.
3. Wildcards search file names whereas regular expressions search lines of text. A wildcard must describe the entire file name for it to match (even if it describes it using "*"). A regular expression may describe only part of a line. The regular expression "cat" matches all of these lines:

```
cat
scatter
"My dear, you force me into a cataclysmic decision."
```

All three contain "cat," which matches the expression.

TYPES OF REGULAR EXPRESSIONS

There are three types of regular expressions:

- *Basic* regular expressions were developed first. They're used in commands like grep and in the editors vi and emacs.
- *Extended* regular expressions added more features to the basic regular expressions (although a couple of features were also removed). They're mostly used in programming commands (such as awk or lex), but you can also find them in egrep, some versions of man, or as an option in emacs or some versions of vi .
- POSIX regular expressions add still more features. When the international standards committees got around to standardizing regular expressions as a part of UNIX, they added their own features. Unless your UNIX system regularly runs in a language other than English, very few of the features of POSIX regular expressions will matter to you. For that reason, I won't be discussing the POSIX-specific features at all.

The basic regular expressions are called basic because they were invented first. They were part of the very first UNIX editor, ed. (Searching for regular expressions in ed also gave rise to the name for grep.) In some older man pages, you'll see references to "*ed*-style regular expressions." This simply means basic regular expressions.

Table 8.1 shows the metacharacters for basic regular expressions.

Table 8.1 ■ Basic Regular Expression Metacharacters

.	Match any single character.
^	Refers to the beginning of the line.
$	Refers to the end of the line.
[abc]	Match one of the characters in the brackets.
[^abc]	Match any character *except* one of the characters in the brackets.
expr	Match any number of *expr* in a row. The *expression* can be any expression: a character, a bracket expression, or a patternexpression grouped with \(and \).
\c	Turn off the special meaning of the characters ., ^, $, \, [, and *; turn on the special meaning of the characters (,), {, and }, and the numbers 1 to 9. Other characters don't have special meanings.
expression\{n,m\}	Match between *n* and *m* repetitions of *expression* in a row.
\(expression\)	Treat *expression* as a group, for the purposes of using * or \{ and \}.

■ FOR EXAMPLE:

You can see that these are the metacharacters for regular expressions:

```
. ^ $ [ * \
```

There are some that are special only when a \ is before them. These always come in pairs:

> \ (\ ) \ { \ }

LAB 8.1 EXERCISES

These exercises use grep *to search a file for lines that contain a specific pattern. This is an extension of chapter 7, but the emphasis here is on the expressions, not the mechanisms of* grep.

For this set of exercises, create the file todo with the following content (there is an empty line between "To Do" and the first entry):

```
To Do:

Pay fine $99.32
Coat to dry cleaners [open 9-6]
* Buy oats
Friday: Take out garbage
Saturday: Paint garage door, if dry
* Sat: Show kids goat at zoo
```

8.1.1 MATCH A STRING

Type the following commands:

```
grep at todo
```

a) What is a string?

_____

_____

Enter the following command:

```
grep " at" todo
```

b) Why does the second string need to be quoted?

_____

_____

c) What is the difference between the output of the first and second commands?

_____

_____

Enter the following command:

```
grep "door.
* Sat:" todo
```

d) What is the third command trying to do?

_____

_____

e) Does the third command work? If not, why not?

_____

_____

8.1.2 MATCH THE BEGINNING OR END OF A LINE

Type the following commands:

```
grep dry todo
grep 'dry$' todo
```

a) How does the `$` character change the output?

_____

_____

Type the command:

```
grep '$99' todo
```

b) Does "`dry$`" mean the same thing as "`$dry`"?

_____

_____

Type the following commands:

```
grep '$' todo
grep '^$' todo
```

c) What does the regular expression `^$` match?

_____

_____

8.1.3 MATCH A SINGLE CHARACTER

Enter the following command:

```
grep . todo
```

a) What does the "`.`" regular expression match?

_____

_____

b) Explain the results of the command.

_____

_____

Enter the following command:

```
grep o.t todo
```

c) From the output, what does the "o.t" regular expression match?

_____

_____

8.1.4 MATCH ONE CHARACTER IN A SET

Enter the following command:

```
grep '[Dd]' todo
```

a) What does the "[Dd]" expression match?

_____

_____

b) Are the apostrophes around "[Dd]" required?

_____

_____

c) What does the expression "[A-Z]" match?

_____

_____

Enter the following command:

```
grep '^[^A-Z]' todo
```

d) What does the "`^[^A-Z]`" expression match? What does the second "`^`" character mean?

_____

_____

Enter the following command:

```
grep '[\*]' todo
```

e) What does the "`[\*]`" expression match?

_____

_____

8.1.5 MATCH REPEATED CHARACTERS

Enter the following command:

```
grep 'garb*age' todo
```

a) What does the expression "`garb*age`" match?

_____

_____

Enter the following commands:

```
grep "9*" todo
grep "99*" todo
grep "999*" todo
```

b) Which expression(s) matched only the line containing "99"?

_____

_____

c) Why do you need that many 9s?

_____

_____

Enter the following command:

```
grep '9\{2,2\}' todo
```

d) What does the expression "9\{2,2\}" match?

_____

_____

e) What expression would match all North American phone numbers (three digits, a "-", and four more digits)?

_____

_____

8.1.6 GROUP EXPRESSIONS

Enter the following command:

```
grep "Sat\(urday\)*:" todo
```

a) In the line that appears, what part did the expression match?

_____

_____

b) What does the "\(urday\)*" expression mean?

_____

_____

Enter the following command:

```
grep "\(.\)\1" todo
```

c) What does the "\(.\)\1" expression match?

_____

_____

8.1.7 MATCH METACHARACTERS

a) Write a regular expression that finds the lines containing the "." or the "$" characters.

_____

_____

b) Write a regular expression that finds the "[" character.

_____

_____

c) Write a regular expression that finds the "*" character.

_____

_____

**LAB
8.1**

LAB 8.1 EXERCISE ANSWERS

This section gives you some suggested answers to the questions in Lab 8.1, with discussions related to those answers. Your answers may vary, but the most important thing is whether or not your answers work. Use these discussions to analyze differences between your answers and those presented here.

If you have alternative answers to the questions in these exercises, you are encouraged to post your answers and discuss them at the companion Web site for this book, located at:

```
http://www.phptr.com/phptrinteractive
```

8.1.1 ANSWERS

Type the following commands:

```
grep at todo
grep " at " todo
grep "door.
* Sat:" todo
```

a) What is a string?

Answer: A string is a sequence of characters.

Any sequence of characters is considered a string, whether it consists of letters, numbers, or even spaces.

b) Why does the second string need to be quoted?

Answer: It needs to be quoted because it contains a space.

Remember that the shell interprets the arguments before the `grep` command gets them. If this search were being done inside a program (such as `more`), you wouldn't need the quotation marks.

c) What is the difference between the output of the first and second commands?

Answer: The first command matches any line that contains " " in it. The second matches any line that contains " at ".

The first search will find any line that contains "at." The second search will find any line that contains "at" as a separate word in the middle of a line. It won't find a line that starts with "at" (because there won't be a space at the beginning of the word), or a line that ends with "at" (because there won't be a space at the end of the word).

d) What is the third command trying to do?

Answer: The third command is trying to match a regular expression on two lines in a row.

e) Does the third command work? If not, why not?

Answer: No, it doesn't work. Regular expressions only apply in a single line.

When a program looks for a regular expression, it does so one line at a time. Most UNIX utilities read a file one line at a time. Each line is checked for the regular expression; if there's a match, the program does what it needs to do (i.e., grep prints the line), and then goes on to the next line. If there's no match, the program just goes on to the next line.

When it searches a line, a regular expression normally moves along the line, searching to see if it matches.

The result is that, almost always, regular expressions only match within a single line.

■ FOR EXAMPLE:

The command grep "the" is being used to search a line consisting of the words "tithe often." The program is looking for three letters that match "the." As soon as a letter doesn't match, it can check the word against the next three-letter pattern in the line.

First the program compares "the" to the beginning of the line, letter by letter:

```
the
tithe often
```

The program compares the first letter in the expression against this part of the line. The "t" in "the" matches the "t" in "tithe" so it compares the second letter in the expression ("h") against the second letter for this part of the line. Well, "h" doesn't match "i". The word "the" doesn't match the three letters of the line starting with the first character.

However, maybe "the" matches the three letters of the line starting with the *second* character. (Remember, regular expression programs cannot actually think. They have to try every possibility, even if a person would know it doesn't work, so imagine that the program slides the expression "the" over by one character to check if it matches this part of the line:

```
 the
tithe often
```

Just as before, it compares the "t" in "the" against the first character in the part of the line it's now checking. The "t" is not the same as "i" so the program doesn't even bother comparing "h" against the next letter.

Instead, it moves along the line. Maybe "the" matches the three letters of the line starting with the *third* character:

```
  the
tithe often
```

It compares the "t" in "the" against the third letter of the line "tithe often" and they are the same. Having succeeded in matching one letter, the program compares the second letter of "the" against the fourth letter of the line. (It's rather like checking lottery numbers; if the program were a person, there would be some excitement at this point.) Because the "th" in "the" matches the "th" in "tithe" the program checks the next letter in the expression against the next letter in the line. The letter "e" matches the letter "e" and the program considers the line as containing a match to the expression.

There are exceptions. (There are always exceptions.) The simplest way to search a single file for an expression that spans two lines is to load the file into emacs. If it's not feasible to use emacs, there are other methods, but none of them are easy, and they're beyond the scope of this book. (Each method involves a different program, one of perl, awk, or sed.)

 For more details on using Perl, awk, or sed for this kind of match, visit the companion Web site associated with this book, located at:

```
http://www.phptr.com/phptrinteractive
```

8.1.2 ANSWERS

Type the following commands:

```
grep dry todo
grep 'dry$' todo
```

a) How does the $ character change the output?

Answer: Instead of matching all lines containing "dry", the expression "dry$" matches only the line where "dry" is the last word on the line.

The "$" character forces grep to look only at the end of the line. Instead of the search sailing the length of the line, it is anchored at one end. The other anchor character, "^", fixes the search at the beginning of the line.

Type the command:

```
grep '$99' todo
```

b) Does "dry$" mean the same thing as "$dry"?

Answer: No. The "$" anchor character only anchors an expression if it is at the end of the expression.

The "$" character only acts as an anchor if it's at the end of the expression, just as the "^" character only acts as an anchor if it's at the beginning of the expression.

If this seems odd and inconsistent, remember that regular expressions only search a single line. What does it mean to search for something *before* the beginning of the line, or *after* the end of the line? It doesn't make sense. For that reason, the characters "^" and "$" are treated as metacharacters only at the appropriate end of a regular expression.

Type the following commands:

```
grep '$' todo
grep '^$' todo
```

c) What does the regular expression "^$" match?

Answer:The expression "^$" matches only empty lines.

The "^" at the beginning of the expression matches the beginning of a line. The "$" at the end matches the end of a line. There are no characters in between. The only lines where the beginning is immediately after the ending are the empty lines.

8.1.3 ANSWERS

Enter the following command:

```
grep . todo
```

a) What does the "." regular expression match?

Answer:The "." regular expression matches any single character.

This `grep` command matched all lines in the file except the empty line.

b) Explain the results of the command.

Answer:Any line that had a character on it matched the "." regular expression.

Think again of how the regular expression is checked against the line. A "." matches any single character. When comparing against the empty line, the "." is compared against nothing. The match fails. On any other line, the "." matches the very first character, and no more has to be checked.

If you need to strip the empty lines out of a file, you can use a `grep .` command.

If you want to find all lines that are only a certain number of characters, you can use that number of dots.

■ *FOR EXAMPLE:*

You would use the following to find all lines four characters long:

```
grep "^....$" *
```

The anchors must be there, or the search will also find all lines that are more than four characters long.

Enter the following command:
```
grep o.t todo
```

c) From the output, what does the "o.t" regular expression match?

Answer: The "o.t" matches "o", followed by any character, followed by "t". In the sample text, that's:

```
Coat to dry cleaners [open 9-6]
* Buy oats
Friday: Take out garbage
* Sat: Show kids goat at zoo
```

The words "Coat", "oats", "out", and "goat" all match. The character represented by "." doesn't have to be a character: it could be the space between words (perhaps "go to"), or a tab character.

You can use the "." regular expression to find words for crossword puzzles. The file /usr/dict/words contains a list of words, one to a line. For instance, to find all four-letter words starting with "k" with a "p" as the third letter, you would do the following:

```
$ grep "^k.p.$" /usr/dict/words
```

This might be the result:

```
kepi
kept
kips
```

If the definition is "a French military hat," then "kepi" is the word you need.

8.1.4 ANSWERS

Enter the following command:

```
grep '[Dd]' todo
```

a) What does the "[Dd]" expression match?

Answer: The "[Dd]" expression matches either the letter "D" or the letter "d".

Just as with shell wildcards, square brackets indicate one of a set of characters.

 There is a distinction between a regular expression and a pattern, but it's rather technical. In casual use, they're often used interchangably, as I have here. If you want to know, a pattern is one of the set of all possible character combinations that can be generated by a particular expression. For our purposes, the expression is what you check with and the pattern is what you check against. So "[Dd]" is an expression that matches the patterns "D" and "d".

b) Are the apostrophes around "[Dd]" required?

Answer: They're not required for the regular expression, but they're used to prevent interpretation of "[Dd]" by the shell.

This is a precaution, simply because the regular expression is being given as an argument to grep. Because the square brackets are also shell metacharacters, it's safer to put apostrophes around them to prevent the shell from treating them specially. You could also use "\[Dd]". In this case, the precaution is probably wasted; it would only be a problem if you had a file in that directory named D or one named d.

If you were using regular expressions to search text in vi or emacs or more, the apostrophes wouldn't be needed at all.

c) What does the expression "[A-Z]" match?

Answer: The expression "[A-Z]" matches any capital letter.

Just as with shell wildcard bracket expressions, a "-" character represents a range of characters in ASCII order. In this case, the range is all capital letters. The anchor "^" restricts the match to the beginning of the line.

Enter the following command:

```
grep '^[^A-Z]' todo
```

d) What does the "^ [^A-Z]" expression match? What does the second "^" character mean?

Answer: The expression "^ [^A-Z]" matches all lines that begin with a character that is not a capital letter. When "^" is the first character inside a square bracket expression, it reverses the meaning: The expression matches everything except the characters in the brackets.

The meaning of ^ changes inside square brackets. (The meanings of many metacharacters change inside square brackets.) When a bracket expression starts with "[^", the rest of the list consists of characters that are *not* matched. To match everything that *isn't* a number, use "[^0-9]". To match everything that *isn't* a punctuation mark, use "[^!` ', . "':;?]."

Inside square brackets, the order of the list is important. The regular expression programs use the order to figure out what you really mean. By making the order of the list important, bracket expressions have a way to match characters that are important in bracket expressions. For example, to match "^" so it's not an anchor character, you have to have it someplace other than the beginning of the regular expression. To match "^" as part of a bracket expression, you have to have it someplace other than the beginning of the bracket expression.

■ FOR EXAMPLE:

The regular expression "[:^)]" matches any one of the colon, caret, or right parenthesis characters. The "^" character is matched because it's not the first character in the brackets.

Enter the following command:

```
grep '[\*]' todo
```

e) What does the "[*]" expression match?

Answer: It matches either "\" or "*"; most metacharacters have their special meanings turned off inside a bracket expression.

Inside a bracket expression, the regular expression metacharacters "." and "*" and "\" have no special meaning.

(In fact, this is also true for shell wildcard bracket expressions: The characters "?" and "*" have no special meanings inside bracket expressions.) Other characters, however, become special. The "^" at the beginning of a bracket expression reverses the meaning of the list. The "]" indicates the end of the bracket expression. The "–" character indicates a range of characters.

There are ways to match each of these in a bracket expression, as shown in Table 8.2.

Table 8.2 ■ Matching Metacharacters in Bracket Expressions

Character	To Match It
^	Don't make it the first character. Example: [!^] matches ! or ^, but [^!] matches any charcter except !.
]	Make it first (though it can follow a ^). Example: []] matches], but [^]] matches any character except].
[	Don't make it first. Example: [][] matches] or [. Avoid following this character with ":", ".", or "=".
–	Make it first or last in the expression. Example: []-] matches] or -. Example: [^]-] matches any character except] or -.

The reason to avoid following "[" in a bracket expression with any of ":", ".", or "=" is that POSIX regular expressions use these. If you need to search for ":" or "[", place the "[" second. The pattern "[:[]" matches either ":" or "[".

8.1.5 ANSWERS

Enter the following command:

```
grep 'garb*age' todo
```

a) What does the expression "garb*age" match?

Answer: The expression matches both "garage" and "garbage" because "b*" matches zero or more occurrences of "b".

This expression wouldn't match the string "gar age", for example. The "garb*age" specifies that only repetitions of "b" can come between "gar" and "age", although it matches if there are no "b"s at all.

The * affects only the single character before it, unless you group a set of characters with "\(" and "\)" (discussed in Exercise 8.1.6).

Enter the following commands:

```
grep "9*" todo
grep "99*" todo
grep "999*" todo
```

b) What does the "9*" expression match?

Answer: The expression "9*" matches all lines in the file, because it matches zero or more occurrences of "9".

The tricky part about "*" is that it stands for "zero or more." Any line can have zero of a particular character, even the empty lines.

Unlike the regular expression metacharacters so far, * (and the metacharacters in the next few exercises) affects the character *before* it.

If there are no characters before the * character, it matches itself. The regular expression "*" matches an asterisk. The regular expression "**" matches zero or more asterisks: The second asterisk is following a character, so it has its special meaning.

If you really mean "all characters on a line," use the expression ".*". If you mean all lines of one or more characters, use "..*".

c) What does the "99*" expression match?

Answer: The expression "99" matches lines containing at least one 9, because it matches a 9 followed by zero or more 9s.*

Some people expect "9*" to match any string containing a "9". Why doesn't it?

Answer: Unlike shell wildcards, the "" metacharacter also matches zero occurrences of the character.*

In order to match a specific number of occurrences of a character, basic regular expressions provide the "\{\}" pair.

Enter the following command:

```
grep '9\{2,2\}' todo
```

d) What does the expression "9\{2,2\}" match?

Answer: The expression matches "99"—a sequence of two 9s.

When you're searching a lot of text files for (say) all capitalized short forms (like QWERTY, CRT, or IRS), it's convenient to be able to eliminate all of the one- and two-letter capital letters. You could search for three letters or more with "[A-Z][A-Z][A-Z][A-Z]*", but that's longer to type than "\{". It also doesn't let you limit the maximum number in the sequence.

Although they're bothersome to type, the "\{" and "\}" pairs help when trying to find repeated characters. This expression is usually described as "\{n,m\}", where n and m are numbers. It matches only sequences of n or more characters, to a maximum of m. So "9\{2,4\}" matches sequences of two, three, or four 9s in a row.

■ FOR EXAMPLE:

Using grep, the expression "9\{2,4\}" will also find sequences of more than four 9s. Suppose there are five 9s in a row. The first four are a pattern of four 9s, and the last four are a pattern of four 9s. The way to find exactly four 9s is to mark an ending to the expression.

```
grep 9\{2,4\}[^9] *
```

Now the expression is "two, three, or four 9s, followed by a character that is not a 9." However, this example won't find two 9s at the end of a line. At the end of a line, there is no last character that isn't a 9.

If you don't want to set one of the limits, leave the number out: The expression "9\{3,\}" matches three or more 9s in a row. The expression "9\{,4\}" matches zero, one, two, three, or four 9s in a row. (Extended regular expressions add convenient short forms for "zero or one occurrences" and "one or more occurrences" of a character.)

Another possible use is to find all lines over a certain length.

■ *FOR EXAMPLE:*

To find all files that contain lines over 60 characters long:

```
grep '.\{61,\}' *
```

You don't need to use "^" or "$" here because you're just concerned with lines over a certain length. (You would need to anchor the expression if you wanted to find lines *under* a certain length.)

Whether you use the "\{\}" expression depends on the sorts of searches you do. You may find you don't need it or you may find it's incredibly useful.

e) What expression would match all North American phone numbers (three digits, a "-", and four more digits)?

Answer: The expression "[0-9]\{3,3\}-[0-9]\{4,4\}" *matches all North American phone numbers.*

In this case, the expression is three digits, a "-", and four more digits. The real power of regular expressions comes from combining them. The "-" in the middle of the expression makes it match phone numbers and not social security numbers.

8.1.6 ANSWERS

Enter the following command:

```
grep "Sat\(urday\)*:" todo
```

a) In the line that appears, what part did the expression match?

Answer: The expression matched both "Sat:" *and* "Saturday:".

A grouping is most useful when it's in the middle of an expression. If you only wanted to match "Sat," then the expression could have been "Sat."

b) What does the "\(urday\)*" expression mean?

Answer: The expression "\(urday\)*" *matches zero or more occurrences of the string* "urday".

Both of the repetition metacharacters ("*" and "\{\}") can be used for groups as well.

Enter the following command:

```
grep "\(.\)\1" todo
```

c) What does the "\(.\)\1" expression match?

Answer: The expression matches any character that occurs twice.

This expression is different from ".." because the second character *must* be the same as the first one, no matter what it is. The group doesn't have to be a single character, either: The expression "\(..\)\1" finds any pattern with a repeated pair of characters.

This structure, called a *back reference*, is almost never used in searches, but is often used in search-and-replace functions in editing. Basic regular expressions can support up to nine of them in one expression (\1 through \9).

This back referencing is one of the reasons why you cannot put a "\ (\)" pair inside another "\ (\)" pair. That is, you cannot have a group inside another group. There would be no way to tell which group the back references referred to.

(In extended regular expressions, where there are no back-references, you can put groups inside other groups.)

8.1.7 ANSWERS

a) Write a regular expression that finds the lines containing the "." or the "$" characters.

Answer:The regular expression "[. $]" matches these characters.

Remember that the characters ".", "$", "\", and "[" are not special inside brackets. You could also use brackets to answer the previous question: the expression "[[ ]" would also match the character "[".

b) Write a regular expression that finds the "[" character.

Answer:The regular expression "\ [" matches this character.

The character "\" is a metacharacter that turns off the special meaning of the next character. To match a "\" character, use two backslashes in a row: "\\".

c) Write a regular expression that finds the "*" character?

Answer:The regular expression "" matches the "*" character.*

If you only want to match the "*" character, you can use the regular expression "*". However, if there are any other characters in the expression, it's safer to use "*".

LAB 8.1 SELF-REVIEW QUESTIONS

To test your progress, you should be able to answer the following questions. The data to be used for these questions is in the file movies, which is reproduced here.

```
All That Jazz

Jaws

M*A*S*H

Redneck Zombies
Romeo and Juliet

The Wiz
```

1) The expression "*" matches which of the following:
   a) _____The empty lines
   b) _____All lines in the file
   c) _____The line containing "M*A*S*H"
   d) _____All of the above

2) The expression "^ [^^]" matches which of the following:
   a) _____No line in this file
   b) _____All lines in the file
   c) _____All lines except the empty lines
   d) _____Any line beginning with a capital letter

3) Which of these expressions would find the line with only one "z"?
   a) _____z
   b) _____^[^z]*z[^z]*$
   c) _____z\{1,1\}
   d) _____z[^z]*

Quiz answers appear in Appendix A, Lab 8.1

L A B 8.2

EXTENDED REGULAR EXPRESSIONS

LAB OBJECTIVES

After this lab, you will be able to:

✓ Match Zero or One Characters

✓ Match Alternative Strings

✓ Group Extended Expressions

Extended regular expressions are nearly identical to basic regular expressions. They add some capabilities and use some different metacharacters.

- Instead of using "\ (" and "\ )" to group expressions, extended regular expressions use " (" and ")".

- Instead of using "\ {" and "\ }" to indicate repetition, extended regular expressions use "{" and "}".
- There are no back references. The expression "\1" matches "1".
- There are metacharacters for zero or one occurrences, "?", and for one or more occurrences, "+".
- There is a metacharacter to choose between strings or grouped expressions, "|".

Bracket expressions are the same as in basic regular expressions.

The metacharacters for extended regular expressions are shown in Table 8.3.

Table 8.3 ■ Extended Regular Expression Metacharacters

.	Match any single character.
^	Refers to the beginning of the line.
$	Refers to the end of the line.
[abc]	Match one of the characters in the brackets.
[^abc]	Match any character *except* one of the characters in the brackets.
expr*	Match any number of *expr* in a row. The *expr* can be any expression: a character, a bracket expression, or a pattern grouped with (and).
expr?	Match zero or one occurrence of the pattern expr.
expr+	Match one or more occurrences of the pattern expr.
\c	Turn off the special meaning of the characters ., ^, $, \, [, *, ?, +, |, (,), {, and }. Other characters don't have special meanings.
expr1|expr2	Match either pattern *expr1* or *expr2*.
pattern{n,m}	Match between *n* and *m* repetitions of *pattern* in a row.
(pattern)	Treat pattern as a group, for the purposes of using *, ?, +, |, or { and }.

There are more metacharacters when using extended regular expressions, but they're more consistent than the basic regular expression characters.

.   *   ^ $?   [+ | (   )   {   }

The \ character always turns off the special meaning, instead of sometimes giving a character a special meaning.

LAB 8.2 EXERCISES

 These exercises use the todo *file that you created for Lab 8.1.*

8.2.1 MATCH REPEATED CHARACTERS

Enter the following commands:

```
egrep '9?' todo
egrep '99?' todo
egrep '9+' todo
```

(If the egrep command isn't on your system, use grep -E instead.)

a) What's the difference between "9?" and "99?"

_____

_____

b) What's the difference between "9?" and "9+"?

_____

_____

c) How would you write "9?" using basic regular expressions? How would you write "9+"?

_____

_____

d) Which line would match the expression "`^[^9]*9{1,1}[^9]*$`"?

_____

_____

8.2.2 MATCH ALTERNATIVE STRINGS

Enter the following command:

```
egrep "Friday|Saturday" todo
```

a) What lines are matched?

_____

_____

b) Could you write this expression using basic regular expressions? If so, how?

_____

_____

8.2.3 GROUP EXTENDED PATTERNS

Enter the following command:

```
egrep "(Fri(day)?)|(Sat(urday)?)" todo
```

a) What lines are matched?

_____

_____

b) How would you extend this regular expression to match all of the days of the week or just their first three letters?

_____

_____

c) How would you match a "(" character in an extended regular expression?

_____

_____

LAB 8.2 EXERCISE ANSWERS

This section gives you some suggested answers to the questions in Lab 8.2, with discussions related to those answers. Your answers may vary, but the most important thing is whether or not your answers work. Use these discussions to analyze differences between your answers and those presented here.

If you have alternative answers to the questions in these exercises, you are encouraged to post your answers and discuss them at the companion Web site for this book, located at:

`http://www.phptr.com/phptrinteractive`

The most important thing to realize is whether your answers work. There are often several ways to achieve the same result.

8.2.1 ANSWERS

Enter the following commands:

```
egrep '9?' todo
egrep '99?' todo
egrep '9+' todo
```

**LAB
8.2**

a) What's the difference between "9?" and "99?"?

Answer: The pattern "9?" matches any line containing a sequence of zero or one 9s in a row (i.e., every line in the file). The pattern "99?" matches any line containing a 9 followed by zero or one 9 (i.e., every line containing a 9).

Like "*", the "?" and "+" characters are special when they occur after another character or pattern. The "?" matches zero or one of the characters; you can think of it as asking, "Is this present or isn't it?" The "+" character matches at least one; you can think of it as "the character plus any repetitions."

In "99?", the extra 9 changes the pattern to "one or two 9s." This isn't quite the same as "9+", but for the text in this file, the results are identical.

b) What's the difference between "9?" and "9+"?

Answer: The "9?" matches zero or one 9. There must be at least one 9 for "9+" to match.

The "+" character requires at least one occurrence of the preceding character. The expression "9?" matches almost any string. It matches "zoo" just as well as it matches "9".

The fact that egrep displays the entire line hides what's actually being matched. Unless you anchor the regular expression so it indicates the entire line, egrep searches each character on the line, looking for a match. Because "9?" is one of those patterns that matches zero occurrences, it matches every line, even the empty ones. The "9+" expression requires at least one 9 to match.

c) How would you write "9?" using basic regular expressions? How would you write "9+"?

Answer: You can write "9?" as "9\{0,1\}". You can write "9+" as "9\{1,\}".

The "?" and "+" metacharacters are conveniences. In extended regular expressions, you could also write "9?" as "9{0,1}", and "9+" as "9{1,}".

d) Which line would match the expression "^[^9]*9{1,1}[^9]*$"?

Answer: This pattern specifies a line containing only one 9:

```
Coat to dry cleaners [open 9-6]
```

This regular expression uses anchors and bracket expressions to make sure there is only one 9 on the line. The anchors make sure the expression extends over the entire line, not just a part of the line. The "{1,1}" specifies a single 9 (although it isn't necessary; using just "9" would work as well). The bracket expressions before and after the 9 specify no other 9s on the line.

When you need to find a single occurrence of a pattern on a line, anchor the expression at the beginning and end of the line.

8.2.2 ANSWERS

Enter the following command:

```
egrep "Friday|Saturday" todo
```

a)   What lines are matched?

*Answer: This pattern matches the lines containing either "*Friday*" or "*Saturday.*"*

```
Friday: Take out garbage
Saturday: Paint garage door, if dry
```

You could also extract the "day" part and write this regular expression as "(Fri|Satur)day." This is harder to read, though, and often isn't worth the trouble. The parentheses must be there to group the patterns. Without them, the expression is "Fri|Saturday," which matches "Fri" or "Saturday".

b)   Could you write this expression using basic regular expressions? If so, how?

Answer: This expression cannot be done using basic regular expressions.

This is the single biggest advantage of extended regular expressions: the ability to say "this *or* that." Because the editors vi and emacs use basic regular expressions, you may find yourself thinking in terms of basic regular expressions only. Sometimes you must use extended regular expressions, and the " | " expression is one of those times.

8.2.3 ANSWERS

Enter the following command:

```
egrep "(Fri(day)?)|(Sat(urday)?)" todo
```

a)   What lines are matched?

Answer: This expression matches any line containing "Fri," "Friday," "Sat," or "Saturday":

```
Friday: Take out garbage
Saturday: Paint garage door, if dry
* Sat: Show kids goat at zoo
```

The | bar is rather like a bracket expression, but for longer strings: it allows you to match one of a list of words or expressions.

This is another expression that cannot be written in basic regular expressions. In basic regular expressions, you cannot put groups inside groups.

b)   How would you extend this regular expression to match all of the days of the week or just their first three letters?

Answer: A regular expression to match each day of the week is as follows:

```
Sun(day)?|Mon(day)?|Tue(sday)?|Wed(nes-
    day)?|Thu(rsday)|Fri(day)|Sat(urday)?
```

You can have more than two alternatives for a | expression. You can actually shorten the expression a bit because each one has "day" in it. This is a little bit shorter to type but harder to read:

```
(Sun|Mon|Tue|Wed|Thu|Fri|Sat)((s|nes|r)?day)?
```

This expression is not as precise an expression. The regular expression in the answer matches only the days of the week. This regular expression would match such nonsense words as "Satnesday" and "Monrday."

Which regular expression you use to find the days of the week depends on what you're searching and how many wrong matches you're willing to tolerate.

c) How would you match a " (" character in an extended regular expression?

Answer:To match a " (" character, put a backslash before it, like this:"\ (".

This tends to confuse people because in basic regular expressions, the \ turns on some metacharacters. In extended regular expressions, the \ always turns off the special meaning of the next character. If the next character doesn't have a special meaning, the backslash is ignored.

LAB 8.2 SELF-REVIEW QUESTIONS

To test your progress, you should be able to answer the following questions. Suppose you have a file of phone numbers; the phone number comes after a : character. Some of the data is reproduced as follows:

```
Adams, Mike:576-8122 (h), 887-2336 (w)
Barb Adelaide:881-7294
Adelaide, King :519-741-0692
Andrews, Jodie:887-7671
Carter, Lance:881-2999
Anne Finch:887-6345, 887-9999 (fax)
```

I) The extended regular expression " (" will find all of the lines with parentheses in them.
    a) _____True
    b) _____False

2) Which regular expression finds both work and fax numbers?
    a) _____(w|fax)
    b) _____w|fax
    c) _____(w)|(fax)
    d) _____\(w\)|\(fax\)

3) Which regular expression would find everyone whose last name starts with "A"?
    a) _____(^A[^,]*)|(A[^:]*)
    b) _____((A[^,]*)|(A*)):
    c) _____(^A[^:]*,)|(A[^ :]*):
    d) _____(A[^:]*)|(A[^:]*):[^:]*$

Quiz answers appear in Appendix A, Lab 8.2

C H A P T E R   8

TEST YOUR THINKING

 The projects in this section are meant to have you utilize all of the skills that you have acquired throughout this chapter. The answers to these projects can be found at the companion Web site to this book, located at:

`http://www.phptr.com/phptrinteractive`

Visit the Web site periodically to share and discuss your answers.

The file renovation contains a list of your expenses for renovating your house. Each line has the name of a supplier, a colon, the supply, another colon, and the cost.

```
Murcheson Lumber:10 6' 2x4:$32.91
Murchesn Lumber:1 lb. nails:$2.14
Kepler Build-All:8 sheets 4x8 drywall:34.24
Krazy Achmed's Paint-It:2 gallons primer:$15.93
Krazy Achmed's Paint-It:4 rolls drywall tape:$8.93
Kepler Build-All:5 lbs. Drywall Screws:$8.76
Mulder's Tool Shack:drywall gun:85.23
Happy's Hardware Hut:5 gallons drywall mud:$14.29
```

1) Write the regular expression to match all of the costs.

2) Write the regular expression to find all of the Murcheson Lumber expenses (even with misspellings).

3) Write the regular expressions to find all of the drywall costs.

4) Write a single regular expression to find all of the nail and screw costs.

5) Write the regular expressions to find all of the costs under $10.00, and all of the costs over $10.00.

CHAPTER 9

THE VI EDITOR

The vi *(visual) editor is on almost every UNIX system. It's the standard editor. And whether you like it or hate it, you will need to use it. Probably sooner, not later.*

When you think of a text editor, you probably think of a word processor or something similar: The editor displays as much of the file as fits on the screen. You move the cursor around, and you edit text. Sometimes you add text; sometimes you delete text. An editor that uses the entire screen to display text is called a *screen editor*. The vi editor, which this chapter explores, is just such an editor.

L A B   9.1

STARTING AND QUITTING VI

LAB OBJECTIVES

After this Lab, you will be able to:

✓ Start vi

✓ Add Text

✓ Save the File

✓ Exit vi

The vi editor was the first screen editor available for UNIX systems. Before that, there were only line editors, which displayed text one line at a time. (The editor ed, which I've already referred to as the "standard UNIX text editor," is a line editor.) The name vi is short for "visual" and is pronounced either "vee-eye" or "vye." (I have known people who insisted on pronouncing it "six" under the impression it was a Roman numeral six, but no one ever understood them.) The vi editor is actually a screen editor built on top of a line editor. (The line editor version is called ex.) Because it uses its own commands for some things and ex commands for others, there are two different styles of commands in vi. These will be explained later.

The vi editor is also a *mode editor*. This means it has different operating modes. What works as a command in one mode may not be a command in another mode. The vi editor has two modes, as follows:

- *Text input mode* is the mode used to add text to a file. Anything you type in input mode goes into the file.
- *Command mode* is the mode used to give commands. Anything you type in command mode is a command. For example, you can save the file, quit vi, search the text, and so on, using commands.

To switch from input mode to command mode, press the Escape key. There are several commands to switch from command mode to input mode; each command inserts the text at a different location (at the end of the line, at the beginning of the line, before the cursor, after the cursor, and so on).

With a mode editor, some or all commands are letters or phrases. For example, the command to go to the end of the file is the letter G. In a modeless editor (such as emacs), you can always enter text, and commands are always "magic" key combinations (such as Control-D).

Even though vi is not the "standard" editor, it (or a nearly identical copy) is available on every UNIX system. For that reason, even if you prefer emacs, you should know the basics of vi.

If you have problems, press the Escape key. That ends the current command. Then you can try again.

Some commands in vi are letters; these are indicated by the instruction, "Type the command." Other commands must be finished by pressing Enter; these are indicated by the instruction, "Enter the command."

LAB 9.1 EXERCISES

9.1.1 START VI

Enter the following command:

```
vi
```

a) What is the name of the file you are editing?

_____

_____

b) What do the "~" characters represent?

_____

_____

c) What mode are you in?

_____

_____

Enter the following command:

```
:quit
```

d) What happened?

_____

_____

9.1.2 ADD TEXT

Start `vi` again.

Type the following command:

```
a
```

a) What mode are you in?

_____

_____

Type the following line; press Enter at the end of the line.

```
Memo:  Everybodyxx
```

b) What does the `a` command do?

_____

_____

c) Backspace over the "xx". What happens?

_____

_____

Press the Escape key.

d) What does Escape do? What happens if you press Escape again?

_____

_____

9.1.3 SAVE THE FILE

Enter the `quit` command.

     a) What happens?

_____

_____

Enter the following command:

    `:write`

    b) What happens?

_____

_____

Enter the following command:

    `:w memo`

    c) What message does `vi` print?

_____

_____

Using the `a` command, add the following text:

    `Congratulations to Chris, the former playboy.`

Press the Escape key and enter the following command:

    `:w`

    d) What name is the file saved under this time?

_____

_____

9.1.4 EXIT VI

Use the a command to add the following lines of text.

```
Chris is now the proud father of a little boy.
The early arrival (early this morning, two weeks early)
means that Chris won't be in the office this week or next
    week.

Best wishes from all of us!
```

Press the Escape key and then enter the :quit command.

a) What happens when you try to quit this time?

_____

_____

Enter the following command:

```
:wq
```

b) What happens?

_____

_____

Open the file for editing again (with the command vi memo).

Use the a command to add any text at all.

Now press the Escape key and enter the following command:

```
:q!
```

c) What's the difference between the :q command and the :q! command? (Use cat to examine the memo file.)

_____

_____

LAB 9.1 EXERCISE ANSWERS

 This section gives you some suggested answers to the questions in Lab 9.1, with discussions related to those answers. Your answers may vary, but the most important thing is whether or not your answers work. Use these discussions to analyze differences between your answers and those presented here.

If you have alternative answers to the questions in these exercises, you are encouraged to post your answers and discuss them at the companion Web site for this book, located at:

```
http://www.phptr.com/phptrinteractive
```

9.1.1 ANSWERS

Enter the following command:

```
vi
```

a) What is the name of the file you are editing?

Answer: The file has no name yet.

When you started vi this time, you didn't name a file to be edited. There was no file name. (Some versions of vi "make up" a file name for you, and display this temporary file name on the bottom line of the screen.)

Figure 9.1 shows the vi screen.

Normally you know what file you're editing, and you just name it on the command line. The command vi memo would open the file memo for editing, even if the file didn't exist yet. It displays the name of the file and its size on the bottom line, the status line. You can name more than one file; when you're done editing or reading one, use the :next command to start editing the next file in the list.

When you don't name a file, some versions of vi immediately open a temporary file and display the name of the temporary file on the status line.

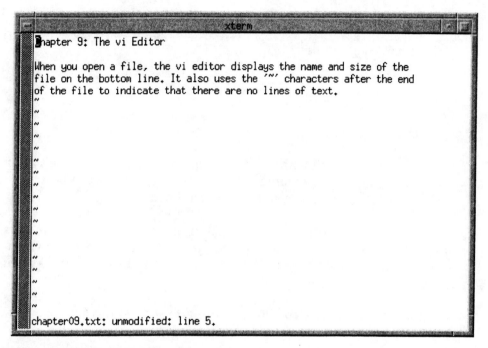

Figure 9.1 ■ **The vi screen**

b) What do the "~" characters represent?

Answer: The "~" characters represent lines of the screen that do not have lines of text.

How do you distinguish between a screen full of empty lines, or an empty vi screen that shows there are no lines in the file? The answer in vi is that if there are no lines of text, vi shows you a ~ character instead.

Admittedly, it's still difficult to distinguish between an empty file and a file that consists of lines that have a single ~ character. (However, a file consisting of one ~ to a line is much less common than a file that starts with more than 25 empty lines.)

You *can* tell them apart: When you open a file in vi, the bottom line of the screen (the *status line*) displays the file's name and its size in bytes.

c) What mode are you in?

Answer: You are in command mode.

All vi sessions start in command mode.

Enter the following command:

    :quit

d) What happens?

Answer:The vi session ends.

This command started with a ":". Not all commands do. There's a set of commands that do. All commands that start with a ":" must be ended by pressing Enter. These colon commands can be fairly long.

Another thing to notice is that as soon as you typed ":", the cursor moved to the status line and displayed your command text. On the bottom line of the screen, you can backspace over mistakes in the command.

You don't have to type the entire word "quit"; you can shorten most colon commands to one or two letters. From now on, we'll use :q to quit.

The colon commands are also called "ex commands." They're actually commands used by the ex line editor, which formed the basis for vi. The ex commands always start with ":" and must be ended by pressing Enter.

9.1.2 ANSWERS

Start vi again. Type the following command:

    a

a) What mode are you in?

Answer:You are in input mode.

The a command puts you in input mode. Any text you type is inserted *after* the cursor.

If you type a very long line in input mode, the text will "wrap" around the screen and show up on the next line. This is something vi does so you can see the entire line; it does not mean that you have started a new line.

To start a new line in vi, you must press Enter.

Type the following line; press the Enter key at the end of the line.

    Memo: Everybodyxx

b) What does the a command do?

Answer: The a *command enters input mode, and inserts the text immediately after the cursor's current position.*

Commands such as a are called "vi commands." Vi commands tend to be short, one or two letters. vi does *not* display them on the screen.

c) Backspace over the "xx". What happens?

Answer: The cursor moves, but the characters "xx" do not disappear.

One of the peculiarities of vi is that it doesn't erase characters you backspace over. It's something you learn to live with.

On some terminals, vi makes the deleted characters go away when you press Escape; on others, vi doesn't make them go away until you give some other command that makes vi redraw the screen.

Press the Escape key.

d) What does Escape do? What happens if you press Escape again?

Answer: Pressing the Escape key leaves input mode and goes back to command mode. Pressing Escape again may make the terminal beep but has no other effect.

In command mode, the Escape key interrupts whatever command you're currently running and it beeps.

You can also leave input mode by pressing the Interrupt key (Control-C). If you press Control-C, the terminal will beep.

9.1.3 ANSWERS

Enter the :quit command.

a) What happens?

Answer: *vi prints an error message and doesn't quit.*

The error message looks something like this:

```
No write since last change (":quit!" overrides)
```

If you have made changes and haven't saved them yet, vi warns you when you try to quit. You have the choice of saving the file or quitting without saving.

Enter the following command:

```
:write
```

b) What happens?

Answer: *vi prints an error message asking for a file name.*

The error message looks something like this:

```
No current filename
```

When you edit a file with most text editors (including vi), you're really editing a copy of the file. This copy is held in a storage area, a *buffer*. To make your changes permanent, you have to write them to the disk. The :write command writes the buffer to the disk, replacing the previous version of the file with your new edited version.

In this case, vi doesn't know what the name of the file is, because you didn't specify one when you started vi.

The :write command can be abbreviated :w, and we'll use the :w command from now on.

Enter the following command:

```
:w memo
```

c) What message does `vi` print?

Answer:The message reads something like:

```
"memo" [New File] 2 lines, 17 characters
```

This is the name of the file being written, whether it's a new file, and its size.

Using the `a` command, add the following text:

```
Congratulations to Chris, the former playboy.
```

Press the Escape key and enter the following command:

```
:w
```

d) What name is the file saved under this time?

Answer:The file is saved under the name memo.

`vi` "remembers" the file's name. The file's name is the name you supplied on the command line when you started `vi`. If you didn't supply a name on the command line, the file's name is the name you use the first time you save the file.

9.1.4 ANSWERS

Use the `a` command to add the following lines of text:

```
Chris is now the proud father of a little boy.
The early arrival (early this morning, three weeks early)
means that Chris won't be in the office this week.
```

```
Best wishes from all of us!
```

Press the Escape key and then enter the `:quit` command.

a) What happens when you try to quit this time?

Answer: `vi` *prints an error message like this one:*

```
No write since last change (:quit! overrides)
```

`vi` warns you if you try to quit without saving any changes.

Enter the following command:

```
:wq
```

b) What happens?

Answer: vi *saves the file and exits.*

You can save *and* exit with one command. Although :w is short for the :write command and :q is short for the :quit command, the :wq command is not a short form for any longer command name. It writes the file and quits.

Open the file for editing again (with the command vi memo).
Use the a command to add any text at all.
Now press the Escape key and enter the following command:

```
:q!
```

c) What's the difference between the :q command and the :q! command? (Use cat to examine the memo file.)

Answer: The :q *command checks to see if the file has been changed; if it has, then* vi *doesn't quit. The* :q! *command always quits, whether you've changed the file or not.*

Many of the vi commands use ! as a kind of intensifier. When a command is followed by !, vi doesn't do any of the usual safety checks, it just performs the command.

The commands covered so far are summarized in Table 9.1

Table 9.1 ■ vi Session Commands

Command	Meaning
a	Enter text input mode.
Escape	Leave text input mode and enter command mode.
Control-C	Interrupt current command; also leaves text input mode.
:quit	Quit if there are no unsaved changes. Can be abbreviated :q
:quit!	Quit even if there are unsaved changes. Can be abbreviated :q!
:write [name]	Write current text into the file *name*. Can be abbreviated :w [name]
:write! [name]	Write current text into the file *name*, even if it's not the file you're currently editing. Can be abbreviated :w! [name]
:wq	Write the file and quit.
:next	Go to next file in the argument list if there are no unsaved changes. Can be abbreviated :n
:next!	Go to the next file in the argument list even if there are no unsaved changes. Can be abbreviated :n!

LAB 9.1 SELF-REVIEW QUESTIONS

To test your progress, you should be able to answer the following questions.

1) The `vi` editor has modes.
   a) _____True
   b) _____False

2) Pressing Escape twice leaves you in the same mode you started in.
   a) _____True
   b) _____False

3) When you open a file in `vi`, which of the following does it show you?
   a) _____The file's name (if it already exists).
   b) _____The file's size (if it already exists).
   c) _____Where the lines of the file end, by filling the rest of the lines with '~'.
   d) _____All of the above.

4) Which of the following is true of commands that start with ":"?
   a) _____They must be completed by pressing Enter.
   b) _____They are not displayed on the screen.
   c) _____They are part of `vi`, not `ex`.
   d) _____They are always short.

5) The :w command is short for :`write`, and :`q` is short for :`quit`, so :`wq` is short for :`writequit`.
   a) _____True
   b) _____False

Quiz answers appear in Appendix A, Lab 9.1

L A B 9.2

INSERTING TEXT

LAB OBJECTIVES

After this lab, you will be able to:

✓ Insert Text

✓ Append Text

This lab assumes you still have the file todo from Chapter 8, "Regular Expressions." To perform this lab, start vi with the file todo as the argument:

```
vi todo
```

LAB 9.2 EXERCISES

9.2.1 INSERT TEXT

Type the following command:

```
a
```

a) What happens to the cursor? What mode are you in now?

_____

_____

Type the following letters:

```
hings t
```

b) Where are the letters inserted?

_____

_____

Press the Escape key.

c) What mode are you in now?

_____

_____

9.2.2 APPEND TEXT

Type the following command:

```
i
```

a) What happens to the cursor? What mode are you in now?

_____

_____

Type the following letters (end with a space):

```
I have
```

b) Where are the letters inserted?

_____

_____

Press the Escape key and then type the following command:

    I

Type the following letters (end with a space):

    Ten

c) Where are the letters inserted?

_____

_____

Press the Escape key and then type the following command:

    A

Type the following letters (start with a space):

    Today

d) Where are the letters appended?

_____

_____

LAB 9.2 EXERCISE ANSWERS

This section gives you some suggested answers to the questions in Lab 9.2, with discussions related to those answers. Your answers may vary, but the most important thing is whether or not your answers work. Use these discussions to analyze differences between your answers and those presented here.

If you have alternative answers to the questions in these exercises, you are encouraged to post your answers and discuss them at the companion Web site for this book, located at:

http://www.phptr.com/phptrinteractive

9.2.1 ANSWERS

Type the following command:

    a

a) What happens to the cursor? What mode are you in now?

Answer: The cursor moves one character to the right. It may change shape. You are now in input mode.

In some versions of vi and on some terminals, the cursor will change shape to indicate that you are in input mode. A version of vi called elvis also gives you the option of displaying a message at the bottom of the screen to remind you that you are in input mode.

Type the following letters:

    hings t

b) Where are the letters inserted?

Answer: The letters are inserted after the current cursor position.

The text should now look like this:

    Things to Do:

There are only six commands that enter input mode. The difference between them is where the text is inserted. The a command inserts the new text *after* the cursor's current position.

Press the Escape key.

c) What mode are you in now?

Answer: You are now in command mode.

To exit input mode, press Escape. Control-C (interrupt) will also work.

9.2.2 ANSWERS

Type the following command:

```
i
```

a) What happens to the cursor? What mode are you in now?

Answer: The cursor may change shape. You are now in input mode.

Type the following letters (end with a space):

```
I have
```

b) Where are the letters inserted?

Answer: The letters are inserted before the cursor's current position.

The line should now look like this:

```
Things I have to Do
```

Press the Escape key and then type the following command:

```
I
```

Type the following letters (end with a space):

```
Ten
```

c) Where are the letters inserted?

Answer: The letters are inserted at the beginning of the line.

The line should now look like this:

```
Ten Things I have to Do
```

Press the Escape key and then type the following command:

```
A
```

Type the following letters (start with a space):

```
Today
```

d) Where are the letters appended?

Answer: The letters are appended at the end of the line.

The line should now look like this:

```
Ten Things I have to Do Today
```

The commands to enter input mode are summarized in Table 9.2.

Table 9.2 ▪ vi Commands to Enter Input Mode

a	Insert the text after the current cursor position.
A	Insert the text at the end of the current line.
i	Insert the text at the current cursor position.
I	Insert the text at the beginning of the current line.
o	Insert the text on a new line before the current line.
O	Insert the text on a new line after the current line.

As you can see, the uppercase versions of commands are usually related to the lowercase versions, but exactly how depends on the command.

vi *doesn't insert line breaks for you when typing; you have to press the Enter key yourself. You can get* vi *to wrap lines for you by entering the* ex *command* :set wrapmargin 8. *This causes* vi *to insert a new line whenever a word gets within 8 characters of the right side of the screen. (You can use other numbers, of course.) To turn this off, use the command* :unset wrapmargin.

LAB 9.2 SELF-REVIEW QUESTIONS

To test your progress, you should be able to answer the following questions.

1) The cursor may change shape to tell you you're in input mode.
   a) _____True
   b) _____False

2) Each of the commands to enter text input mode inserts the text in a different place.
   a) _____True
   b) _____False

3) In the following table, match the command with the location where text is inserted.

   a) i   i) Beginning of line
   b) A   ii) End of line
   c) 1   iii) After the cursor
   d) a   iv) At the cursor

Quiz answers appear in Appendix A, Lab 9.2

L A B 9.3

MOVING THE CURSOR

> ## LAB OBJECTIVES
>
> After this lab, you will be able to:
> ✓ Move the Cursor on the Line
> ✓ Move the Cursor Through the File
> ✓ Move the Cursor by Context
> ✓ Move the Screen Display

For the exercises in this lab, open the file memo again using the command vi memo.

LAB 9.3 EXERCISES

9.3.1 MOVE THE CURSOR ON THE LINE

In command mode, type the following commands:

```
$
h
^
l
```

a) What does each of these commands do?

_____

_____

b) What happens when you try to use 1 to go past the end of a line?

_____

_____

9.3.2 MOVE THE CURSOR THROUGH THE FILE

In command mode, type the following commands:

```
j
k
L
H
M
```

a) What does each of these commands do?

_____

_____

Add approximately 40 lines of text; the content doesn't matter. (Hold down the Enter key until all text has disappeared from view.)

Press Escape to enter command mode again, and then type the following commands:

```
G
1G
```

b) Where does the cursor go with each command?

_____

_____

Press the Control-G key combination.

  c) What information is displayed?

_____

_____

Go back to the beginning of the file.

Press Control-F and Control-B.

  d) What do Control-F and Control-B do?

_____

_____

**LAB
9.3**

9.3.3 MOVE THE CURSOR BY CONTEXT

Use the 1G command to return to the beginning of the file.

Type the following commands:

```
www
b
```

  a) What happens each time you press w? When you press b?

_____

_____

  b) What happens when you get to the end of a line?

_____

_____

9.3.4 MOVE THE SCREEN DISPLAY

Use the j command to move the cursor to the middle of the screen.

Type the following commands:

```
Control-Y
Control-E
z
```

**LAB
9.3**

a) What does each command do?

_____

_____

LAB 9.3 EXERCISE ANSWERS

This section gives you some suggested answers to the questions in Lab 9.3, with discussions related to those answers. Your answers may vary, but the most important thing is whether or not your answers work. Use these discussions to analyze differences between your answers and those presented here.

If you have alternative answers to the questions in these exercises, you are encouraged to post your answers and discuss them at the companion Web site for this book, located at:

http://www.phptr.com/phptrinteractive

9.3.1 ANSWERS

In command mode, type the following commands:

```
$
h
^
1
```

a) What does each of these commands do?

Answer:*The* $ *command moves the cursor to the* end *of the line.*

The h *command moves the cursor one character (or row) to the* left.

The ^ *command moves the cursor to the* beginning *of the line.*

The l *command moves the cursor one character (or row) to the* right.

The four letter commands (h, j, k, and l) are the basic movement commands. It pays to learn them, because they occur in other programs too, particularly in games where you have to move the cursor. They can be difficult to learn at first. (For instance, why doesn't l go "left"?)

The letters were chosen not because they're easy to remember but because they're easy to *type*. When the your hands are resting on the typists' "home row," the first three fingers of your right hand are on "j," "k," and "l," The "h" key is just a key to the left.

You may find it easy to remember ^ and $ because they correspond to the same meanings for characters in regular expressions. ^ is the beginning of the line and $ is the end.

The ^ *command actually takes you to the first nonblank character on the line. So if the line started with spaces, such as "* The*", the* ^ *command takes you to the "*T*". To go to the beginning of the line, use* 0 *(zero).*

b) What happens when you try to use l to go past the end of a line?

Answer:*vi beeps and doesn't allow you to move to the next line using* l.

Remember that underneath it all, vi is actually a line editor. It operates on text one line at a time. The h and l commands stop moving the cursor when they reach the end of the line.

9.3.2 ANSWERS

In command mode, type the following commands:

```
j
k
L
H
M
```

a)   What does each of these commands do?

The j *command moves the cursor one line* down.

The k *command moves the cursor one line* up.

The L *command moves the cursor to the* last *line of the screen.*

The H *command moves the cursor to the* first *line of the screen.*

The M *command moves the cursor to the middle line of the screen.*

The G *command moves the cursor to the last line of the file.*

It may be easier to learn the four basic commands by memorizing j and k. The letter "j" dips down below the line while the letter "k" reaches up above the other letters. So the j command goes down and k goes up. If you keep your index and middle fingers resting on "j" and "k," then you can see that the command to go left (h) is to the left of "jk." The command to go right (l) is to the right of "jk."

Incidentally, pressing Enter in command mode is the same as the j command. It moves the cursor down one line. Pressing the Space key in command mode is the same as l and pressing Backspace is the same as h. The arrow keys on the keyboard may work as well, although this depends on the type of your terminal.

The L, H, and M commands move the cursor within one screenful of text. They aren't essential to using vi, but can save you some repetitious typing.

Add approximately 40 lines of text; the content doesn't matter. (Hold down the Enter key until all text has disappeared from view.)

Press Escape to enter command mode again, and then type the following commands

```
G
1G
```

b)   Where does the cursor go with each command?

Answer: The G *command moves the cursor to the last line in the file. The* 1G *command moves the cursor to the first line in the file.*

The G command is used to move throughout a file. The G command by itself always goes to the end of the file.

To move to a particular line in the file, supply a line number before the command. In this case, the line was line 1. This may be why the default behavior for G is to go to the end of the file: You may not know the number of the last line, but you know the number of the first line. The first line is always line number 1.

Press the Control-G key combination.

  c) What information is displayed?

  Answer: Control-G displays the file name and information:

```
"memo" line 1 of 54 --1%--
```

(Your information will be slightly different, depending on how many lines you added to the file.) When you need information about the file you're editing, use the Control-G command.

It will show you other information too: if you're not allowed to write to the file, it will display "read only."

Go back to the beginning of the file.

Press Control-F and Control-B.

  d) What do Control-F and Control-B do?

  Answer: Control-F moves forward in the file by one screen, while Control-B moves backwards.

It's fairly easy to remember Control-F (for forward) and Control-B (for backward). They don't actually move an entire screenful of text; two lines are kept so you can keep your place in the file.

With all of these movement commands, you can *repeat* them by first typing the number of repetitions.

■ *FOR EXAMPLE:*

The command 8j moves the cursor down by 8 lines. The command 4Control-F moves the cursor forward by 4 screenfuls. The command 3l moves the cursor right by 3 characters.

9.3.3 ANSWERS

Use the 1G command to return to the beginning of the file.
Type the following commands:

```
www
b
```

a) What happens each time you press w? When you press b?

Answer: The w command moves to the beginning of the next word. The b command moves back to the previous word beginning.

There are a set of commands that move by *context*. They have rules for figuring out what is and isn't a word and what is and isn't a sentence or a paragraph. For example, a paragraph ends with an empty line. A sentence ends with certain punctuation characters or when a paragraph ends.

b) What happens when you get to the end of a line?

Answer: The cursor moves to the next word, even if it's on another line.

Unlike the h, j, k, and l commands, the b and w commands move to the next line.

There are other context movement commands. The) command moves to the beginning of the next *sentence*. The } command moves to the beginning of the next *paragraph*. (A paragraph is the line after an empty line.) The (and { commands move by the same amounts, in the opposite direction.

9.3.4 ANSWERS

Use the j command to move the cursor to the middle of the screen.
Type the following commands:

```
Control-Y
Control-E
z
```

a) What does each command do?

Answer: The Control-Y command moves one line backward through the file, but it doesn't move the cursor from the current line.

The Control-E command moves one line forward through the file but it doesn't move the cursor from the current line.

The z command redraws the screen so the line with the cursor is the top line.

If scrolling the screen with Control-Y or Control-E would make the cursor disappear off the screen the cursor stays on the top or bottom line of the screen.

**LAB
9.3**

Like most of the other movement commands, typing a number before the Control-Y or Control-E command moves that many lines. For example, 3Control-E moves the display 3 lines.

The z command redraws the screen so that the line with the cursor is at the top of the display. This command is sometimes useful when you're reading through a file. If you type a number before the z command, that *line number* is placed at the top of the screen. (The G command behaves slightly differently. You should experiment with it and see if you can spot the differences.)

The movement commands in this lab are summarized in Table 9.3

Table 9.3 ■ Movement Commands in vi

[n]j	Move cursor down *n* lines (default 1).
[n]k	Move cursor up *n* lines (default 1).
[n]l	Move cursor right *n* characters (default 1).
[n]h	Move cursor left *n* characters (default 1).
[n]Enter	Same as j.
[n]Space	Same as l.
[n]Backspace	Same as h.
$	Move cursor to right end of line.
^	Move cursor to first nonblank character on left of line.

Table 9.3 ■ Movement Commands in vi (Continued)

0	Move cursor to first row of line.
[n]G	Move cursor to line *n* of file (default is end of file).
[n]w	Move cursor to beginning of *n*th next word (default 1)
[n]b	Move cursor to *n*th previous word beginning (default 1)
[n])	Move cursor to beginning of *n*th next sentence (default 1).
[n](	Move cursor to *n*th previous sentence beginning (default 1).
[n]}	Move cursor to beginning of *n*th next paragraph (default 1).
[n]{	Move cursor to *n*th previous paragraph beginning (default 1).
[n]Control-F	Move cursor forward *n* screenfuls of lines (default 1).
[n]Control-B	Move cursor backward *n* screenfuls of lines (default 1).
[n]Control-E	Move screen forward *n* lines without moving cursor (default 1).
[n]Control-Y	Move screen backward *n* lines without moving cursor (default 1).
H	Move cursor to top line of screen.
L	Move cursor to last line of screen.
M	Move cursor to middle line of screen.
z	Redraw screen so line with cursor is at top.

LAB 9.3 SELF-REVIEW QUESTIONS

To test your progress, you should be able to answer the following questions.

1) For all of the movement commands described in this section, starting them with a number causes them to be repeated that many times.
   a) _____True
   b) _____False

2) In the following table, match the command to its movement.

   a) i   **i)** One row right

   b) k   **ii)** One row left

   c) l   **iii)** One line up

   d) h   **iv)** One line down

3) In the following table, match the command to its movement.

   a) Control-B   **i)** Cursor moves one screen forward

   b) Control-E   **ii)** Cursor moves one screen backward

   c) Control-F   **iii)** Screen moves one line forward; cursor doesn't move

   d) Control-Y   **iv)** Screen moves one line backward; cursor doesn't move

4) Which command moves to the end of the file?
   a) _____Control-G
   b) _____$
   c) _____G
   d) _____Control-L

5) The Control-G command displays information about the file.
   a) _____True
   b) _____False

Quiz answers appear in Appendix A, Lab 9.3

L A B   9.4

DELETING TEXT

LAB OBJECTIVES

After this lab, you will be able to:

✓ Delete a Line

✓ Delete a Word or Character

✓ Write Over Text

✓ Undo the Change

The process of writing usually involves creating and then deleting. As Mark Twain once said, "Writing is easy. All you have to do is cross out the wrong words." The vi editor provides several ways to cross out the wrong words or the wrong lines or the wrong letters.

All of the deletion commands operate on the idea of a range. You can delete from *here* to *there*. Many of the commands here have already defined the range (such as the current line or word or character). There are other ways of *addressing* the delete commands that let you specify exactly the range you want to remove.

To perform the exercises in this lab, open the file memo again with the following command:

```
vi memo
```

LAB 9.4 EXERCISES

9.4.1 DELETE A LINE

With the cursor on the first line, type the following commands:

```
dd
5dd
```

a) What does the dd command do?

_____

_____

b) What effect does the 5 have on the command?

_____

_____

Move to the line after "Best wishes."

Enter the following command:

```
:.,$delete
```

Exit without saving the changes.

c) What does the command :.,$delete do?

_____

_____

9.4.2 DELETE A WORD OR CHARACTER

Use vi to open the file memo again.

Move the cursor to the line beginning with "Memo:".

Type the following command:

    dw

> **a)** What does the dw command do?

Type the following command:

    dl

> **b)** What does the dl command do?

Type the following command:

    x

> **c)** What does the x command do?

Enter the following command:

    d

Exit without saving the changes.

d) What does the d command do?

_____

_____

9.4.3 WRITE OVER TEXT

Type the following command:

    re

a) What does the r command do?

_____

_____

Go back to the beginning of the line and then type the following command:

    RAttention!

b) What does the R command do?

_____

_____

c) What happens when you press Enter and continue typing text?

_____

_____

9.4.4 UNDO A CHANGE

Press Escape and then type the following command:

    u

a) What does the u command do?

_____

_____

b) What happens when you type u twice?

_____

_____

LAB 9.4 EXERCISE ANSWERS

This section gives you some suggested answers to the questions in Lab 9.4, with discussions related to those answers. Your answers may vary, but the most important thing is whether or not your answers work. Use these discussions to analyze differences between your answers and those presented here.

If you have alternative answers to the questions in these exercises, you are encouraged to post your answers and discuss them at the companion Web site for this book, located at:

`http://www.phptr.com/phptrinteractive`

9.4.1 ANSWERS

With the cursor on the first line, type the following commands:

```
dd
5dd
```

a) What does the dd command do?

Answer: The dd command deletes the current line.

To delete the entire line you're on, use the command dd.

b) What effect does the 5 have on the command?

Answer:The 5 causes it to delete the next 5 lines, starting with the current line.

The delete command is another command you can repeat. This is useful for getting rid of a block of text.

Move to the line after "Best wishes."

Enter the following command:

    :.,$delete

Exit without saving the changes.

c) What does the command `:.,$delete` do?

Answer:The `:.,$d` command deletes from the current line to the end of the file.

This is a colon command, so it behaves differently from the vi commands. The basic command is `:delete`, which can be abbreviated `:d`. The " `.,$` " is called an *address*. It's the range of lines you want affected by the command.

To delete lines 1 through 10, use the range "`1,10`". The command would be `:1,10d`.

The addresses "**.**" and "$" stand for "the current line" and "the last line."

To delete line 55, use the command `:55d`. Note that the when you're using these ranges, you must use the colon command, `:d`, and not the vi command `d`.

9.4.2 ANSWERS

Use vi to open the file memo again.
Move the cursor to the line beginning with "Memo:".
Type the following command:

    dw

a) What does the dw command do?

Answer: The dw command deletes from the current cursor position to the beginning of the next word.

The line now looks like this:

```
: Everybody
```

Type the following command:

```
dl
```

b) What does the command do?

Answer: The dl command deletes the next character to the right of the cursor.

The line now looks like this:

```
Everybody
```

The actual delete command is d (one "d"). The delete command can be followed by any movement command, and it will delete from the cursor to the destination.

■ FOR EXAMPLE:

The command d$ deletes to the end of the line. The command dG deletes to the end of the file.

(There are other commands in vi that can be followed by a movement command. Doubling the command, such as typing dd, is how you tell vi that those commands should affect the entire current line instead of waiting for some kind of movement command.)

Type the following command:

```
x
```

c) What does the x command do?

Answer: The x command deletes the next character to the right of the cursor.

The line now looks like this:

```
Everybody
```

The x command is just a convenient short form for d1. The command *nx* deletes the next *n* lines.

Enter the following command:

    d

Exit without saving the changes.

d) What does the command do?

Answer: The command deletes two lines of text, starting with the current line.

Remember that in command mode, pressing the Enter key is a movement command: It moves the cursor down one line. When you combine the d command with a movement command, you delete everything from the cursor's current position to the destination of the movement command. Pressing d and then the Enter key is the same as typing dj.

LAB 9.4

9.4.3 ANSWERS

Type the following command:

    re

a) What does the r command do?

Answer: The r command replaces the character under the cursor with the next character you type. In this case, "E" is replaced by "e".

The r command is useful for fixing a single-character mistake. If you need to fix a longer chunk of text, you should either use R (as described in the next question) or delete the mistaken text and insert new text.

Go back to the beginning of the line and then type the following command:

    RAttention!

b) What does the R command do?

Answer: The R command puts you into input mode and overwrites text as you type.

The R command is useful for correcting a long piece of text.

c)   What happens when you press Enter and continue typing text?

Answer: You can add new lines but you cannot write over the next line.

The R command "remembers" the line you're replacing text on. It replaces text on the current line until you have written over all of it; from that point on, you're in input mode. However, the R command only changes the line you were on. You cannot keep "overwriting" through the lines of the file, you can only rewrite the line your cursor began on.

9.4.4 ANSWERS

Press Escape and then type the following command:

    u

a)   What does the u command do?

Answer: The u command undoes the last change you made to the file.

For a command that makes many changes (like a global search-and-replace), the u command undoes *all* of the changes.

b)   What happens when you type u twice?

Answer: The second u command undoes the first u command.

vi stores only one set of changes. If you give the u command twice, you don't "back out" of the second last set of changes. Instead, you undo the undo.

Table 9.4 summarizes the commands covered in this Lab.

Table 9.4 ■ vi Deletion, Change, and Undo Commands

`[n]dd`	Delete the next *n* lines, starting with the current line (default is 1 line).
`[n]d[movement]`	Delete from the current cursor position to the destination of the *movement* command.
`:addrd[elete]`	Delete the lines described in the ex-style *addr*.
`[n]rc`	Replace the next *n* characters with the character *c* (default 1).
`R`	Delete the rest of the line and enter input mode.
`u`	Undo the last command that changed the file.

LAB 9.4 SELF-REVIEW QUESTIONS

To test your progress, you should be able to answer the following questions.

1) The command to delete a line is `D`.
    a) _____True
    b) _____False

2) A command that can be followed by a movement (like `d`) affects the entire current line if you double it.
    a) _____True
    b) _____False

3) In the following table, match the command to the results.

a) `4dd`	**i)** Delete from current line to end of file
b) `dG`	**ii)** Replace letter under the cursor with "q"
c) `d$`	**iii)** Delete current line and three after it
d) `rq`	**iv)** Delete to end of current line

4) In the following table, match the results to the command.

a) Delete letter under cursor   **i)** u

b) Replace text and enter input mode   **ii)** x

c) Undo last change   **iii)** dh

d) Delete current line and line above   **iv)** R

5) Giving the undo command four times is the same as not giving it at all.
   a) _____True
   b) _____False

Quiz answers appear in Appendix A, Lab 9.4

L A B   9.5

SAVING A FILE

LAB OBJECTIVES

After this lab, you will be able to:

✓ Save the File Under a New Name

The basic save-the-file commands, `:write` and `:wq`, were discussed in Lab 9.1. This lab deals with names of files. The vi editor stores two file names for you, the current file and the "other" file. You can use them in commands. (This is different from supplying many file names as command-line arguments.)

The file you are currently editing is the current file, as soon as you give it a name. If you are editing more than one file in a session, the *last* file you edited becomes the "other" file. Most of the commands that result in other files are not discussed in this chapter. (If you're interested, look up the `:next`, `:edit` and `:rewind` commands in the vi man page.)

LAB 9.5 EXERCISES

9.5.1 SAVE THE FILE UNDER A NEW NAME

Open the file memo and enter the following commands:

```
:w newmemo
:w
```

a) What name is the file saved under the first time? The second time?

_____

_____

Enter the following command:

```
:w newmemo
```

b) What happens?

_____

_____

Enter the following commands:

```
:w %
:w! #
```

c) What happens?

_____

_____

**LAB
9.5**

LAB 9.5 EXERCISE ANSWERS

This section gives you some suggested answers to the questions in Lab 9.5, with discussions related to those answers. Your answers may vary, but the most important thing is whether or not your answers work. Use these discussions to analyze differences between your answers and those presented here.

If you have alternative answers to the questions in these exercises, you are encouraged to post your answers and discuss them at the companion Web site for this book, located at:

```
http://www.phptr.com/phptrinteractive
```

9.5.1 ANSWERS

Open the file memo and enter the following commands:

```
:w newmemo
:w
```

a) What name is the file saved under the first time? The second time?

Answer: The first time, the file is saved as newmemo. *The second time, it's saved as* memo.

Enter the following command:

```
:w newmemo
```

b) What happens?

Answer: vi *responds with an error message like this one:*

```
"newmemo" File exists - use ":w! newmemo" to over-
    write.
```

vi tries to keep you from accidentally overwriting a file that already exists, unless it's the file you're actually editing.

Enter the following commands:

```
:w %
:w! #
```

c) What happens?

Answer: The :w % *command saves the file as* memo; *the* :w! # *command saves the file as* newmemo.

vi can keep track of two file names easily: the current file and another file (called the *alternate file*). In an ex command, the percent sign (%) is a short form for the current file, and the pound sign (#) is a short form for the alternate file name.

The % character gets used in some ex commands as an address for the whole file, instead of using the address "1,$".

LAB 9.5 SELF-REVIEW QUESTIONS

To test your progress, you should be able to answer the following questions.

1) Even if you save a file under a new name, vi keeps using the original name.
   a) _____True
   b) _____False

2) Match the character with its meaning in a colon command.

   a) !   **i)** The alternate file name

   b) #   **ii)** The current file

   c) %   **iii)** Do not check; do it anyway

3) To write over an existing file that isn't being edited, use the ! after the : w command.
   a) _____True
   b) _____False

Quiz answers appear in Appendix A, Lab 9.5

L A B 9.6

SEARCHING TEXT

LAB OBJECTIVES

After this lab, you will be able to:

✓ Find a Character on the Line

✓ Search for a Regular Expression

✓ Search for a Word Beginning or Ending

✓ Repeat a Search

LAB 9.6

Most of the work you do editing a file involves deleting and changing text. (This was the point of the last lab.) However, you must delete the correct text. The vi editor gives you two different ways of finding the correct text.

The first technique finds a character on a line. This is useful when you need to skip over much of the line to get to a particular character. It's especially useful combined with a delete command—you can delete all of the text from the cursor's current position to a particular character.

The second technique searches the entire file for a regular expression. You can search forward in the file (toward the end) or backward (toward the beginning). This command you will use often. You won't remember the line number for a section of a file you need to examine or change, but you will often remember a particular word or phrase in that section of the file.

LAB 9.6 EXERCISES

9.6.1 FIND A CHARACTER ON THE LINE

Open the file memo.

Move the cursor to line 6 (the line beginning, "The early").

Type the following command:

```
fe
```

a) What does the command do?

_____

_____

Type the following command:

```
2fe
```

b) What effect does the 2 have?

_____

_____

Type the following command:

```
Fe
```

c) How is F different from f?

_____

_____

9.6.2 SEARCH FOR A REGULAR EXPRESSION

Enter the following commands:

```
/y
?y
```

a) Which command searches forward in the text? Which one searches backwards?

_____

_____

b) What happens when you try to search past the end (or beginning) of the file?

_____

_____

c) Does `vi` use basic regular expressions or extended regular expressions?

_____

_____

**LAB
9.6**

9.6.3 SEARCH FOR A WORD BEGINNING OR ENDING

Enter the following command:

```
/y\>
```

a) What does the "`\>`" expression match?

_____

_____

9.6.4 REPEAT A SEARCH

Type the following command:

```
n
```

a) What does the n command do? What direction does it search? What does it search for?

_____

_____

Enter the following commands:

```
/
?
```

b) What do these commands do? What direction do they search? What do they search for?

_____

_____

c) What do you think would happen if you used / as the very first search on opening a file?

_____

_____

LAB 9.6 EXERCISE ANSWERS

 This section gives you some suggested answers to the questions in Lab 9.6, with discussions related to those answers. Your answers may vary, but the most important thing is whether or not your answers work. Use these discussions to analyze differences between your answers and those presented here.

If you have alternative answers to the questions in these exercises, you are encouraged to post your answers and discuss them at the companion Web site for this book, located at:

```
http://www.phptr.com/phptrinteractive
```

9.6.1 ANSWERS

Open the file memo.
Move the cursor to line 6 (the line beginning, "The early").
Type the following command:

```
fe
```

a) What does the command do?

Answer: The f *command searches the line for the next occurrence of a letter to the right of the cursor.*

The f command moves the cursor to the next occurrence of the letter you're searching for.

Type the following command:

```
2fe
```

b) What effect does the 2 have?

Answer: The 2 *causes the command to search for the second "e" to the right.*

However, like the h and l movement commands, the f command only searches the current line. If you specify too large a number of repetitions, the cursor doesn't move.

If you want to search all of the lines in the file, you must use the / command.

Type the following command:

```
Fe
```

c) How is F different from f?

Answer:The F command searches to the left of the cursor; the f command searches to the right.

There are several different line-search commands. The f and F commands move the cursor to the character you're searching for. The t and T commands search the line, but move the cursor to the character *before* the one you're searching for. (This is especially useful when you're using the command as the movement part of a delete command; you can delete all of the characters up to but not including the one you're searching for.)

9.6.2 ANSWERS

Enter the following commands:

```
/y
?y
```

**LAB
9.6**

a) Which command searches forward in the text? Which one searches backwards?

Answer:The / command searches forward in the text. The ? command searches backwards.

Here we used "y" but any basic regular expression can be used.

b) What happens when you try to search past the end (or beginning) of the file?

Answer: vi "wraps" the search.

c) Does vi use basic regular expressions or extended regular expressions?

Answer: vi uses basic regular expressions.

As mentioned before, any basic regular expression can be used.

Basic regular expressions in vi have some quirks and some additional metacharacters. Searching for "/" and "?" can surprise you.

Because the "/" and "?" characters tell vi which direction you're searching, they're considered special characters. When searching forward for a "/" character, you must escape the slash, and when searching backwards for a "?" character, you must escape the question mark.

■ FOR EXAMPLE:

To find the string "/?" searching forward, type:

```
/\/?
```

To find the same string searching backward, type:

```
?\/\?
```

You may find it easier just to put a backslash before all occurrences of "/" and "?".

9.6.3 ANSWERS

Enter the following command:

```
/y\>
```

a) What does the "\>" expression match?

Answer:The "\>" expression matches the end of a word.

There are two new search expressions added in vi, \< and \>. They match the beginning and end of a word, respectively.

Without them, you need three searches to make sure you've found all of the occurrences of "the," for example. One search looks for "the" surrounded by spaces or other punctuation marks (the surrounding spaces and punctuation marks are needed to make sure you don't find words like "brothel"); the next search looks for "the" at the beginning of a line and followed by spaces or punctuation marks; and the last search looks for "the" at the end of a line. So these three searches:

```
/[ `!@#$%^&*()|\{}:"';<>?,./]the[ `!@#$%^&*()|\{}:"';<>?,./]
/^the[ `!@#$%^&*()|\{}:"';<>?,./]
/[ `!@#$%^&*()|\{}:"';<>?,./]the$
```

can be replaced with the search

```
/\<the\>
```

9.6.4 ANSWERS

Type the following command:

```
n
```

a) What does the n command do? What direction does it search? What does it search for?

Answer: The n command repeats the last search, looking in the same direction for the same regular expression.

The command n is supposed to stand for "next." This is a vi command, so you don't need to press the Enter key.

Enter the following commands:

```
/
?
```

b) What do these commands do? What direction do they search? What do they search for?

Answer: The / command repeats the last search, but always searches forward. The ? command repeats the last search but always searches backward.

When you type the search commands (/ or ?) without a regular expression, vi repeats the last search you made.

Typing the command letter twice does the same thing: //and ?? repeat the search, each in its own direction. The reason is that you can add modifiers to the search commands: Adding a z at the end of the command causes vi to display the matching line as the first line on the screen. Some character needs to come between the regular expression and the z to indicate that "z" isn't part of the regular expression. (This is why you must escape "/" in a forward search and "?" in a backward search: so that vi knows it's part of the regular expression and not the end of the regular expression.

If you do add a modifier like z to the end of the search, it is *not* remembered by the n command. You must repeat it when you repeat the search, either with //z or with ??z.

The search commands are summarized in Table 9.5.

Table 9.5 ■ vi Search Commands

fc	Search forward in line for character *c*.
Fc	Search backward in line for character *c*.
tc	Search forward in line for character *c*, but put cursor one character before it.
Tc	Search backward in line for character *c*, but put cursor one character before it.
/regexp	Search forward for *regexp*.
?regexp	Search backward for *regexp*.
/regexp/z	Search forward for *regexp*, and display screen so matching line is at top.
?regexp?z	Search backward for *regexp*, and display screen so matching line is at top.
/	Search forward for last *regexp* searched for.
?	Search backward for last *regexp* searched for.
n	Repeat last search.

**LAB
9.6**

LAB 9.6 SELF-REVIEW QUESTIONS

To test your progress, you should be able to answer the following questions.

1) `vi` uses basic regular expressions, with some additions.
   a) _____True
   b) _____False

2) In the following table, match the command with what it does.

   a) `/\<the\>`   **i)** Search forward for the word "the"

   b) `?^[^A-Z]`   **ii)** Repeat last search

   c) `n`   **iii)** Search backward for a line not beginning with capital letters

   d) `/[A-Z]$`   **iv)** Search forward for lines ending in a capital letter

3) In the following table, match the command with what it does.

   a) Delete from cursor to first ;   **i)** `fG`

   b) Search left on line for "G"   **ii)** `dt;`

   c) Delete from cursor up to but not including first ;   **iii)** `df;`

   d) Search right on line for "G"   **iv)** `FG`

4) The command `//z` repeats the last search, and puts the matching line on the first line of the screen.
   a) _____True
   b) _____False

Quiz answers appear in Appendix A, Lab 9.6

L A B   9.7

SEARCHING AND REPLACING

LAB OBJECTIVES

After this lab, you will be able to:

✓ Replace a Word on the Current Line
✓ Replace a Word Multiple Times
✓ Replace a Word Throughout the File

A search-and-replace command is essential in any decent text editor. For any large body of files, there will often be times when you need to replace one word (perhaps a product name) with another word (the new product name), or one version number with another, or one date with another. Without a search-and-replace function, you'll need to find each occurrence, delete the old word or text, and enter the replacement text. That's tedious work and prone to error—the best kind of work to hand over to a computer program.

One advantage that vi and other UNIX text editors have over common word processors is that the searches and replacements can make use of regular expressions. With regular expressions, you have much more flexibility in identifying the words you want to replace or in the words you want to replace them with.

LAB 9.7 EXERCISES

9.7.1 REPLACE THE FIRST OCCURRENCE ON THE CURRENT LINE

Move the cursor to line 6 and enter the following command:

```
:s/early/late/
```

a) What happens?

_____

_____

b) What happens if you repeat the command?

_____

_____

c) What happens if you enter just :s and press Enter?

_____

_____

9.7.2 REPLACE ALL OCCURRENCES ON THE CURRENT LINE

On the same line, enter the following command:

```
:s/late/early/g
```

a) What happens? What effect does the g have on the command?

_____

_____

9.7.3 REPLACE A WORD THROUGHOUT THE FILE

Enter the following command:

```
:%s/boy/girl
```

a) What happens?

_____

_____

Enter the following command:

```
:%s/Chris/&topher/g
```

b) What happens? What special meaning does "&" have in the replacement string?

_____

_____

LAB 9.7 EXERCISE ANSWERS

9.7.1 ANSWERS

Move the cursor to line 6 and enter the following command:

```
:s/early/late/
```

a) What happens?

Answer: The first occurrence of "early" is replaced with "late."

The `:s` command is the "substitute" command. The pattern between the first two slashes is replaced by the pattern between the second and third slashes. (You don't actually need the third slash.)

If you're searching for a string that contains a lot of slashes, you don't have to use slashes in the substitute command. Any punctuation character will do. This eliminates a lot of backslashes: the command `:s/\/ usr\/home\//\/home\/project/` *becomes* `:s?/usr/home?/ home/project?`.

b) What happens if you repeat the command?

Answer: The first of the remaining occurrences of "early" are replaced with "late."

Each time you repeat the command, the first occurrence of "early" is replaced.

Watch out if the string you're replacing is part of the string you're replacing it with.

■ FOR EXAMPLE:

You have the line "a elephant a ear" and you want to replace the word "a" with "an." The first command you give is:

```
:s/a/an
```

This gives you "an elephant." You repeat the command, and this gives you "ann elephant a ear." The third time you repeat it, you get "annn elephant a ear."

To actually replace the *word* "a" in this case, you might want to replace "a " with "an" or replace "a\>" with "an". Either way, the search pattern ("a " or "a\>") doesn't match "an".

c) What happens if you enter just `:s` and press Enter?

Answer: The first of the remaining occurrences of "early" is replaced with "late."

Just like the search command, the substitute command remembers the last pattern you searched and replaced.

9.7.2 ANSWERS

On the same line, enter the following command:

```
:s/late/early/g
```

a) What happens? What effect does the g have on the command?

Answer: The g causes all occurrences of "late" on the line to be replaced with "early."

Like the search commands / and ?, you can add modifiers to the end of the substitute command. (If you add modifiers, you *must* have the third slash there.) There are only three allowed modifiers, and only two of them are useful. The most useful is g, which replaces *all* occurrences on the line, not just the first.

The other modifier is c, which asks for confirmation of each replacement. (You can use it with g.) For each replacement, vi prints the line on the screen. If you want it replaced, press y or Y; any other character means the pattern is *not* replaced.

9.7.3 ANSWERS

Enter the following command:

```
:%s/boy/girl
```

a) What happens?

Answer: The first occurrence of "boy" on a line is replaced with "girl" throughout the file.

The substitute command is an ex command, which means you can specify the range of lines affected by the command as the address. The address "%" means the entire file. (So does the address "1,$".) Without the g modifier at the end of the command, the substitute command still replaces only the first occurrence of the pattern. If you're replacing something throughout the file, you're more likely to use a command like :%s/boy/girl/g.

Enter the following command:

```
:%s/Chris/&topher/g
```

**LAB
9.7**

b) What happens? What special meaning does "&" have in the replacement string?

Answer: The word "Chris" is replaced with "Christopher." The "&" is a short form for "the search pattern that was matched."

There are several metacharacters that are only available in the replacement section of a search and replace. The character "&" stands for the entire pattern that was matched. Back references (described in Chapter 8, "Regular Expressions") are another. You can use back references to rearrange words. The character "~" stands for "the previous replacement text."

■ FOR EXAMPLE:

To turn "peg leg" into "peg leg Pete," you can use & to stand for the entire matched string:

```
:s/peg leg/& Pete/
```

This is the same as the command `:s/\(peg leg\)/\1 Pete/`.

To transpose the words "peg" and "leg," use the following command:

```
:s/\(peg\) \(leg\)/\2 \1/
```

The backreference \2 is replaced by the *second* group in the regular expression, and \1 is replaced by the first group.

If you suddenly realized there were two more occurrences of "peg leg" on the next line, you can repeat the replacement by moving the cursor down to the next line and doing `:s` twice. Or you can use the ~ character and the g modifier:

```
:s//~/g
```

This repeats the last search (because you haven't specified a new search pattern), uses the old replacement text (because you've inserted the "~" character), and replaces all of the occurrences on the line (because you've added the g at the end of the command).

Table 9.6 summarizes the commands in this lab.

Table 9.6 ■ vi Search-and-Replace Commands

Command	Effect
`:s/`*regexp*`/`*replacement*`/`	Replace first occurrence of *regexp* on this line with *replacement*.
`:s/`*regexp*`/`*replacement*`/g`	Replace all occurrences of *regexp* on this line with *replacement*.
`:%s/`*regexp*`/`*replacement*`/`	Replace first occurrence of *regexp* on a line throughout file.
`:%s/`*regexp*`/`*replacement*`/g`	Replace all occurrences of *regexp* throughout file.

LAB 9.7 SELF-REVIEW QUESTIONS

To test your progress, you should be able to answer the following questions.

1) The `:s` command is short for substitute.
    a) _____True
    b) _____False

2) Each repetition of the `:s` command replaces the first occurrence of the pattern.
    a) _____True
    b) _____False

3) In the following table, match the command with its results.

    a) `:s/A/z/g`   **i)** "Aardvark" becomes "AArdvark"

    b) `:s/\(A\)/\1\1/`   **ii)** "Aardvark" becomes "AAardvark"

    c) `:s/[Aa]/&&&/g`   **iii)** "Aardvark" becomes "zardvark"

    d) `:s/\(A\)a\(rdvark\)/\1\1\2/`   **iv)** "Aardvark" becomes "AAAaaardvaaark"

Quiz answers appear in Appendix A, Lab 9.7

LAB 9.8

MOVING TEXT

LAB OBJECTIVES

After this lab, you will be able to:

✓ Move a Line of Text

✓ Copy Text

The boss has reviewed your document, and everything's fine, except that the paragraph near the middle should be at the beginning, and the introduction should be the conclusion, and the last paragraph should be repeated in the introduction.

Rather than retype all of that text, you can move it or copy it. The two actions are nearly identical.

When you delete text in vi, it is placed into a temporary storage area (called a *buffer*). You can copy the text out of the buffer back into the body of the file. You can copy it out of the buffer more than once, creating multiple copies of the text.

You don't even have to delete the text to place it into the buffer.

**LAB
9.8**

9.8.1 MOVE A LINE OF TEXT

Enter the following commands:

```
4G
4dd
j
p
```

a) What happens? What does the p command do?

_____

_____

b) Try it again, but use P. How is it different?

_____

_____

9.8.2 COPY TEXT

Go to the first line of the file and give the following commands:

```
yy
p
```

a) What does the yy command do?

_____

_____

Enter the following commands:

```
:1,2w tmpfile
:r tmpfile
```

b) What does the `1,2w tmpfile` command do?

_____

_____

c) What does the `:r tmpfile` command do?

_____

_____

LAB 9.8 EXERCISE ANSWERS

This section gives you some suggested answers to the questions in Lab 9.8, with discussions related to those answers. Your answers may vary, but the most important thing is whether or not your answers work. Use these discussions to analyze differences between your answers and those presented here.

If you have alternative answers to the questions in these exercises, you are encouraged to post your answers and discuss them at the companion Web site for this book, located at:

`http://www.phptr.com/phptrinteractive`

9.8.1 ANSWERS

Enter the following commands:

```
4G
4dd
j
p
```

a) What happens? What does the p command do?

Answer: The p command inserts the text you deleted after the line the cursor is on.

When you delete text, it's stored in a buffer. (Not the same buffer as the one that holds the entire file. "Buffer" is a generic computer term for a storage space.) The p and P commands put the contents of that buffer into the file.

Whether the deleted text is inserted after the line or on the current line depends on what text was deleted. A deleted line is inserted as a new line; a deleted part of a line is inserted on the current line. If the last delete command had been dw (deleting a word), then the word would be inserted after the cursor, on the current line.

b) Try it again, but use P. How is it different?

Answer: The P command inserts the text you deleted before the line the cursor is on.

The P command inserts the text before the cursor, but is otherwise identical to the p command.

9.8.2 ANSWERS

Go to the first line of the file and give the following commands:

```
yy
p
```

a) What does the yy command do?

Answer: The yy command copies the current line of text instead of deleting it.

If you only want to *copy* the text, you can use the y command instead of the d command. The y command (it stands for "yank") yanks a copy of the text into the same buffer that the delete command uses. It is one of those commands that can take a movement command after it, so (for example), the command 4yw yanks the next four words into that buffer.

You can "put" as many copies of the text as you want into the file; it doesn't go away until you delete (or yank) something else.

Enter the following commands:

```
:1,2w tmpfile
:r tmpfile
```

**LAB
9.8**

b) What does the `1,2w tmpfile` command do?

Answer: It saves the first two lines of the file in the file `tmpfile`.

The address "`1,2`" is an ex-style address, which can be used with the ex commands. You can use the Control-G command to find the line numbers you need.

c) What does the `:r tmpfile` command do?

Answer: The `:r` *command reads in the file* `tmpfile` *and inserts it into the file you're editing.*

The `:r filename` command can be used to insert any file into the current file. This is another way to copy or move text. It's useful if you think you might be deleting or yanking text before you paste in the text you're moving. (Remember that any delete or yank command will change what's in the buffer.)

Table 9.7 summarizes the commands in this lab.

Table 9.7 ■ vi Text Copying and Moving Commands

Command	Effect
[n]yy	"Yank" *n* lines of text for copying.
[n]p	Put the contents of the buffer *after* the cursor, *n* times (default 1).
[n]P	Put the contents of the buffer *before* the cursor, *n* times (default 1).
:r filename	Read in the file *filename* on the line after the cursor.

LAB 9.8 SELF-REVIEW QUESTIONS

To test your progress, you should be able to answer the following questions.

1) The p command puts deleted or yanked text back into the file.
   a) _____True
   b) _____False

2) The y command behaves like the d command, except it doesn't delete text, it only copies it.
   a) _____True
   b) _____False

3) The :r command inserts a file into the buffer.
   a) _____True
   b) _____False

   Quiz answers appear in Appendix A, Lab 9.8

CHAPTER 9

TEST YOUR THINKING

 The projects in this section are meant to have you utilize all of the skills that you have acquired throughout this chapter. The answers to these projects can be found at the companion Web site to this book, located at:

`http://www.phptr.com/phptrinteractive`

Visit the Web site periodically to share and discuss your answers.

Use the file `verse`, shown here, for these projects:

```
12 botles of milk on teh wall
12 botles of milk
There'll be 11 botles of mikl on teh wall
If one of those botles should happen to fall
```

1) What commands would be required to correct the errors and resort the lines so it reads:

```
12 bottles of milk on the wall
12 bottles of milk
If one of those bottles should happen to fall
There'll be 11 bottles of milk on the wall
```

2) How would you go about creating the file `song`, which contains 15 verses for each number of bottles from 15 to 1?

CHAPTER 10

WORKING WITH TEXT FILES

 UNIX is rich in tools for working with text files. Once you've created a file, there are dozens of tools to change it, extract its contents, and format it.

CHAPTER OBJECTIVES

In this chapter, you will learn about:

In the early days, UNIX was used primarily for text processing in Bell Labs. Most documents were text files instead of specially formatted word processor files. Because all of the information was in text files, special tools were created to deal with text. While these utilities won't help you with a word processor file or a spreadsheet, many files on a UNIX system, such as your stored e-mail, are just text.

This chapter is about some of those specialized text-manipulation tools: `sort`, `wc`, `spell`, `fold`, and `fmt`.

Another very useful tool is `diff`, which compares two text files.

**LAB
10.1**

L A B   10.1

SORTING

LAB OBJECTIVES

After this lab, you will be able to:

✓ Sort a File

✓ Sort by Keys

✓ Sort a File Numerically

The sort command sorts a file or a sequence of files. It sorts lines. It can sort based on either the entire line or based on a part of the line (i.e., it can sort based on the third word of the line). The part of the line used for sorting is called the *key*. Normally a key is a word.

Normally, keys are separated by any white space (tabs or spaces). The line "Two words" contains two keys: the first key is "Two" and the second key is " words." Even though the space separates the two keys, it's considered part of the second key.

LAB 10.1 EXERCISES

To do this lab, you need a file to be sorted.

Create a file named days that contains the following lines. Note that some of the days are separated from the month by two spaces and some by one. These spaces will be important in the exercises.

```
Jan  1 New Year's Day
Feb 14 Valentine's Day
Mar 15 Ides of March
Mar 15 Bethany's birthday
Apr  1 April Fool's Day
May 17 Memorial Day
May 24 Sandi's birthday
Jul 1  Independence Day
Aug 5  My birthday
Sep  3 Labor Day
dec 25 Christmas
Dec 26 Boxing Day
```

10.1.1 SORT A FILE

Run the following commands:

```
sort days
sort -f days
```

a) In the first case, how are the lines sorted? Why is "dec 25" at the end of the list?

_____

_____

b) How does the -f option change the output?

_____

_____

Run the following command:

```
sort -r days
```

c) Now how are the lines sorted?

_____

_____

Run the following command:

```
sort -M days
```

(Some versions of `sort` do not support -M.)

d) How is this output different?

_____

_____

10.1.2 SORT BY KEYS

Run the following commands:

```
sort -k 3 days
sort -k 3b days
```

a) What word in the line are they sorted by?

_____

_____

b) How does the output of these two commands differ? Why?

_____

_____

Run the following command:

```
sort -k 1M,1 -k 2r days
```

c) What does this command do? (Hint: look at the May entries.)

_____

_____

10.1.3 SORT NUMERICALLY

Run the following commands:

```
sort -k 2n days
sort -n -k 2 days
```

a) What does the n modifier do to the sort?

_____

_____

b) Does it have the same effect in the second command?

_____

_____

c) What would the following command do?

```
sort -rn -k 2 -k 1M,1
```

_____

_____

LAB 10.1 EXERCISE ANSWERS

This section gives you some suggested answers to the questions in Lab 10.1, with discussions related to those answers. Your answers may vary, but the most important thing is whether or not your answers work. Use these discussions to analyze differences between your answers and those presented here.

If you have alternative answers to the questions in these exercises, you are encouraged to post your answers and discuss them at the companion Web site for this book, located at:

```
http://www.phptr.com/phptrinteractive
```

10.1.1 ANSWERS

Run the following commands:

```
sort days
sort -f days
```

a)   In the first case, how are the lines sorted? Why is "dec 25" at the end of the list?

Answer: The lines are sorted in ASCII order. In the ASCII character set, all of the uppercase letters come before any of the lowercase letters.

The output looks like this:

```
Apr  1 April Fool's Day
Aug  5 My birthday
Dec 26 Boxing Day
Feb 14 Valentine's Day
Jan  1 New Year's Day
Jul  1 Independence Day
Mar 15 Bethany's birthday
Mar 15 Ides of March
May 17 Memorial Day
May 24 Sandi's birthday
Sep  3 Labor Day
dec 25 Christmas
```

The ASCII order is the same order used by ls to sort file names. This is the standard order for sorting on UNIX systems. You'll notice that the empty lines show up at the beginning of the sorted file.

Other options will let you sort in different ways. The -d option, for example, does a "dictionary" sort: Only digits, letters, and white space characters are used in the sort. (Normally, sort will happily use a control character in sorting, if you happen to have one in the file.)

b)   How does the -f option change the output?

Answer: The -f option forces sort *to sort upper- and lowercase letters as if they were equal.*

UNIX documentation refers to this as a "folded" sort. Upper- and lower-case letters are treated as equal. Now the `dec 25 Christmas` line is immediately after the `Dec 26 Boxing Day` line.

Combining this option with the `-u` option can have unexpected results. Remember, the `-u` option causes `sort` to discard any duplicate lines (the "u" stands for "unique"). Combining the two options can make `sort` delete lines of the file you didn't intend to have deleted.

■ FOR EXAMPLE:

Suppose you have a file containing the following lines:

```
channel
english
English
```

Normally, the words sort in the order `English channel english` because `English` starts with an uppercase letter. The `-f` option causes `sort` to treat them as identical, and they are sorted in the order `channel English english`. When the `-u` option causes `sort` to discard the duplicate line, it gives you the result:

```
$ sort -uf cases
channel
English
```

Even with `-f`, `E` comes before `e`. It's possible that some versions of `sort` behave differently, but I've never encountered one.

It's difficult to predict how the `-u` option will interact with other options. If more than one line sorts identically, generally the `-u` option prints the *last* matching line from the source text. The exception is with the `-f` option. This part of the `-u` option will surprise you if you use it with the `-k` option.

Run the following command:

```
sort -r days
```

c) Now how are the lines sorted?

Answer: The −r option sorts the file in reverse order.

The output looks like this:

```
dec 25 Christmas
Sep  3 Labor Day
May 24 Sandi's birthday
May 17 Memorial Day
Mar 15 Ides of March
Mar 15 Bethany's birthday
Jul  1 Independence Day
Jan  1 New Year's Day
Feb 14 Valentine's Day
Dec 26 Boxing Day
Aug  5 My birthday
Apr  1 April Fool's Day
```

The −r option reverses the meaning of the sort. In this case, it's reverse ASCII order. If some other option had been given to change the kind of sort (such as -M in the next question), it would reverse the order of that sort.) You can provide other options to control the order of the sort, and −r will reverse that sort as well.

Run the following command:

```
sort -M days
```

d) How is this output different?

Answer: The −M option causes sort *to treat the sorting keys as month names.*

The output looks like this:

```
Jan  1 New Year's Day
Feb 14 Valentine's Day
Mar 15 Ides of March
Mar 15 Bethany's birthday
Apr  1 April Fool's Day
May 17 Memorial Day
```

```
May 24 Sandi's birthday
Jul  1 Independence Day
Aug  5 My birthday
Sep  3 Labor Day
Dec 26 Boxing Day
dec 25 Christmas
```

The -M option is only available on System V systems, such as Solaris 2.3 and later and UnixWare.

According to the documentation, the sorting key is treated as a three-letter case-insensitive name. You'll note that despite this, the line dec 25 still sorts *after* Dec 26. This is the same as the problem in sorting with -f. Even though it says case insensitive, uppercase letters sort first.

You can fix this by forcing the sort command to pay attention to the second key, the day of the month. This is the topic of the next Exercise.

10.1.2 Answers

Run the following commands:

```
sort -k 3 days
sort -k 3b days
```

a) What word in the line are they sorted by?

Answer: These sort on the third word of the line, key 3.

The -k option specifies which key is used for sorting. The -k option has a complicated format because you can specify how many words will make up the key and how each key is supposed to be sorted. In this case, the first command sorts starting with the third word on the line. The second command sorts starting with the third word on the line, but it ignores any space or tab characters at the beginning of the third word.

Remember that spaces sort before any letters. As I mentioned at the beginning, even though spaces mark the beginning of a new word (or key), the spaces are part of the key. So the third key of lines

```
Jul 1   Independence Day
Aug 5   My birthday
```

both start with " ", while the third key of

```
Apr  1 April Fool's Day
```

starts with " A".

b) How does the output of these two commands differ? Why?

Answer: *The second command ignores the spaces after the second word on each line, so only the words are used to sort.*

You can use b as an option to modify the entire sort, or you can use it as we have here, as a modifier for just this record. By using -b, -f, and -d, you can get a normal alphabetic sort, the kind you learned in school.

Run the following command:

```
sort -k 1M,1 -k 2r days
```

c) What does this command do? (Hint: look at the May entries.)

Answer: *This command sorts by month in the first field and reverse order by the date in the second field.*

The file is sorted by the first key and when two lines have the same first key, they are sorted by the second key. (You can have more keys, and the sorting continues in the same way.)

The record specification can get quite precise. You can even specify how many words you want in the record and how many characters of the record you want to use in the sort. The format is:

```
-k start record[modifers][,end record[modifiers]]
```

You already know about the starting record. The option -k 3 specifies a key starting with the third record. If you don't specify the end of the record, sort uses from there to the end of the line. The key in -k 3 goes to the end of the line.

The option -k 1M, 1 is a sort key that starts and ends with the first record, and the first record is sorted as a month name. The option -k 2r is a sort key that starts with the second record and goes to the end of the line; it's sorted in reverse order.

The options -b, -d, -f, -i, -n, and -M can be used to modify the sort order of keys. The -i option tells sort to ignore nonprinting characters, such as control characters.

All of these options can also be used to modify the entire sort command.

10.1.3 ANSWERS

Run the following commands:

```
sort -k 2n days
sort -n -k 2 days
```

a) What does the n modifier do to the sort?

Answer:The -n modifier causes sort to treat the record as a number.

In the first command, the spaces are significant in the key: the key " 3" sorts before " 1 ".

The -n option automatically ignores leading white space, so you don't need -b with a record that's being sorted as a number.

b) Does it have the same effect in the second command?

Answer: In this case, yes.

There is a case where they aren't identical. The numeric modifier ignores leading white space when it modifies a record (the -k option), but *not* leading white space at the beginning of a line.

■ *FOR EXAMPLE:*

If you have these lines, where the first line begins with a space but the second doesn't:

```
    9
    8
```

The command `sort  -n` sorts them in the order they appear above, because white space at the beginning of the line is important. The command `sort  -k  1n` sorts the 8 before the 9.

c) What would the following command do?

```
sort -rn -k 2 -k 1M,1
```

Answer: The command sorts the input in reverse order (-r), treating all keys as numbers unless otherwise specified (-n). It sorts based on the second key (-k 2), and then if two lines have the same second key, on the first key, which it treats as month names (-k 1M, 1).

That is about as complex a sort command as you'll run into. There are only two more options that may be of use.

First, you can write the output to a file specified with the -o option.

Second, you may not want to use white space to separate the "words" used for sorting. You can pick a different character by using the -t option.

■ FOR EXAMPLE:

You want to set up a file that contains names, area codes, and phone numbers. You don't want to sort it using spaces to separate keys because names contain different numbers of words. Instead, you separate keys with colons, like this:

```
Snoopy:415:896-0010
The Red Baron:519:211-6913
```

Now you can use the colon to separate keys, and you can sort by name, area code, or phone number. To sort by area code:

```
sort -t : -k 2
```

Normally, sort *treats a group of white space characters as indicating just one new key, no matter how many spaces and tabs there are in a row. If you make space or tab the delimiter, each occurrence of that character starts a new record. Two spaces in a row become an empty record.*

All of the sort options are summarized in Table 10.1.

Table 10.1 ■ Sort Options

Effect	Option
Ignore leading white space	-b
Remove duplicate lines	-u
Reverse order of sort	-r
Treat key as a number	-n
Treat key as a three-letter month name	-M
Treat upper and lowercase letters as equal	-f
Use character *c* as key delimiter	-t *c*
Use dictionary order: use only letters, digits, and white space	-d

LAB 10.1 SELF-REVIEW QUESTIONS

To test your progress, you should be able to answer the following questions.

1) In ASCII sorting, a line that starts with "E" comes before a line that sorts with "f".

   a) _____True

   b) _____False

2) In the following table, match the option with its effect:

   a) -r   **i)** Eliminate duplicate lines

   b) -f   **ii)** Use dictionary sort

   c) -u   **iii)** Sort in reverse order

   d) -d   **iv)** Sort upper- and lowercase letters as identical

3) Because a space marks the start of a new field or record, it doesn't count as part of the record.

   a) _____True

   b) _____False

4) Which of the following options would you use to sort on the fourth word of the line and only the fourth word?

   a) _____-k 4

   b) _____-k 4,5

   c) _____-k 3,4

   d) _____-k 4,4

5) For which of the following reasons is the option -t ` ` (space) not the same as sort's normal behavior?

   a) _____It doesn't include tab characters.

   b) _____It won't treat more than one space in a row as a single field separator.

   c) _____It will cause sort to ignore all space characters.

   d) _____(a) and (b)

   e) _____(a) and (c)

Quiz answers appear in Appendix A, Lab 10.1

L A B 10.2

COUNTING WORDS

LAB OBJECTIVES

After this lab, you will be able to:

✓ Count Lines, Words, or Bytes

✓ Display Counts for a File

Sometimes it's useful to know how many words or lines there are in a file. The wc command tells you just that.

The wc command is simple minded. It doesn't use any magic formulas to calculate its numbers. According to wc, a word is one or more characters that begin and end with white space (a space, a tab character, the beginning or end of a line). For example, the wc command treats both "musician" and "the-artist-formerly-known-as-Prince" as one word.

A "line" is an end-of-line character. If you have two paragraphs separated by an empty line, like this:

```
"I love you," he said. "Madly, passionately, deeply."

"You forgot to take out the trash again?" she replied.
```

These count as three lines: the first line, the empty line, and the last line.

Most versions of wc don't distinguish between bytes and characters.

The syntax is straightforward:

```
wc [-c|-m|-C] [-lw] [file ...]
```

If you specify more than one *file*, the wc utility summarizes each command and provides a total.

The -C and -m options are not found on all systems, although they are found on Solaris.

LAB 10.2 EXERCISES

10.2.1 COUNT LINES, WORDS, OR BYTES

Run the following commands:

```
wc -l days
wc -w days
wc -c days
```

a) What information does each command display? You may have to open the file with an editor to confirm your ideas.

_____

_____

b) What additional information do you get when you supply more than one file name on the command line?

_____

_____

c) What is the default when no options are given?

_____

_____

LAB 10.2 EXERCISE ANSWERS

 This section gives you some suggested answers to the questions in Lab 10.2, with discussions related to those answers. Your answers may vary, but the most important thing is whether or not your answers work. Use these discussions to analyze differences between your answers and those presented here.

LAB 10.2

If you have alternative answers to the questions in these exercises, you are encouraged to post your answers and discuss them at the companion Web site for this book, located at:

```
http://www.phptr.com/phptrinteractive
```

10.2.1 ANSWERS

Run the following commands:

```
wc -l days
wc -w days
wc -c days
```

a) What information does each command display? You may have to open the file with an editor to confirm your ideas.

Answer: The -l option displays the number of lines in the file. The -w option displays the number of words in the file. The -c option displays the number of bytes in the file.

The wc command (which stands for "word count") is just a small useful utility for finding word and line counts in files or groups of files. Although ls -l would give you the same size (byte) counts, there are no other tools that can conveniently give you the number of lines or words.

The -c option counts the number of *bytes*, not the number of *characters*. Remember that on systems with non-English character sets, such as Japanese Kanji, a character may take up more than one byte of storage. On those systems, the number of bytes *isn't* the number of characters. The Solaris version of wc provides the -m and the -c options, which do count the number of characters, even in non-English character sets. The two options are identical.

> *You can use* `wc -l` *to count the number of files in a directory:*
> *use* `ls -1 | wc -l`.

b) What additional information do you get when you supply more than one file name on the command line?

Answer: When more than one file is specified, `wc` *also displays the total count.*

The total count makes it easy to tally all the words in a directory or a set of files, or to sum up the sizes of all files in the directory.

c) What is the default when no options are given?

Answer: The `wc` *command displays lines, words, and bytes, in that order.*

LAB 10.2 SELF REVIEW QUESTIONS

To test your progress, you should be able to answer the following questions.

1) The command `wc -c *` will list the size of all files in the directory, if there are no subdirectories.
    a) _____True
    b) _____False

2) It is possible to have a file so the output of `wc -w` is 0.
    a) _____True
    b) _____False

3) The command `wc -m mysteryfile` gives a result of 389, but the command `wc -c mysteryfile` gives a result of 412. What is the reason for this?
    a) _____The `wc` command is broken.
    b) _____The file contains multibyte (non-English character set) characters.
    c) _____There are many empty lines in the file.
    d) _____Many of the words are hyphenated.

4) Which option would you use to determine the number of lines in a file?
    a) _____`-c`
    b) _____`-C`
    c) _____`-l`
    d) _____`-m`
    e) _____`-w`

Quiz answers appear in Appendix A, Lab 10.2

L A B   10.3

CHECKING SPELLING

LAB OBJECTIVES

After this lab, you will be able to:

✓ Run Spell

✓ Create a Personal Dictionary

The `spell` command checks a text file for misspelled words.

The `spell` command has this syntax:

```
spell [-bivx] [+localdict] [file ...]
```

The *file* arguments are files to be checked.

The options are not particularly useful. The -b option uses British spelling instead of American spelling; it's very useful to Britons, but not to Americans. The -i option is for use with documents written for the `troff` text formatting system. (Most people do not use `troff` any more.) The -v and -x options control how `spell` decides if a word is in its dictionary.

The *+localdict* option allows you to specify local dictionary files. It's the topic of Exercise 10.3.2.

LAB 10.3 EXERCISES

10.3.1 RUN SPELL

Run the following command:

```
spell days
```

a) What words are misspelled? Do any words show up twice?

_____

_____

b) Are the words actually misspelled?

_____

_____

_____

10.3.2 CREATE A PERSONAL DICTIONARY

Run the following commands:

```
spell days | sort -dfu > mydict
spell +mydict days
```

(Your system may require the option `-f mydict` instead.)

a) What does the first command do?

_____

_____

b) Are any words misspelled now?

_____

_____

LAB 10.3 EXERCISE ANSWERS

This section gives you some suggested answers to the questions in Lab 10.3, with discussions related to those answers. Your answers may vary, but the most important thing is whether or not your answers work. Use these discussions to analyze differences between your answers and those presented here.

If you have alternative answers to the questions in these exercises, you are encouraged to post your answers and discuss them at the companion Web site for this book, located at:

```
http://www.phptr.com/phptrinteractive/
```

10.3.1 ANSWERS

Run the following command:

```
spell days
```

a) What words are misspelled? Do any words show up twice?

Answer: This is the output from my version of spell; *other versions may have slightly different results.*

```
1
Year's
14
Valentine's
15
15
Bethany's
1
Fool's
17
24
Sandi's
1
5
3
25
26
```

The only words here are the words with punctuation in them and the numbers.

My version of `spell` doesn't understand punctuation, but some versions do. They will accept 's at the end of a correctly spelled word.

Most versions of the `spell` command have no memory, either. An unknown word is printed each time it appears.

b) Are the words actually misspelled?

Answer: No; all of the words are correctly spelled.

For each word, the `spell` program checks its dictionary. (The dictionary is traditionally the file `/usr/dict/words`.) If `spell` cannot find the word in the dictionary, it writes the word to the screen. The words show up in the order that they appear in the file. Sometimes it's more accurate to call them unknown words instead of misspelled words. It won't catch misspellings that are themselves words: It won't catch "your" when you mean "yore" or "metal" when you mean "mettle."

The `spell` program, like all spell-checking programs, is only as good as its dictionary. You probably have words you use frequently that are not in the dictionary (i.e., your name, or the name of your company, or your address.) To keep the `spell` program from identifying those words each time they occur, you need to add your own personal dictionary.

10.3.2 ANSWERS

Run the following commands:

```
spell days | sort -dfu > mydict
spell +mydict days
```

a) What does the first command do?

Answer: The command produces a sorted list of the "misspelled" words, removes the duplicates, and saves them in the file `mydict`.

The `spell` command requires the words in the dictionary to be sorted, one word to a line, without any spaces on the line. To get this, you need to sort the output of `spell` and remove the duplicates.

If some words actually were misspelled, you would have to remove them from `mydict` with an editor or have corrected them before running the `spell` command.

The only catch is that all the versions of `spell` I checked treat uppercase letters as special. If a word in the dictionary is spelled with uppercase letters, the `spell` command insists that the word must be spelled with uppercase letters to be correct.

b)   Are any words misspelled now?

   Answer: No; the `spell` *command also checks them against the file* `mydict`.

I often create small local dictionaries for directories full of technical documents. I save the sorted output of `spell` and then edit it to make sure I haven't accidentally preserved a spelling mistake. (Once the mistake is in the dictionary, it's very hard to notice again.)

If you read the Solaris `spell` man page, you'll find extensive instructions on creating new hashed dictionaries. ("Hashing" is a technique used to speed up searches in data.) Although hashed dictionaries are faster than simple text dictionaries, they're more difficult to create and to update. Unless your local dictionaries are huge and contain thousands of words, it's not worth the effort of creating a new hashed dictionary.

THE `ISPELL` COMMAND

Although the `spell` command is on most systems, it is not on all systems. If your system doesn't have `spell`, you may have an alternative program called `ispell` (the interactive spell command).

The `ispell` command opens up each file and presents each misspelled word to you in context. You have the choice of fixing the word once or throughout the file, or of ignoring this instance of it, or ignoring it throughout the file.

Many people find `ispell` more convenient than spell (although it has options so you can use it as you use the older `spell` command). If your system does not have it, ask your system administrator if it can be installed. It's free software, so cost shouldn't be a problem.

LAB 10.3 SELF-REVIEW QUESTIONS

To test your progress, you should be able to answer the following questions.

1) The `spell` command is only as good as its dictionary.
    a) _____True
    b) _____False

2) To add words to a personal dictionary, you don't need to sort them first.
    a) _____True
    b) _____False

3) You are spell checking a document to be sent to the Queen of England or some member of her staff. Which option would you use?
    a) _____-b
    b) _____-i
    c) _____-v
    d) _____-x

Quiz answers appear in Appendix A, Lab 10.3

L A B 10.4

FORMATTING FILES

LAB OBJECTIVES

After this lab, you will be able to:

✓ Fold Lines

✓ Format Paragraphs

As you edit text, you'll often find that the lines become odd lengths: a line you shortened stays short, while a line where you added a necessary clause becomes much longer than the screen will display. There are several programs that adjust the length of lines in a file.

You may also notice that tab characters do not display as nicely as you would like. There are also programs to turn tab characters into the correct number of spaces, and back again.

LAB 10.4 EXERCISES

Before starting this lab, you'll need a file that contains long and short lines. Create the following file, and call it ode:

```
The force that through the house fuse drives the power
(With apologies to Dylan Thomas)

The force that through the house fuse drives the power
```

```
Is the voltage; it blasts the watts through ohms
(That's the resistance).
And I was dumb to tell my doubting wife
I knew my way around the broken fusebox
```

10.4.1 FOLD LINES

The `fold` command inserts line breaks in lines.

Enter the following commands:

```
fold -w 40 ode
fold -s -w 40 ode
```

a) What's the length of the longest line in the output?

_____

_____

b) Where do the line breaks get inserted in the first command? The second?

_____

_____

c) What happens to the short lines?

_____

_____

10.4.2 FORMAT PARAGRAPHS

Enter the following command:

```
fmt -w 40 ode
```

a) What's the length of the longest line in the output?

_____

_____

b) Where do the line breaks get inserted?

_____

_____

c) What happens to the short lines? To empty lines?

_____

_____

LAB 10.4 EXERCISE ANSWERS

This section gives you some suggested answers to the questions in Lab 10.4, with discussions related to those answers. Your answers may vary, but the most important thing is whether or not your answers work. Use these discussions to analyze differences between your answers and those presented here.

If you have alternative answers to the questions in these exercises, you are encouraged to post your answers and discuss them at the companion Web site for this book, located at:

```
http://www.phptr.com/phptrinteractive
```

10.4.1 ANSWERS

Enter the following commands:

```
fold -w 40 ode
fold -s -w 40 ode
```

a) What's the length of the longest line in the output?

Answer: The longest line is 40 characters.

Here's what `fold -w40` does to the first two lines:

```
The force that through the house fuse dr
ives the power
(With apologies to Dylan Thomas)
```

The `-w 40` option sets the line length (the "width" of the output) to 40 characters. The `fmt` command reads the text and, if a line is more than 40 characters long, inserts a line break after character 40.

Without the `-w` option, `fold` breaks lines when they're 80 characters long. (The normal terminal display is 80 characters wide.)

b) Where do the line breaks get inserted in the first command? The second?

Answer: Without the `-s` option, line breaks are inserted after 40 characters, even if that's in the middle of a word. With the `-s` option, line breaks replace the last space before the 40th character.

In the very first line, `fold` without the `-s` option inserts the line break in the middle of the word "drives."

Here's what `fold -s -w40` does to the first two lines:

```
The force that through the house fuse
drives the power
(With apologies to Dylan Thomas)
```

This time, the line break is inserted after the space, and before the beginning of "drives."

c) What happens to the short lines?

Answer: Short lines aren't affected.

The `fold` command only inserts line breaks, it doesn't join together existing lines. For that, you need a different command.

10.4.2 ANSWERS

Enter the following command:

```
fmt -w 40 ode
```

a) What's the length of the longest line in the output?

Answer: The longest line is "the resistance). And I was dumb to tell," which is 40 characters long.

The `-w 40` option behaves just as it does for the `fold` command: it sets the maximum line length to 40 characters.

**LAB
10.4**

 On some BSD systems, `fmt` uses a different command format. If it doesn't recognize -w, use the command `fmt 30 40 ode` instead. The first number is the minimum line length (`fmt` shouldn't start looking for a space until the line is 30 characters long), and the second number is the maximum line length (`fmt` shouldn't let a line get more than 40 characters long).

b) Where do the line breaks get inserted?

Answer: Line breaks are inserted at the first space before the length limit.

In fact, for long lines, the `fmt` command acts like the `fold -s` command: it inserts line breaks at the last space before the limit. If a single word is longer than the line, `fmt` doesn't break it. (This may be useful to know if you type a lot of jawbreaking medical terminology.)

c) What happens to the short lines? To empty lines?

Answer: Short lines are joined together. Empty lines aren't touched.

This is what makes `fmt` a text formatter: It actually joins short lines together as well as breaking long lines. This process of breaking and joining lines is referred to in many UNIX programs as "filling" text.

Lines with the same indent (the number of spaces or tabs at the beginning of the line) are treated as being part of the same paragraph, and the fmt leaves the indent the same.

Empty lines are treated as the start of a new paragraph.

The fmt program treats a *change* in text indent as the start of a new paragraph. Often, this isn't what you want in a text file. The fmt program isn't really a very smart formatter.

■ FOR EXAMPLE:

If you have this text in a file:

```
Before you install the software:
 * Log out of other sessions.
 * Back up your important files.
Once you do this, you can begin.
```

The fmt command turns this into:

```
Before you install the software:
 * Log out of other sessions. * Back up your important
 files.
Once you do this, you can begin.
```

The two indented lines are joined because they have the same indent, and it's a different indent than the first and last lines.

FORMATTING INSIDE AN EDITOR

Inside the vi editor, you can format a file with the following command:

```
:%!fmt
```

The :%! command runs a command (fmt in this case) on the entire file. You can format just the paragraph the cursor is in (actually, from the line with the cursor to the end of the paragraph) with the following command:

```
!}fmt
```

The ! } command runs a command on the current paragraph.

OTHER COMMANDS

The tools in this chapter are only a few of the text tools available. There are others, and many of them seem useless until you need exactly that tool. None of the tools mentioned here are discussed in this book, but you might want to know that they exist, in case you need them.

- The program comm looks at two sorted files and tells you what lines are in both files, what lines are only in the first file, and what lines are only in the second file.
- The cut command extracts a part of each line from a file. You can ask it only to take the tenth through 15 characters or the third word.
- The diff command compares two text files and tells you what changes need to be made to turn the first file into the second file.
- The expand command turns all tab characters into the correct number of spaces; the unexpand command turns groups of spaces into tab characters. (The default setting for tab characters in UNIX is every eight characters.)
- The join command combines two files based on a word (or key) they have in common.
- The paste command "glues together" lines of files. You can think of it as a side-by-side version of cat.
- The tr command turns one character into another, for instance, it turns all lowercase letters into uppercase.
- The uniq command strips out all duplicate lines in a sorted file.

Many of these require the file to be sorted first.

There are other general purpose tools, too. They are definitely beyond the scope of this workbook:

- The sed utility is a filter version of a line editor. If you are comfortable with ex commands in vi, you will find this easy to use.

**LAB
10.4**

- Awk and `perl` are programming languages specialized for handling text.

LAB 10.4 SELF-REVIEW QUESTIONS

To test your progress, you should be able to answer the following questions.

1) The `fold -w 72` command won't break a word in the middle.
   a) _____True
   b) _____False

2) Without other options, the `fmt` command sets the maximum line length to which of the following?
   a) _____50 characters
   b) _____60 characters
   c) _____70 characters
   d) _____80 characters

3) When does the `fmt` command stop "filling" lines (assumes there is a new paragraph)?
   a) _____When there is an empty line
   b) _____When the next line has a larger indentation than the current line
   c) _____When the next line has a smaller indentation than the current line
   d) _____All of the above

Quiz answers appear in Appendix A, Lab 10.4

CHAPTER 10

TEST YOUR THINKING

 The projects in this section are meant to have you utilize all of the skills that you have acquired throughout this chapter. The answers to these projects can be found at the companion Web site to this book, located at:

`http://www.phptr.com/phptrinteractive/`

Visit the Web site periodically to share and discuss your answers.

Suppose you have written a new `spell` command but you need to create an entirely new dictionary. (Dictionary files can be copyrighted, and you do not have permission to reproduce an existing dictionary.)

1) What steps would you use to create a dictionary based on text files already on your system? Consider:

   a) How would you generate lists of words?

   b) How you would turn existing text files into lists of words, one per line?

   c) How you would generate a list you could check for spelling?

2) Can you summarize the commands you would need for this job?

CHAPTER 11

PRINTING TEXT FILES

 The great thing about paper is that even people without computers can read it. Fortunately, UNIX provides tools for formatting and printing text files.

CHAPTER OBJECTIVES

In this chapter, you will learn about:

Despite the predictions of office automation experts, the paperless office hasn't happened yet. In fact, offices produce a blizzard of paper, so the prediction isn't likely to come true soon. Paper is just too portable, too convenient, and too standard. Reading a paper takes less electricity than reading the same text on line, it doesn't strain your eyes, and you can take paper to places where a computer won't go.

To do Labs 11.1 and 11.3, your printing system must be set up. You can do Lab 11.2 even if you don't have printers connected to your system.

You'll also need a text file to be printed. Name it `toprint`, and it should be at least 80 lines long. Most lines should contain some text; a file of 80 empty lines isn't sufficient. For Lab 11.2, some of the text lines should be fairly long—at least 70 characters. (You can build this file by using `cat` to join all of the example files.)

L A B 11.1

PRINTING A FILE

LAB OBJECTIVES

After this lab, you will be able to:

✓ Identify Your Print Command

✓ Print a File

PRINTERS

There are several different styles of printers, but the two you're most likely to encounter are ink (or bubble) *jet* printers and *laser* printers. From the standpoint of standard UNIX printing commands, there's not much difference between them.

The UNIX printing commands were developed when the only printers were line printers. Line printers normally print six lines of text per inch, so an 8.5 x 11-inch sheet of paper is 66 lines high.

Inkjet printers spray ink onto the page, creating the shapes of the letters or the picture you're drawing. Laser printers melt a chemical (called toner) onto the paper. They've just about taken over printing, because the output is more attractive, more readable, and they print faster than any line printer. Laser printers and inkjet printers usually print slightly larger text than the line printers used to; laser and inkjet printers get 60 or 61 lines to an 11-inch sheet of paper. Most inkjet printers are compatible with the Hewlett-Packard Laserjet. Most laser printers are compatible with the Hewlett-Packard Laserjet or Adobe PostScript or both.

To get the fancy effects a laser printer can provide, the file must be written in the special control language for that printer; there's one language for Laserjet-compatible printers and another for PostScript printers. (The language for PostScript printers is PostScript.) You'll never write a file directly in a printer language; that's always done by another program. However, it can be useful to know whether a file is written for a Laserjet printer or a PostScript printer, because they cannot print each other's files.

Both kinds of laser printers can print text files. For special effects (such as changing the point size or drawing pictures), the file must be written in the language of the printer. Another program does that for you.

LOCAL COMMANDS

Because printing varies so much from site to site, always ask if there are local commands to print files. The commands in this chapter are standard, but your system may have a program specially written for you. For example, in our office, we use a special program called 2print (written by one of the programmers) that prints text files so that two pages are shrunk onto one. This saves paper when printing text files, and is not much more difficult to read. It also "knows" about our printers.

A local command, if one exists, is almost certainly better for your needs. Ask other users or the system administrator.

LAB 11.1 EXERCISES

11.1.1 IDENTIFY YOUR PRINT COMMAND

Enter the following commands:

```
command -v lp
command -v lpr
```

If your system doesn't have the command command, use one of the alternatives described in Chapter 6, "Emergency Recovery."

a) Which command do you have, `lp` or `lpr`?

_____

_____

11.1.2 PRINT A FILE

Enter the following command:

```
lp toprint
```

(If your print command is `lpr`, use `lpr toprint` instead.)

a) What's the output of the `lp` command?

_____

_____

b) Examine the printed copy. Is there an extra page at the beginning?

_____

_____

LAB 11.1 EXERCISE ANSWERS

This section gives you some suggested answers to the questions in Lab 11.1, with discussions related to those answers. Your answers may vary, but the most important thing is whether or not your answers work. Use these discussions to analyze differences between your answers and those presented here.

If you have alternative answers to the questions in these exercises, you are encouraged to post your answers and discuss them at the companion Web site for this book, located at:

```
http://www.phptr.com/phptrinteractive
```

11.1.1 ANSWERS

Enter the following commands:

```
command -v lp
command -v lpr
```

a) Which command do you have, lp or lpr?

Answer: The answer depends on your system. You may have only lp, only lpr, or both.

Recent UNIX systems have both lp and lpr, although the system administrator may install and enable only one. (The command lp stands for "line printer.") Historically, lp was on System V UNIX systems, and lpr was on Berkeley systems. Solaris and Linux systems use lp.

Both commands do essentially the same thing: they send files to a *spooler.* Because a UNIX system has more than one user, the printer may already be busy when you want to print your job. A job spooler is just a storage queue for jobs that may not be able to run immediately. (The term "spooler" and the strategy of using a spooler are taken from older mainframe computers.)

Another program called a *print daemon* runs constantly, looking for spooled jobs. When it finds a spooled job, it sends the job to the correct printer.

There are other daemon programs running on the system that provide services like printing. The word "daemon" is an old term for "guardian angel."

11.1.2 ANSWERS

Enter the following command:

```
lp toprint
```

a) What's the output of the lp command?

Answer: The lp command prints a "job id" number. If the print spooler is not running, the lp command prints an error message.

Assuming your printer system is running correctly, you'll see a message like this:

```
job id: homer-251c
```

This job number identifies your print request. If you later want to cancel or change your request, you need to refer to it by its job number. In this case, the request is named "homer-251c." (On some systems, the job number includes the name of the printer; on other systems, it doesn't. In this case, the printer is named "homer".)

The lp command stores a request to print the file toprint in a directory called the *spool directory*. If the printer's not busy, the request will be noticed within seconds and the file will be printed. If the printer is busy, the file may not be printed for some time. (Someone may be printing out the phone book first.)

If you change the file between the time you use the lp command and the time it prints, the version that gets printed is the *new* version. If you delete the file, nothing gets printed. You can change this by giving lp the -c option, which copies the file and prints the copy.

If you have a file already in a printer language, such as PostScript, you can print it directly using lp, if you have the same kind of printer. To print the file, use the -b option, which tells lp that it isn't a text file.

b)   Examine the printed copy. Is there an extra page at the beginning?

Answer: Depends on how your system administrator set it up. You may have a banner page that identifies the print job.

On systems with many users, the printer daemon is often set up to print a front page that identifies the print job. Typically it contains your log-in name, the file name, and the date and time.

You can set the title on the banner page with the -t option. If the title includes spaces, remember to put it in quotation marks.

On Solaris 2.0+ systems and on UnixWare, you can eliminate the front page with the option -o nobanner (unless the system administrator has turned off this option). If many people use the same printer, you should keep the banner page. It helps identify where your job starts and where it ends.

TROUBLESHOOTING PRINTING

A couple of hints if you're having problems printing a particular file:

- If you get the message "No default destination" then it's possible that your printer system has not been set up, or that there is no default printer. If the system has not been set up, you cannot print. If it has been set up but there's no default printer, you can check for specific printers and print to one; see Lab 11.3, "Managing Print Jobs."
- If your output begins with a line like "%! Adobe-PS" then you're trying to print a PostScript file on a printer that isn't PostScript compatible.

LAB 11.1 SELF-REVIEW QUESTIONS

To test your progress, you should be able to answer the following questions.

1) The `lp` command sends files directly to the printer.
   a) _____True
   b) _____False

2) The system administrator starts the printer daemon, and it searches for files to print.
   a) _____True
   b) _____False

3) Which of the following is the option to turn off the banner page?
   a) _____-nobanner
   b) _____-o nobanner
   c) _____-o nofront
   d) _____-c

4) If you print a file with `lp -c` and then change the file, what happens?
   a) _____The file is not printed.
   b) _____The version that prints is the changed version.
   c) _____The version that prints is the original version.
   d) _____There is no banner page.

Quiz answers appear in Appendix A, Lab 11.1

L A B   11.2

FORMATTING TEXT FILES FOR PRINTING

LAB OBJECTIVES

After this lab, you will be able to:

✓ Set the Page Lengths and Margins

✓ Change Page Headings

✓ Print in Columns

Using the default settings, most printed text files don't look very attractive. The text starts immediately at the left margin and runs from page to page without any top or bottom margins. If you're using a laser printer, it might look even worse. The UNIX system provides a file called `pr` that formats files for printing.

If you look at the man page, the syntax of the `pr` command looks complex. The important options are:

```
pr [+page][-column][-dFmt][-h header][-l lines] [-o
   offset] [file...]
```

The +*page* option starts printing on a later page—the *page* is a number. Normally `pr` starts on page 1.

The -column option formats the text in columns; the *column* is also a number, the number of columns on the page.

The -d option double spaces the output.

The -F option folds lines in the text, as if you had run the file through fold before giving it to pr. (The fold command was mentioned in Chapter 10, "Working with Text Files.")

The -h option prints text (specified as *header*) at the top of each page.

The -l option sets the number of lines on a page. The *lines* argument is a number, the number of lines on the page.

The -m option "merges" files. Rather than printing one file after another, the files are printed side by side, each in its own column.

The -o option creates a left margin by shifting the text over by a number of spaces. The *offset* is a number.

The -t option eliminates the page header and the trailing blank lines.

There are more options. See the pr man page for them. The pr command works well in conjunction with fmt, described in Chapter 10, "Working with Text Files."

LAB 11.2 EXERCISES

11.2.1 SET THE PAGE LENGTHS AND MARGINS

Run the following command:

```
pr toprint | more
```

a) How does pr change the formatting of the file?

_____

_____

Run the following command:

```
pr -l 60 toprint > sixty
```

b) How many lines are there between header lines?

Run the following command:

```
pr -o 10 toprint | more
```

c) How does the -o 10 option change the formatting of the file?

11.2.2 CHANGE PAGE HEADINGS

Run the following command:

```
pr -h "test file for formatting" toprint | more
```

a) What parts of the header have changed? What parts have not changed?

Run the following command:

```
pr -t toprint | more
```

b) How does the -t option affect the header line?

11.2.3 PRINT IN COLUMNS

Run the following command:

```
pr -2 toprint > columns
```

a) How many columns are there in the output?

_____

_____

b) What happens to lines that are too long?

_____

_____

Run the following command:

```
pr -m toprint toprint | more
```

c) How does `pr` arrange the files?

_____

_____

LAB 11.2 EXERCISE ANSWERS

This section gives you some suggested answers to the questions in Lab 11.2, with discussions related to those answers. Your answers may vary, but the most important thing is whether or not your answers work. Use these discussions to analyze differences between your answers and those presented here.

If you have alternative answers to the questions in these exercises, you are encouraged to post your answers and discuss them at the companion Web site for this book, located at:

```
http://www.phptr.com/phptrinteractive
```

11.2.1 ANSWERS

Run the following command:

```
pr toprint | more
```

**LAB
11.2**

a) How does `pr` change the formatting of the file?

Answer: The `pr` program breaks the file into chunks that fit onto a page.

The `pr` program is not a word processing program; it's a filter that goes through the text file, chopping it into segments that fit onto a printed page. Each "chunk" is given a header line and sent to the standard output. The `pr` command can do other formatting tasks: you can specify page offsets and the number of lines on a page. You can even double-space output and print the file in columns.

By default, `pr` places two empty lines, a header line, and two more empty lines at the top, and five empty lines at the bottom of the "page." Also by default, `pr` assumes there are 66 lines on a sheet of paper.

Run the following command:

```
pr -l 60 toprint > sixty
```

b) How many lines are there between header lines?

Answer: With the `-l 60` option, there are 60 lines between header lines.

If you're using a laser printer, the output is only 60 or 61 lines per page, not 66. This can lead to a tremendous waste of paper if you've formatted for 66 lines. Using the option `-l 60` makes the output readable on most laser printers.

Run the following command:

```
pr -o 10 toprint | more
```

c) How does the `-o 10` option change the formatting of the file?

Answer: The `-o 10` option inserts 10 spaces at the left margin.

The `-o` option actually stands for "offset." It doesn't really provide margins, it merely moves the text over a few spaces. When using `fmt` to format text, a width of 60 gives you a 10 character margin on each side (if you use `pr -o 10`).

The usual command line to format and print a text file is:

```
fmt -w 60 file| pr -o 10 | lp
```

If you have a laser printer, you'll need to add the `-1  60` option to the `pr` command.

11.2.2 ANSWERS

Run the following command:

```
pr -h "test file for formatting" toprint | more
```

a) What parts of the header have changed? What parts have not changed?

Answer: The name of the file is replaced by the text "test file for formatting." The date and time remain the same.

Without this option, the heading on the file is the date and time, the name of the file, and the page number. The option replaces only the name of the file with the argument to the –h option.

This option is useful when the name of the file isn't a useful guide to the content of the text. If you are printing many files with similar contents, it's more useful to replace the heading "/project/tests/output/ 030998" with "March 9, 1998 output/provisional data." The option doesn't *remove* the header line.

Run the following command:

```
pr -t toprint | more
```

b) How does the –t option affect the header line?

Answer: The –t option eliminates the header and trailer space entirely.

The header is normally five lines (two empty lines, the header line, two more empty ones) and the bottom of the page is five empty lines. With the –t option, the header and the footer (or trailer) are omitted entirely. You might need it if you're formatting the file for some other reason (i.e., the -n option numbers lines, so you might use `pr -n -t` to produce a version of the file with numbered lines).

The header and trailer are also omitted if you specify a page length that's 10 lines or less.

11.2.3 ANSWERS

Run the following command:

```
pr -2 toprint > columns
```

a) How many columns are there in the output?

Answer: There are two columns

The -2 option specifies two columns. Columns are separated by one space. The columns are all the same width. You can have as many columns as you can fit on the page; -3 specified three columns, -4 four columns, and so on.

b) What happens to lines that are too long?

Answer: Long lines are cut off.

You can fix this with the -F option, which folds long lines.

Run the following command:
```
pr -m toprint toprint | more
```

c) How does `pr` arrange the files?

Answer: The files are printed side by side, one in each column.

The -m option is an excellent way to do side by side comparisons of files. There's one column for each file; you cannot specify the number of columns. The largest number of files you can specify with -m is nine.

LAB 11.2 SELF-REVIEW QUESTIONS

To test your progress, you should be able to answer the following questions.

1) The `pr` command formats files for printing.
   a) _____True
   b) _____False

2) By default, `pr` assumes the page is what length?
   a) _____60 lines
   b) _____61 lines
   c) _____66 lines
   d) _____70 lines

3) The command `pr -l 20` sets the page length to 20 lines.
   a) _____True
   b) _____False

   Quiz answers appear in Appendix A, Lab 11.2

LAB
11.2

L A B   11.3

MANAGING PRINT JOBS

LAB OBJECTIVES

After this lab, you will be able to:

✓ Determine the Status of a Print Job

✓ Cancel a Print Job

✓ List Available Printers

✓ Print to a Specific Printer

Sooner or later, you will want to know more about your print job. You may want to know whether it has printed yet (without walking down the hall). You may discover a terrible error in a huge file and you want to stop the file from printing. You may want to be able to print to one special printer, such as a color printer or the only PostScript printer.

Most of these commands require you to actually have a file waiting to be printed. On Solaris and UnixWare systems, the easiest way to do this is with the command lp -H hold toprint. *Record the print-request number.*

The -H hold option queues up a print job but does not proceed with it until you give the command lp -H resume -i *print-request*. If your system doesn't support the -H option, then you'll need to save these exercises until you have one or more pending requests.

LAB 11.3 EXERCISES

11.3.1 DETERMINE THE STATUS OF A PRINT JOB

Run the following command:

```
lpstat | more
```

a) If you have output, describe it.

_____

_____

Run the following command:

```
lpstat -o
```

b) What does the -o option do?

_____

_____

Run the following command:

```
lpstat -u yourloginid
```

c) Is the output different from only lpstat without the -u option? If so, how?

_____

_____

11.3.2 CANCEL A PRINT JOB

Enter the following command:

```
cancel print-job
```

(Replace *print-job* with the job id number of the held print job.)

a) What is the output of the `cancel` command?

_____

_____

Queue two held print jobs. Enter the following command:

```
cancel -u yourloginid
```

b) According to `lpstat`, which print job was removed from the queue?

_____

_____

11.3.3 LIST AVAILABLE PRINTERS

Enter the following commands:

```
lpstat -d
lpstat -a
```

a) Is this the printer that prints your files?

_____

_____

b) Are the results the same for the two commands?

_____

_____

11.3.4 Print to a Specific Printer

Pick a different printer on the system.

Enter the following command:

```
lp -H hold -d printername toprint
```

a) Which option must you use with `lpstat` to see the file in the queue?

_____

_____

LAB 11.3 EXERCISE ANSWERS

This section gives you some suggested answers to the questions in Lab 11.3, with discussions related to those answers. Your answers may vary, but the most important thing is whether or not your answers work. Use these discussions to analyze differences between your answers and those presented here.

If you have alternative answers to the questions in these exercises, you are encouraged to post your answers and discuss them at the companion Web site for this book, located at:

```
http://www.phptr.com/phptrinteractive
```

11.3.1 Answers

Run the following command:

```
lpstat | more
```

a) If you have output, describe it.

Answer: Sample output is shown here:

```
$ lpstat

homer-251c ringo      629 bytes toprint
```

This is a list of all jobs that haven't printed or haven't finished printing yet on your default printer. The first job in the list is the job that's printing, and the rest are displayed in the order they will print. On some systems, the command lpstat prints *all* jobs waiting for your default printer; on other systems, the command prints only your jobs waiting for your default printer. On some high-security sites, you're not allowed to see other users' jobs; this can be controlled by the system administrator.

The output has four parts: The job id ("homer-251c"), your log-in id ("ringo"), and the size and name of the file. If you have more than one file in the queue, you'll see more entries.

Your default printer may be the only printer on the system, or it may be one of many.

The BSD command lpq *is equivalent to the* lpstat *command.*

Run the following command:

    lpstat -o

b)   What does the -o option do?

Answer: The -o *option causes* lpstat *to list the status of all printers.*

Here's an example of

```
$ lpstat-o
chaucer:
homer:
homer-251c ringo        629 bytes toprint
homer-251d john      891131 bytes graphic.ps
homer-2520 pete        9452 bytes proposal
spenser:
spenser-357 paul       2882 bytes bands.txt
spenser-359 george       99 bytes zen_reading
```

In this output, there are three printers: chaucer, homer, and spenser. Chaucer has no jobs waiting, homer has three, and spenser has two.

Run the following command:

```
lpstat -o yourloginid
```

c) Is the output different from only `lpstat` without the -u output? If so, how?

Answer: The -u option restricts the output to your requests only. On some systems, that is different from `lpstat` (no options) output.

The command `lpstat -u yourloginid` shows only your print jobs for your default printer. Depending on your system's security setup, the default `lpstat` command may show all jobs waiting for that printer or only your jobs.

**LAB
11.3**

Enter the following command:

```
cancel print-job
```

a) What is the output of the `cancel` command?

Answer: Sample output is shown here:

```
$ cancel homer-251c
832bobo2013829 dequeued
```

Notice that the name of the "dequeued" file isn't necessarily the same as the request. On most systems, the name reported by the `cancel` command is the name of the file that held the print request, not the name of the job id.

The BSD command `lprm` *is equivalent to the* `cancel` *command*

Queue two held print jobs. Enter the following command:

```
cancel -u yourloginid
```

b) According to `lpstat`, which print job was removed from the queue?

Answer: Both print jobs were removed.

You can tell even without the `lpstat` command, because two items are listed as being "dequeued";

```
$ cancel -u ringo
832bobx4413039 dequeued
832bobx4413040 dequeued
```

The `-u` option removes all jobs for a particular user (in this case, you). The system administrator can use the `-u` option to remove anyone's print jobs from the queue, but you have permissions for your jobs only.

11.3.3 ANSWERS

Enter the following commands:

```
lpstat -d
```

a) Is this the printer that prints your files?

Answer: It is almost certainly the printer that prints your files.

The `lpstat -d` option lists the system default printer. This is the printer that *everyone* uses, unless they specify otherwise.

```
lpstat -a
```

b) Are the results the same for the two commands?

Answer: They may be. The `-d` option lists the system default printer, and the `-a` option lists all printers that are accepting print jobs.

The two items will be the same if there is only one printer, and if it is accepting print jobs.

11.3.4 ANSWERS

Pick a different printer on the system.
Enter the following command:

```
lp -H hold -d printername toprint
```

a) Which option must you use with `lpstat` to see the file in the queue?

Answer: You need to use the -o option.

The `-d` option to `lp` specifies the printer to be used. The argument doesn't have to be a particular printer; on many systems there are also *types* of printers (or printer classes, they're sometimes called). You can just specify a printer class to the `-d` option and `lp` and the printing system will pick a printer to use.

If you want to see only one printer using `lpstat -o`, you can specify the printer (or printers). For example, if you only wanted to see what was queued for the printer "chaucer," you can enter the command:

```
lpstat -ochaucer
```

If you want to see what's queued for both chaucer and homer, use the command:

```
lpstat -ochaucer,homer
```

Separate more than one printer name with commas.

If you find yourself using one printer in particular and it's *not* the default printer, you can use environment variables to make another printer your default. Enter the following command:

```
export LPDEST=printername
```

LAB 11.3 SELF-REVIEW QUESTIONS

To test your progress, you should be able to answer the following questions.

1) The `lpstat` command shows you printer status.
   a) _____True
   b) _____False

2) In the following table, attach the command to the action.

   a) `lp`   i) Display status of all printers

   b) `lpstat -o`   ii) Cancel a print job

   c) `cancel`   iii) Print a file

   d) `lpstat -u`   iv) Display all of your pending print jobs

3) Which of the following is the intent of the command `lpstat -u grendel -ospenser,homer`?
   a) _____Show jobs of user grendel waiting on printers spenser and homer
   b) _____Show jobs of users spenser and homer waiting on printer grendel
   c) _____Show status of printers grendel, spenser, and homer
   d) _____Show jobs waiting for users grendel, spenser, and homer

Quiz answers appear in Appendix A, Lab 11.3

LAB 11.3

C H A P T E R   11

TEST YOUR THINKING

 The projects in this section are meant to have you utilize all of the skills that you have acquired throughout this chapter. The answers to these projects can be found at the companion Web site to this book, located at:

`http://www.phptr.com/phptrinteractive`

Visit the Web site periodically to share and discuss your answers.

You have a dozen files that you need to print immediately. The results of the `lpstat` command are shown as follows:

```
$ lpstat-o
crayon:
pen:
pen-2f0c    larry        2896 bytes memo_2.txt
pen-2f0d    larry        1902 bytes memo_3.txt
pen-2f0e    larry         214 bytes phone_num.txt
pen-2f0f    larry         561 bytes joke
pen-2f10    curly     1510231 bytes report.ps
pencil:
pencil-a21  moe          2882 bytes a28933.tmp
```

We'll assume that none of these are your default printer.

1) Which printer should you use? What command would be required?

2) After queuing them up, you discover that the printer you've chosen is the slowest printer in the building. Which printer would be your second choice? How would you move the jobs to the other printer?

3) Suppose all three printers had full queues. What would your options be? How would you proceed?

4) How many lines does your printer fit on a page? How can you determine this? (There is a `pr` command that makes it quite easy.)

5) Select or create two long files. How can you print them side by side? What if the lines in the files are quite long (more than 80 characters)? How would this change your approach? You may need to use more than one command to format the files. How many files can you fit side by side?

CHAPTER 12

COMMANDS AND JOB CONTROL

 UNIX lets you run more than one command at a time. Because only one command can have access to the keyboard and monitor at a time, UNIX provides special techniques for controlling those other commands. There are other tricks in giving commands that are also useful.

CHAPTER OBJECTIVES

In this chapter, you will learn about:

Sometimes it's useful to run more than one command at a time. Running more than one command at a time has several meanings. It can mean naming more than one command at a time on the command line, or it can mean running a command and going on to another before the first command is finished. Both are possible on UNIX systems.

You can also schedule commands to run later, when the system isn't as busy, or even to run commands on a regular basis.

L A B   12.1

MULTIPLE COMMANDS ON A LINE

LAB OBJECTIVES

After this lab, you will be able to:

✓ Run Multiple Commands on a Line

✓ Group Commands

✓ Use One Command's Output as Arguments

Although we discussed the basic structure of a command line back in Chapter 2, "The Command Line," the UNIX shell provides a lot more flexibility and features for running commands. One is simply the ability to place more than one command on a line so they will all be run. This is useful when you want to queue up two or more commands to run.

A second feature is the ability to group commands. You can run a group of commands in the background, for example, or you can gather all of the output from a group of commands at once. This is a feature you might not immediately think of, but one that is useful when you need it.

The last feature is a kind of counterpart to the pipe. In a command pipeline, the output of one command is used as the input to the next. With command substitution, the output of one command is used as the *arguments* to another command.

LAB 12.1 EXERCISES

12.1.1 RUN MULTIPLE COMMANDS ON A LINE

Enter the following command line:

```
cd;pwd
```

a) What happens? What's the effect of the `;` character in a command line?

_____

_____

12.1.2 GROUP COMMANDS

Enter the following command line:

```
{ cd -; pwd; }; pwd
```

a) What effect do the braces have on the command?

_____

_____

Enter the following command line:

```
(cd -;pwd);pwd
```

b) What effect do the parentheses have on the command?

_____

_____

12.1.3 USE ONE COMMAND'S OUTPUT AS ARGUMENTS

Enter the following commands:

```
echo The current directory is `pwd`.
echo The current directory is $(pwd).
```

a) What do these commands do?

_____

_____

b) Is there a difference between the `` ` ` `` and `$()` forms of the command?

_____

_____

LAB 12.1 EXERCISE ANSWERS

This section gives you some suggested answers to the questions in Lab 12.1, with discussions related to those answers. Your answers may vary, but the most important thing is whether or not your answers work. Use these discussions to analyze differences between your answers and those presented here.

If you have alternative answers to the questions in these exercises, you are encouraged to post your answers and discuss them at the companion Web site for this book, located at:

```
http://www.phptr.com/phptrinteractive
```

12.1.1 ANSWERS

Enter the following command line:

```
cd;pwd
```

a) What happens? What's the effect of the `;` character in a command line?

Answer: The system runs the `cd` command (changing directories to your home directory) and then the `pwd` command (displaying your home directory's name).

The `;` character marks the end of a command, so you can use it to join together two (or more) commands. When the shell is interpreting the command line, it treats the `;` character as if you had typed Enter there.

12.1.2 ANSWERS

Enter the following command line:

```
{ cd -; pwd; }; pwd
```

a) What effect do the braces have on the command?

Answer: All three commands run as though the braces weren't there. The second and third `pwd` commands display the same directory.

The shell treats commands within `{ }` characters as a *group*. Use `{ }` characters when you need some other command modifier (such as `|` or `&`) to affect *all* of the commands in the group.

■ FOR EXAMPLE:

The `env` command prints out your environment. To search your environment *and* your hidden start-up files for your log-in name, you could run two `grep` commands:

```
env | grep $LOGNAME
grep $LOGNAME .*
```

You could also group the output of two commands (`ls` and `env`) and search the output with a single command:

```
{ env ; ls .* ; } | grep $LOGNAME
```

The output of the two commands are "merged" because they're a command group, and can be piped together to the `grep` command. You *must* have the space after the opening `{` character, and you *must* have either a `;`

or a & character before the closing } character. One confusing fact is that you don't actually need a space before the closing } or even before the ; or & characters that must be before the closing } character. (If you're interested in *why* { and (are treated differently, you may want to read the ksh man page to discover the difference between a "reserved word" such as { and a metacharacter such as (.)

You may not need this trick often, but when you do, it's extremely useful.

Enter the following command line:

```
(cd -;pwd);pwd
```

b)   What effect do the parentheses have on the command?

Answer: The first two commands run as you expect, but the third command prints the name of the directory you started in. Your current directory hasn't changed.

A command or commands run within () characters is run by another shell, called a *subshell*.

The commands cd / and pwd are run as a pair. The difference between (cd /;pwd) and cd /;pwd is that commands in () characters are run in a different shell program. Your shell starts up a *new* shell program that runs the commands. Changes to the environment of that new shell (like a change in directory) don't affect subsequent commands in your *old* shell. This new shell is called a *subshell*.

Remember that your current working directory is a bit of information that's specific to your shell program. When you log out, you don't expect to start your next UNIX session in the same directory you started in; every new session starts fresh. This is a similar effect.

When you use the () characters around a command, the shell makes a copy of itself and all its information (such as the current working directory). It tells the copy to go and run those commands. The copy is allowed to write to the screen and take input from the keyboard (as normal), but when it's finished, the copy goes away, and it's almost as though it never happened.

You'll still be able to see the effects of commands that affect files, but you won't see the effects of any commands that affect your shell environment. There are several commands that will affect your environment, although we've only discussed cd.

Often, however, it won't matter whether you use {} or () to group your commands.

12.1.3 ANSWERS

Enter the following commands:

```
echo The current directory is `pwd`.
echo The current directory is $(pwd).
```

a)   What do these commands do?

Answer: Assuming your current directory is /usr/home/jan, *both commands print the line:*

```
The current directory is /usr/home/jan.
```

The echo command repeats its arguments. The pwd command prints the current working directory. Both the `pwd` and the $(pwd) insert the output of the pwd command into the arguments of the echo command.

This trick is called *command substitution*. The results of one command (pwd) are substituted into another command (echo).

b)   Is there a difference between the `` and $() forms of the command?

Answer: On most systems, there's no apparent difference.

There are actually three differences between the two, but you're not likely to notice.

- First, if you're using an old C shell or if you're using the Bourne shell, it may not recognize the $() form.
- Second, the backquote version (``) treats backslashes differently depending on context. In the $() form, backslashes are treated exactly as they are in a regular command. In the backquote form, backslashes aren't metacharacters *unless* they are in front of a dollar sign, a backquote, or another backslash.

- Third, you can nest command substitutions using the $() form. That means you can put a command substitution inside a command substitution.

■ FOR EXAMPLE:

If you want to find all files with .txt file extensions and read the ones that contain the word "kiwi", you could run each command separately:

```
$ find / -name "*.txt" -print
./au.txt
./ba.txt
./ca.txt
./de.txt
./nz.txt
./us.txt
```

Then you remember the names of the files to find which ones contain the word "kiwi":

```
$ grep -l kiwi au.txt ba.txt ca.txt de.txt nz.txt
  us.txt
au.txt
nz.txt
```

Now you can use more to look at the files:

```
$ more au.txt nz.txt
```

Or you can use two nested command substitutions:

```
more $(grep -l kiwi $(find / -name "*.txt" -print))
```

Reading from the right end to the left, the find command prints a list of all files on the system with names ending in .txt. The grep -l command uses that list as its set of files to search for the word "kiwi"; the -l option means that grep prints only the names of the files that contain the word. The more command displays the contents of the files listed by grep's output.

You should use the $() form whenever you can.

LAB 12.1 SELF-REVIEW QUESTIONS

To test your progress, you should be able to answer the following questions.

1) The ; character marks the end of a command, just as Enter does.
    a) _____True
    b) _____False

2) Which of the following is the meaning of the command `ls -l` `cat files`?
    a) _____List the contents of the directories `cat` and `files`.
    b) _____List the contents of your home directory.
    c) _____Group the commands `ls` and `cat files`.
    d) _____Treat every line in `files` as a file or directory name, and give a long listing for those names.

3) "Command substitution" involves which of the following characters?
    a) _____ ;
    b) _____ | and &
    c) _____ ` ` or $ ( )
    d) _____ { } or ( )

Quiz answers appear in Appendix A, Lab 12.1

L A B   12.2

SETTING ENVIRONMENT VARIABLES

LAB OBJECTIVES

After this lab, you will be able to:

✓ Set a Variable

✓ Export a Variable to the Environment

✓ Unset a Variable

Throughout this book, there have been references to environment variables. Variables are temporary storage locations with names, and environment variables are variables stored in your environment. Your environment is like a bulletin board for programs. If a program wants to know what kind of terminal you're using, it can peek in the variable named TERM for the value.

There are other pieces of information stored in the environment. Your current directory, for instance, is part of the environment. (In the Korn Shell, it's stored in a variable named PWD.)

Every program gets its own copy of the environment from the program that started it (usually your shell). Because every program has its own copy, if one program changes its own environment, it won't affect the environment of any other program that's already running. For example, if you are running two `xterm` programs on a machine with X installed, changing the value of TERM in one `xterm` has no effect on the value of TERM in the other `xterm`.

Many programs use environment variables. You can store start-up commands for `vi` in an environment variable (the environment variable EXINIT), or the size of your terminal screen (for `more` or `vi`). The `lp` command checks the LPDEST environment variable for the name of your printer. Programs that use start-up files or special data files (such as `spell`) often let you specify an alternative data file using an environment variable. A program's man page describes the environment variables it checks.

LAB 12.2 EXERCISES

12.2.1 SET A VARIABLE

Enter the following commands:

```
VAR=value
echo $VAR
```

a) What is the output of the `echo` command?

_____

_____

Enter the following command:

```
env
```

b) Is VAR listed? Why not?

_____

_____

12.2.2 EXPORT A VARIABLE TO THE ENVIRONMENT

Enter the following command:

```
VAR="another value" env
```

a) Is VAR listed?

_____

_____

Enter the following commands:

```
export $VAR
env
```

b) Is VAR now listed?

_____

_____

12.2.3 UNSET AN ENVIRONMENT VARIABLE

Enter the following commands:

```
VAR=
env
```

a) Is VAR still in the environment?

_____

_____

Enter the following commands:

```
unset VAR
env
```

b) Is VAR still in the environment?

LAB 12.2 EXERCISE ANSWERS

 This section gives you some suggested answers to the questions in Lab 12.2, with discussions related to those answers. Your answers may vary, but the most important thing is whether or not your answers work. Use these discussions to analyze differences between your answers and those presented here.

If you have alternative answers to the questions in these exercises, you are encouraged to post your answers and discuss them at the companion Web site for this book, located at:

```
http://www.phptr.com/phptrinteractive
```

12.2.1 ANSWERS

Enter the following commands:

```
VAR=value
echo $VAR
```

a) What is the output of the echo command?

Answer:The echo *command prints the word* "value".

The = sign assigns a value to a variable. The value is the word "value" in this case. Whenever you refer to the variable's value (and the shell knows you mean the *value* rather than the name of the variable because you put a $ at the beginning), it substitutes "value". (We refer to the name itself as the variable, and $name as a variable reference.)

Because the shell contains a programming language, it keeps track of its own variables. You can use these variables to do simple math, for example. A variable is just a place to store information for a little while.

■ FOR EXAMPLE:

Sometimes you need to move back and forth between three or four directories with long names. You cannot use `cd` – because there are three or four directories, and `cd` – only returns to the previous directory (whichever it was). Instead of typing long directory names again and again, you can assign each of these names to a variable. Here's a single example:

```
project=/net/nfs/osiris/projects/bison
```

Now, to change directories to `/net/nfs/osiris/projects/bison`, enter the command:

```
cd $project
```

If you're going to be in these directories every day for many days, you might want to consider setting up an *alias*.

 Visit the Web companion to this book to learn how to set up an alias. It is located at:

```
http://www.phptr.com/phptrinteractive
```

Enter the following commands:

```
env
```

b) Is VAR listed? Why not?

Answer: The value of VAR is not listed because it's not in the environment yet.

The environment is the list of variables that are available to all of your programs (or at least all programs you start from this particular shell). Every program has its own copy of the environment. A shell variable isn't automatically in the environment, you have to put it there.

The env command prints out many of the variables in your environment. At this point, VAR is just a variable with a value. It's not in the environment because programs other than the shell cannot see it yet. Shell built-ins like `echo` can see it because they're part of the shell. (The `set` command prints out all of the variables in your environment, but it prints out a lot of other information as well.)

Common environment variables are shown in Table 12.1.

Table 12.1 ■ Common Environment Variables

Variable	Description
HOME=/home/johnmc	Your home directory.
LANG=C	Defines the characters that are acceptable in file names. "C" or "POSIX" are common values for English-speaking countries.
LOGNAME=johnmc	Your log-in name. On BSD systems, there is a second environment variable, USER, which also contains your log-in name.
MAIL=/var/mail/johnmc	The file where your mail is stored before you read it.
PATH=/usr/bin:/usr/ccs/bin	Directories that contain programs to be run.
PWD=/home/johnmc	Your current directory.
SHELL=/usr/bin/ksh	The name of your shell. (May not be set if you're using C shell.)
TERM=xterm	Your current terminal type
TERMCAP=/etc/termcap	A file containing descriptions of terminals.
TZ=:US/Eastern	Your time zone.
VISUAL=/usr/bin/vi	Your editor program. When a program starts an editor for you, it uses the editor named in this variable. If this is not set, programs will start vi.

**LAB
12.2**

12.2.2 ANSWERS

Enter the following command:

```
VAR="another value" env
```

a) Is VAR listed?

Answer: Yes. Assigning a value to a variable at the beginning of the command line makes it part of that command's environment.

But if you type env again, it's not there. The assignment is only good for that command line, or for that occurrence of the env program.

Enter the following commands:

```
export $VAR
env
```

b) Is VAR now listed?

Answer: Yes. The export *command makes it part of the environment.*

You can combine the assignment and the export command into one line, like this:

```
export MYNAME=johnmc
```

The variable MYNAME is now part of the environment. As I'm using the term, something that's in the "environment" can be seen by programs other than the shell. Sometimes the shell man page refers to variables that only the current shell "knows about" as environment variables, even though they wouldn't be by this definition. The export command makes the variable available to other programs. You don't need to export a variable when you make it (why bother if no other program needs to know about it?), and you can export a variable later if you need to.

12.2.3 ANSWERS

Enter the following commands:

```
VAR=
env
```

a) Is VAR still in the environment?

Answer: Yes, but now it has no value associated with it.

The value report by env is now:

```
VAR=
```

Computer programmers distinguish between a variable that's there and empty and a variable that isn't there at all. In this case, you've just changed the value of VAR to nothing (there's nothing after the = sign), but you haven't removed it from the environment at all.

Enter the following commands:

```
unset VAR
env
```

b) Is VAR still in the environment?

Answer: No.

The command unset removes the variable from the environment entirely.

You might imagine that the command set should be used to create variables, since unset removes them. The set command can create variables, but its primary job is setting and displaying the options for the shell.

LAB 12.2 SELF-REVIEW QUESTIONS

To test your progress, you should be able to answer the following questions.

1) A variable is a named temporary storage place for information.
   a) _____True
   b) _____False

2) What is the value of the variable name after the following commands?

   ```
   name=jack

   name='$name sprat'
   ```

   a) _____jack
   b) _____jack sprat
   c) _____$name sprat
   d) _____jack jack sprat

3) The variable name is now part of the environment?
   a) _____True
   b) _____False

4) What is the value of the variable name after the command

   ```
   name=
   ```

   a) _____Variable no longer set
   b) _____jack
   c) _____jack sprat
   d) _____$name sprat
   e) _____Set but no value

5) What is the value of the variable name after the command

   ```
   unset name
   ```

   a) _____Variable no longer set
   b) _____jack
   c) _____jack sprat
   d) _____$name sprat
   e) _____Set but no value

   Quiz answers appear in Appendix A, Lab 12.2

L A B 12.3

FOREGROUND AND BACKGROUND

LAB OBJECTIVES

After this lab, you will be able to:

✓ Run a Command in the Background

✓ List All Background Jobs

✓ Move a Job to the Foreground

Up until now, you've had to wait for each command to finish before you could start the next command. Even when you join commands using the ; or | characters, you have to wait for all of the commands to finish before you can go on to the next command line. We call commands like these commands running in the *foreground*. Foreground commands have control of the keyboard and the screen. Before you can enter a new command, you have to wait for the foreground command to finish.

But UNIX offers ways to put jobs in the *background*. A background job is any job that doesn't have control of your terminal. While it runs, you're free to type other commands.

Like all good offers, there's a catch: The command you run in the background shouldn't write to the terminal. You can understand why: The messages from the background job would mix with the messages from the foreground job, and it would be hard to tell them apart. If you were running more than one job in the background and each were writing messages to the screen, there might be no way to distinguish which command sent what message.

While all UNIX systems can run jobs in the background, only some can move jobs between the background and the foreground. This facility is called *job control*. It should be available to you; it's on almost all systems and shells. (It may not be available in the Bourne shell, `/bin/sh`.)

With the prevalence of windowing displays such as X Windows (see Chapter 13, "X Window System"), the ability to move commands between the foreground and the background is not as important as it used to be. It's still useful when a command takes longer than you expected, so you want to put it in the background.

LAB 12.3 EXERCISES

12.3.1 RUN A COMMAND IN THE BACKGROUND

Enter the following command:

```
sleep 5 &
```

Wait 10 seconds, and then press Enter again.

a) What sort of output do you get? What happens the second time you press Enter?

_____

_____

Enter this command, and then press Control-Z:

```
find . -name not_here 2> /dev/null
```

Enter this command; if the number reported when you pressed Control-Z was not 2, use that number instead of 2:

```
bg %2
```

b) What output do you get when you press Control-Z?

_____

_____

c) What happens after you enter the bg command?

_____

_____

12.3.2 LIST ALL BACKGROUND JOBS

a) What output does the command jobs produce?

_____

_____

12.3.3 MOVE A JOB TO THE FOREGROUND

Enter the following command:

```
fg %1
```

a) What happens to the command prompt?

_____

_____

b) What does %1 refer to?

_____

_____

Press Control-Z again.

c) What happens?

_____

_____

LAB 12.3 EXERCISE ANSWERS

This section gives you some suggested answers to the questions in Lab 12.3, with discussions related to those answers. Your answers may vary, but the most important thing is whether or not your answers work. Use these discussions to analyze differences between your answers and those presented here.

If you have alternative answers to the questions in these exercises, you are encouraged to post your answers and discuss them at the companion Web site for this book, located at:

```
http://www.phptr.com/phptrinteractive
```

12.3.1 ANSWERS

Enter the following command:

```
sleep 5 &
```

Wait 10 seconds, and then press Enter again.

a) What sort of output do you get? What happens the second time you press Enter?

Answer: Your output should look something like this:

```
$ sleep 5 &
[1]     23603
```

The [1] is the job id number. It identifies which background job this is. The 23603 is the *process id number.* Should you need to, you can use the process id number to kill the background job, as discussed in Chapter 6,

"Emergency Recovery." You can also use the job id number for this; we'll discuss that a little later in this lab.

If you start another background job before this one finishes, it will become job 2. The job id numbers are reused as they become available, so if job 1 finishes, and you start another job before job 2 is finished, the new job will become job 1.

The second time you press Enter, you should see output something like this:

```
[1] +  Done                        sleep 5 &
```

This means that the job is done. The output is exactly like the output of the `jobs` command for this job only.

Enter this command, and then press Control-Z:

```
find . -name not_here 2> /dev/null
```

Enter this command; if the number reported when you pressed Control-Z was not 2, use that number instead of 2:

```
bg %2
```

b) What output do you get when you press Control-Z?

Answer: The output looks like this:

```
$ find / -name not_here 2> /dev/null
[2] + Stopped (user)            find / -name nosuchfile
  2> /dev/null
```

The Control-Z key combination stops the command. Once the command is stopped, you can choose to kill it, restart it in the background, or restart it in the foreground.

The Control-Z key combination sends the "suspend" signal, just as the Control-C key combination sends the "interrupt" signal. Control-Z only works on systems with job control.

c) What happens after you enter the `bg` command?

Answer: The command is restarted in the background.

The output looks like this:

```
[2] find / -name not_here 2> /dev/null
```

The command is restarted and you're given the job id number again.

12.3.2 ANSWERS

a) What output does the command jobs produce?

Answer:The jobs *command lists the programs currently running in the background. Here's an example of* jobs *output. I've added extra jobs here:*

```
[4]  + Running   sleep 100
[3]  - Done      groff -man spell.r 2> ~/troff.err
[2]    Running   find / -name nosuchfile 2> /dev/null
```

Each of these is a job running in the background. Besides the command itself (on the right), the listing contains other information:

- The *job id* number is in brackets. Job 4 is sleep 100.
- The *current job* is indicated by +. The current job is the job you "moved" into the background most recently.
- The *previous* job is indicated by -. The previous job is the job that used to be the current job.
- The *state* of the job is also given. The groff command is done, but the other two commands are still running.

The -1 option to jobs will cause it to also display the pid number of each job, in case you want to use kill on the command.

The jobs *command only lists jobs started in that terminal window. If you're using X Windows and you have more than one* xterm *window open, you must use* ps -e -u *yourloginid to list all of your processes, including the ones running in the background.*

12.3.3 ANSWERS

Enter the following command:

```
fg %1
```

a) What happens to the command prompt?

Answer:The command prompt goes away.

The command is now in the foreground, so you cannot enter another command until this one finishes.

b) What does %1 refer to?

Answer:The %1 refers to job id number I.

The % character is used to indicate a job id number. Besides the fg and bg commands, this also works for the kill command. You can give a %jobid number to kill instead of the process id number. For example, kill %1 would kill the background job with job id 1.

If you don't specify a job id number, the bg or fg command applies to the current job.

Press Control-Z again.

c) What happens?

Answer:The job is stopped again.

With Control-Z, bg, and fg, you can move commands back and forth, between the foreground and the background.

If that background job asks for input (perhaps you need to answer a yes/no question), it just stops. It's suspended until you move it to the foreground and give it the input it needs, or until you kill it. If a background job tries to write output to the screen, it may get suspended or it may not. (If it does write to the screen, it will probably mess up the display you're currently reading.)

Whether a background job gets suspended when writing output depends on your terminal settings. You may remember that the stty command sets controls for your terminal display. If you give the command `stty tostop`, background jobs that try to write output to the terminal will be suspended. To turn this behavior off (it's not normally on), give the command `stty -tostop`. (With `stty`, placing a – before a setting causes the setting to be turned off.)

LAB 12.3 SELF-REVIEW QUESTIONS

To test your progress, you should be able to answer the following questions.

1) Any number of commands can run in the foreground.
    a) _____True
    b) _____False

2) The Control-Z key combination puts commands in the background.
    a) _____True
    b) _____False

3) Which of the following will the command `fg` do?
    a) _____Bring background job 1 to the foreground.
    b) _____Move the foreground job into the background.
    c) _____Bring the current job to the foreground.
    d) _____Move the current job into the background.

    Quiz answers appear in Appendix A, Lab 12.3

L A B   12.4

SCHEDULING JOBS

LAB OBJECTIVES

After this lab, you will be able to:

✓ Run a Job at a Later Time

✓ Cancel a Scheduled Job

UNIX provides several facilities for running jobs at a later time.

With what you already know, you can set up jobs to run later. The simplest way would be to set up a command like:

```
(sleep 2400; command ) &
```

This has several disadvantages: first, it will go away when you log out (because all of your jobs end when you log out, unless you use the command nohup at the beginning of the command line). Second, the sleep command slows down the entire system. All commands do; this isn't special to the sleep command. Third, it's difficult to calculate how many seconds it is until the time the command should start.

Fortunately, you don't need to do it this way. UNIX systems offer three commands to schedule other jobs: at, batch, and crontab. Both at and batch schedule a job to run once; crontab schedules a job to run regularly. If you want a command to be run every year, every month or even every minute, crontab is the command you use to schedule it.

All three of these commands can be abused. (A job scheduled to run every minute can slow down the system a *lot.*) For that reason, you may not be allowed to run them. (If you are acting as a system administrator, you'll need information on scheduling jobs and on assigning permissions to schedule jobs. See the companion book to this one, *UNIX System Administrator's Interactive Workbook,* by Joe Kaplenk (Prentice Hall, PTR 1999).)

There are no exercises involving crontab here. There are normally no reasons for users to schedule regular jobs.

LAB 12.4 EXERCISES

12.4.1 RUN A JOB AT A LATER TIME

Create a file called file1.

Now enter the following command (after the at command, enter the cp command, press Enter, and then press Control-D):

```
at now + 10 minutes
cp file1 file2
Control-D
```

a) What is the output of the at command?

_____

_____

Enter the following command:

```
atq
```

b) How does the output of the atq command compare with the output of the at command? What does the atq command do?

_____

_____

12.4.2 CANCEL A SCHEDULED JOB

Enter the following command:

```
at -r jobid
```

a) What's the output of the command?

_____

_____

LAB 12.4 EXERCISE ANSWERS

12.4.1 ANSWERS

Create a file called `file1`. Now enter the following command (after the `at` command, enter the `cp` command, press Enter, and then press Control-D):

```
at now + 10 minutes
cp file1 file2
Control-D
```

a) What is the output of the `at` command?

Answer: Sample output is shown here.

```
$ at now + 5 minutes
at> cp file1 file2
at> <EOT>
warning: commands will be executed using /bin/ksh
job 903665655.a at Fri Jun 12 22:48:00 1998
```

The `at` command schedules a job to run at a particular time. There are three parts to an at command:

- The at command, including the time and date when the command is to run.
- The command to be run.
- Control-D to end input.

There are several ways to specify the time. The synopsis for at is:

```
at [-f file] [-m] time [date] [+ increment]
```

The *time* is either a word (one of "now," "noon," or "midnight") or a time in hours and minutes. The time is assumed to be a 24-hr. clock unless you specify "am" or "pm." All of these at commands run at the same time, 1:00 P.M. today (or 1:00 P.M. tomorrow if given after 1:00 P.M.):

```
at 1300
at 100 pm
at 1:00 pm
at 1 pm
at midnight + 13 hours
at noon + 1 hour
at noon + 60 minutes
```

If you say "noon," it's always relative to the very next noon, so if you say it in the evening, it means noon of the next day. If you say "now," you always have to add an extra time increment, using +.

You can also specify a *date*, which is either a word ("today" or "tomorrow") or a date in the form *month day*. The month can have the full name ("December") or just the first three letters ("dec"). Case doesn't matter.

This sounds complicated, but it's intended to be flexible. Most dates and times you enter will be correct.

The warning in the output (Commands will be executed using /usr/bin/sh) means that the Bourne shell will be used to run the commands. For most commands this won't matter much, but it will matter if the command is a shell built-in command. (Remember that you can use command -v to see if a command is a shell built-in; see Chapter 6, "Emergency Recovery.")

The job you run with at doesn't have to be just one command. It can be several commands, on several lines. The at command tries to reproduce the environment you have when you give the command. For instance, it will make sure that the command runs in the same directory as you're in when you give the at command.

The Control-D is necessary because you're typing in the command on the standard input.

If you don't want to type the command in from standard input, you can put the commands to be run in a file, and then specify the file with the -f option. This is useful if it's a complex set of commands that you want to get just right before you set up the job.

The batch *command is similar to* at, *but you don't specify a time. The system runs the command whenever it's not busy. If you don't need a job by a particular time,* batch *is easier to run.*

Enter the following command:

```
atq
```

**LAB
12.4**

b) How does the output of the atq command compare with the output of the at command? What does the atq command do?

Answer: The atq *command lists jobs queued by the* at *command. The* at   -c *command describes a particular job.*

```
$ atq
Rank    Execution Date      Owner   Job Queue  Job Name
1st    Jun 15, 1998 12:00   johnmc  897926400.a.0    a    stdin
```

The "Rank" is the order in which the commands will be run. The "Execution Date" describes when the command will run. "Owner" and "Job" are self-explanatory.

The "Queue" is the list of jobs containing this particular job. There are different job queues. Jobs queued by at go into the "a" queue; jobs queued by batch go into the "b" queue. (There may be other queues on your system.)

The "Job Name" is the file that contained the commands to be run. In this case, they were typed in from standard input, stdin.

The command at -l also displays a list of pending jobs, but the list doesn't contain as much information.

You'll notice that there's no way to actually determine what the commands to be run are. There may not be a way to find out, short of actually finding the job file and reading it (and you won't have permission to do that). Depending on your system, there may be a way. UnixWare systems offer at −d, which displays a description of the command. Other systems offer at −c, which does the same thing.

Table 12.2 shows an example of the output of at −d on a UnixWare system. These are the commands that are executed when the job runs. Lines that begin with : or # are comments; they don't get executed.

The important thing to notice is that only the last command, cp file1 file2, is the command entered to be run. The rest of the commands set up the environment so that when the command runs, it runs under the same conditions as when the at command was given.

Table 12.2 ■ at −d Output

```
### BEGIN          897731160.a.0        BEGIN ###

: at job

: jobname: stdin

: notify by mail: no

export _; _='/usr/bin/at'

export LANG; LANG='C'

export HZ; HZ='100'

export PATH; PATH='/usr/bin:/usr/ccs/bin'

export LOGNAME; LOGNAME='johnmc'

export MAIL; MAIL='/var/mail/johnmc'

export TERMCAP; TERMCAP='/etc/termcap'

export SHELL; SHELL='/usr/bin/ksh'

export HOME; HOME='/home/johnmc'

export TERM; TERM='xterm'
```

Table 12.2 ■ `at -d` **Output (Continued)**

```
export PWD; PWD='/home/johnmc'

export TZ; TZ=':US/Eastern'

cd /home/johnmc/work

#ident       "@(#)/etc/cron.d/.proto.sl 1.1 eiger 11/30/95
51258 NOVELL"

#ident "Header: /sms/sinixV5.4es/rcs/s19-full/usr/src/cmd/
.adm/.proto,v 1.1 91/02/28 15:51:58 ccs Exp "

cd /home/johnmc

ulimit 2097151

umask 22

cp file1 file2



### END          897731160.a.0          END ###
```

12.4.2 ANSWERS

Enter the following command:

```
at -r jobid
```

a) What's the output of the command?

Answer:There is no output if the command succeeds.

When you give the `-r` option, the `at` command removes a job from the queue. You *must* specify the job id; use `at -1` to get the list of jobs.

You can only remove jobs you submitted. The system administrator can remove any job.

LAB 12.4 SELF-REVIEW QUESTIONS

To test your progress, you should be able to answer the following questions.

1) The at and batch commands both schedule jobs to be run later.
   a) _____True
   b) _____False

2) Jobs run with at and batch are run using which of the following?
   a) _____Your current shell
   b) _____The Bourne or POSIX shell
   c) _____The C shell
   d) _____The Korn Shell

3) At one o'clock in the afternoon, you give an at command with the time specification noon + 2 hours. When will the command run?
   a) _____3:00 P.M. today
   b) _____3:00 A.M. tomorrow
   c) _____3:00 P.M. tomorrow
   d) _____The command won't run because the time specification is invalid.

Quiz answers appear in Appendix A, Lab 12.4

CHAPTER 12

TEST YOUR THINKING

The projects in this section are meant to have you utilize all of the skills that you have acquired throughout this chapter. The answers to these projects can be found at the companion Web site to this book, located at:

`http://www.phptr.com/phptrinteractive`

Visit the Web site periodically to share and discuss your answers.

To produce documents in our office, we have a command called `blddoc`. It requires no arguments; it runs in the directory containing the document files and it creates a PostScript file in that directory. It writes error messages to standard error.

The problem is that `blddoc` requires so many system resources that it slows down the computer. Other users complain when `blddoc` is run. If possible, `blddoc` should be run between 11:00 P.M. and 1:00 A.M.

1) How would you schedule `blddoc`? What command line would be best?

Remember that the error messages can contain useful information.

Once the PostScript file has been created, it can be either printed (with `lp`) or it can be copied into another directory (`/usr/spool/pdf`), where a daemon program will discover it automatically and create another file from the PostScript. This new file is the one that is actually shipped to customers.

2)   How does the scheduled command change if you're going to print the Post-Script file? If you're going to copy it into /usr/spool/pdf? If you want to do both and save the error messages from all three operations?

    Error messages from the daemon will be mailed to you, so you don't need to worry about those.

3)   Would this be a useful job to schedule with crontab? If so, why? If not, why not?

C H A P T E R 13

X WINDOW SYSTEM

A Graphic User Interface (GUI) lets you work with pictures instead of command words. The dominant GUI on UNIX is the X Window System.

The X Window System is a Graphic User Interface (GUI) written for UNIX systems. (In fact, it can run on other systems, too, but it's usually found on UNIX systems.) It's called "X" because it was written after the writing of a window system called "W." It was primarily written by graduate students at the Massachusetts Institute of Technology, and all but the most recent versions are free software. The last free version is X11 release 6.

Although the official terms for the X Window System are "X Window System" or "X," most people refer to it as "X Windows" and that's how I'll refer to it.

L A B   13.1

X WINDOW BASICS

LAB OBJECTIVES

After this lab, you will be able to:

✓ Identify Your Display

✓ Identify Your Window Manager

✓ Move a Window

✓ Change a Window's Size

✓ Iconify and Restore a Window

✓ Select and Paste Text

Early computer systems had displays that were "character based," which means they displayed numbers and letters and not much more. If you were lucky, you got a terminal that could do underlining and display different colors. One of the reasons was computing power: If the terminal was responsible for doing all of the display work, then the software on the computer system could concentrate on what letters and numbers to send.

As computers got more powerful, it became possible for the computer software itself to calculate how to draw a picture of a letter on the screen. Various researchers realized that the computer could draw more than just letters; and frankly, some people find command lines harder to work with than pictures. That was the beginning of the design of the *graphic user interface*, a user interface (or shell) that is designed around pictures instead of words. Graphic user interfaces (or GUIs) are common now: they're found on most personal computers.

LAB 13.1 TERMINOLOGY

Before you work with the mouse, cursor, and X Windows, you should learn the terminology. If you've already used Microsoft's Windows, Windows 95, Windows NT, or Apple's System 7 operating systems, this will all be familiar to you.

Button. There are two meanings for "button." It can mean a button on your mouse or pointer device, or it can mean a square or round picture on the screen. Clicking or selecting the button controls the program in some way; it may set an option or it may cause the program to act. If it means a real button on your mouse or pointing device, the term is usually "mouse button." Because most mice have two or three buttons, the buttons are referred to as the left button, the middle button, and the right button. (If you're right-handed, these are pressed with the index finger, the middle finger, and the ring finger.) When a document refers only to the "mouse button," it means the left button.

Click. When you press a button on the mouse, it sends a signal to the computer. This is called "clicking."

Double click. If you press the mouse button twice in quick succession, it's a double click.

Drag. "Dragging" something involves three steps: With the cursor over the picture you want to drag, press the mouse button, drag the mouse so the cursor moves (the picture will follow). When the cursor is at the destination, let go of the mouse button.

Focus. The currently active window. On most systems, you must click on a window or X application to give it the focus, but you can configure your system to automatically give focus to whatever program is under the cursor. (I don't recommend it; I find it gets very annoying when you're trying to work with two programs. It's even more annoying if your system is configured to bring the window with focus to the front of all other windows.)

Icon. An icon is a picture or representation. Usually it refers to a small picture that stands for a larger picture or window.

Iconify. To close (but not exit) a program's window; the window is turned into an icon. Depending on the window manager, the icon may be where the window was or it may be found with the other icons. Some documentation refers to "iconifying" windows and some refers to "minimizing" windows. They mean the same thing.

Menu. A menu is a list of options. To select one item from the menu, click on it. Different programs use different techniques for displaying a menu. You may have to click on a button in the window's decorations or you may have to click the right or middle mouse button.

Select. To select something, click on it. A selected item has the focus.

Window. A window is a picture used to display and work with a particular program. A window usually consists of a main window (or a pane) and some decorations. Figure 13.1 shows the parts of a Motif window. Not all Motif windows have all of these parts.

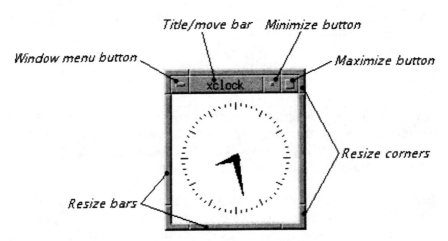

Figure 13.1 ■ Parts of a Motif window.

LAB 13.1 EXERCISES

13.1.1 IDENTIFY YOUR DISPLAY

a) What is the output of the command `echo $DISPLAY`?

_____

_____

b) What is the output of the command `uname -n`?

_____

_____

c) What is the output of the command `hostname`?

_____

_____

13.1.2 IDENTIFY YOUR WINDOW MANAGER

Enter the command

```
$ ps | grep wm
```

a) What currently running commands end in "wm"?

_____

_____

13.1.3 MOVE A WINDOW

Enter the command

```
$ xclock &
```

a) What happens when you drag the title bar?

_____

_____

13.1.4 CHANGE A WINDOW'S SIZE

With the `xclock` command still running:

a) Drag on a corner. What happens?

_____

_____

b) Drag on an edge. What happens?

_____

_____

c) What happens when you click on the expand button (the square button in the upper right corner)? When you click the button again?

_____

_____

d) What happens when you click on the iconify button (the dot button in the upper right corner)?

_____

_____

13.1.5 ICONIFY AND RESTORE A WINDOW

At the end of 13.1.4, the window is iconified. Iconify a new window, if you haven't already.

a) What happens when you click once on the icon?

_____

_____

b) Click elsewhere on the screen. What happens when you double click the icon?

_____

_____

13.1.6 CLOSE A WINDOW

a) Click on the menu button in the upper left corner. What happens?

_____

_____

b) Select Close Window. What happens?

_____

_____

13.1.7 SELECT AND PASTE TEXT

a) What happens when you click on a word? When you double click? When you triple click?

_____

_____

b) Now press the middle mouse button (if you have one). What happens?

_____

_____

_____

13.1.8 DISPLAY WINDOW MANAGER MENUS

a) What happens when you click the left mouse button when the cursor is on the background image (the root window)? When you click the middle mouse button? When you click the right mouse button?

_____

_____

_____

LAB 13.1 EXERCISE ANSWERS

This section gives you some suggested answers to the questions in Lab 13.1, with discussions related to those answers. Your answers may vary, but the most important thing is whether or not your answers work. Use these discussions to analyze differences between your answers and those presented here.

If you have alternative answers to the questions in these exercises, you are encouraged to post your answers and discuss them at the companion Web site for this book, located at:

http://www.phptr.com/phptrinteractive

13.1.1 ANSWERS

a) What is the output of the command echo $DISPLAY?

Answer: The answer varies with each machine. Common values are "localhost:0" and "unix:0".

The display name identifies your machine alone out of all of the machines on your network. The format of the display name is usually

```
name:0.0
```

The *name* is the name of your machine, or the word "localhost." The first number is usually 0, and indicates which X display server you're using. You'll only ever see a number other than zero here if your UNIX system is running more than one display server, and that's quite rare. You may not have the ".0" because it isn't usually necessary. You would only see a number other than zero here if you have multiple monitor screens.

b) What is the output of the command uname -n?

Answer: The answer varies with each machine. It is usually a name.

The uname command prints information about your computer system, such as the version of the operating system and its name on the network. The name printed by uname -n should be the same name as is printed in the *name* section of the display variable, unless your display variable contains "localhost." Any machine can use the word "localhost" if the X display server is running on the same machine.

Every X command needs to know what display it's running on. Normally, you have the DISPLAY environment variable set, so the programs can check the name of your display easily. But if you don't have the environment variable set, or if you're on a different machine, all X commands accept the option -display *displayname*. For example, if today I'm working on the machine "romeo" (using a networking command such as rlogin), I can set the display for my command to be "romeo" with the option -display romeo:0.

This option is also frequently used to make an embarrassing picture appear on someone else's screen. (Though the system administrator can guard against it.)

c)   What is the output of the command `hostname`?

Answer: The answer varies with each machine. It is usually a name.

The `hostname` command prints your computer's name on the network. It's available on systems that don't have `uname`. The name printed by `hostname` should be the same name as is printed in the *name* section of the display variable, again unless your display variable contains "localhost."

13.1.2 ANSWERS

a)   What currently running commands end in "wm"?

Answer: The three common window manager programs are mwm *(the Motif Window Manager),* olwm *(the OpenLook Window Manager), and* twm *(the Tab Window Manager).*

(The `twm` program used to be "Tom's Window Manager" but the current man pages say "Tab Window Manager.")

Besides looking at the list of running programs, there's no consistent way to tell which window manager you're running.

- The `twm` manager displays the name "TWM" at the top of the root menu. (You can see the root menu by clicking the left mouse button while the pointer is on the background image.)
- The `mwm` manager displays the name "MWM" when it asks you to confirm that you want to exit your `mwm` session. (I'm going to use `mwm` only when I'm referring to the actual program, and MWM otherwise.)
- Other window managers present their names at different times.

The `twm` window manager comes free with all distributions of the X Window System. Solaris systems ship with OpenLook; now they also ship with Motif (although you could always buy MWM separately). The most common window manager in use now is MWM.

13.1.3 ANSWERS

a) What happens when you drag the title bar?

Answer: The window moves.

You can also move a window by selecting "Move" in the Window Menu.

13.1.4 ANSWERS

a) Drag on a corner. What happens?

Answer: The window gets larger or smaller.

When you resize a window by dragging on the corner, you can change the window's width or height or both.

Not all windows can be resized. Some programs don't allow their windows to be resized. Or (particularly with drawing programs), dragging on a corner may resize the window but so that the width is still in the same proportion to the height.

b) Drag on an edge. What happens?

Answer: The window changes width or the window changes height, depending on which edge you drag.

If you drag on a side edge, you change the window's width. If you drag on a top or bottom edge, you change the window's height. To change both at once, drag a corner.

c) What happens when you click on the expand button (the square button in the upper right corner)? When you click the button again?

Answer: The window fills the entire screen. When you click the button again, the window returns to its former size.

As the name suggests, the expand button makes the window expand. Clicking the same button again turns it off.

This option is actually described as "Maximize" on the window menu. To reverse it using the window menu, use the "Restore" menu item, not the "Minimize" menu item.

d) What happens when you click on the iconify button (the dot button in the upper right corner)?

Answer: The window changes into an icon.

The standard Motif icon is shown in Figure 13.2. (Some programs, such as `xclock`, have different icon designs.) An icon is a useful way to unclutter your screen. If you know you won't be using that program for a few moments and you need the screen clear for another program (and you don't want to exit the current program), you can turn it into an icon. It takes less screen space that way. (Screen space is sometimes called "real estate.")

Figure 13.2 ■ Standard Motif icon.

13.1.5 ANSWERS

a) What happens when you click once on the icon?

Answer: The icon displays the Window Menu.

You can change the icon back into a window by selecting "Restore." The "Restore" menu item is at the top of the menu. Some menu items are "grayed out" to show that they don't apply right now. For example, the "Iconify" menu item is grayed out because the window is already an icon.

The window menu gives you another way to do all of the window manipulations you've already seen in the previous labs. To iconify a window, select "Iconify," and so on. Normally it's easier to use the buttons and the title bar to move, resize, and iconify the window. A window menu for a Motif icon is shown in Figure 13.3.

Figure 13.3 ■ Motif's icon Window Menu.

b) Click elsewhere on the screen. What happens when you double click the icon?

Answer: The window is restored.

Double clicking on an icon is a short form for opening the Window Menu and selecting "Restore."

13.1.6 ANSWERS

a) Click on the menu button in the upper left corner. What happens?

Answer: The window displays the Window Menu.

A window menu for Motif is shown in Figure 13.3. The "Close" item is on the bottom of the menu.

By the way, most window menus also display key combinations to do the same job. These may or may not work on your system; it depends on how your X system was configured with your terminal's keyboard.

b) Select Close Window. What happens?

Answer: The window goes away.

This is similar to the `kill` command; the window goes away and the program inside it dies. Only use this when you know of no other way to shut down the program inside the window.

13.1.7 ANSWERS

a) What happens when you click on a word? When you double click? When you triple click?

Answer: When you single click on a word, the window gets focus. When you double click, the word is selected. When you triple click, the entire line is selected.

This is a shortcut for selecting text in X windows. You can also drag the pointer over the text you want to select. If you have three buttons on your mouse, the right mouse button *extends* the selected area to the pointer location.

In an `xterm` window, a single click doesn't change where the cursor is: it's still at the command prompt. In other X programs (such as the editor `xedit`), a single click might also move the cursor, it really depends on the application.

b) Now press the middle mouse button (use the right mouse button if you have no middle mouse button). What happens?

Answer: The selected text is pasted into the `xterm` *at the command prompt.*

Unlike Microsoft Windows, you don't need to copy selected text before you paste it. When text is selected, it's automatically copied into the paste buffer.

13.1.8 ANSWERS

a) What happens when you click the left mouse button with the cursor on the background image (the root window)?

Answer: MWM displays the root menu.

The root menu is the menu for controlling MWM itself. The last two items on the menu are "Restart..." and "Quit...". (A "..." following a menu item indicates that selecting the menu item will present you with a dialog box.)

The Restart menu item is useful if you've changed the configuration files and you want the new configuration to take effect immediately. If you don't use the Restart option, the new configuration won't take effect until your next X Windows session.

To quit an X Windows session running mwm, *open the root menu and select the "Quit" option.*

b) What happens when you click the middle mouse button with the cursor on the root window? When you click the right mouse button?

Answer: MWM displays a different menu for each button. This is configurable, so your system may not have different menus.

The nature of these other menus depends entirely on how your system administrator has set up the configuration files for MWM. For example, on my system, the middle button presents a menu called "Personal Tools" and the right button presents a menu called "Sessions." The Personal Tools menu starts specific programs (such as the clock, a picture viewer, and so on); the Sessions menu lists different xterm items, each with different options.

LAB 13.1 SELF-REVIEW QUESTIONS

To test your progress, you should be able to answer the following questions.

1) Which program draws the pictures on your screen?
   a) _____The X display server
   b) _____The X client

2) Which program is responsible for the look and feel of your X session?
   a) _____The X display server
   b) _____The X client
   c) _____The window manager

3) Can you run X programs with *no* display name set?
   a) _____Yes
   b) _____No
   c) _____Yes, but you must provide the display name as an option

4) Match the result to the action:

   a) Resize window's width and height   **i)** Drag on title bar

   b) Move window   **ii)** Click on minimize button

   c) Resize window's width or height   **iii)** Click on maximize button

   d) Turn window into icon   **iv)** Drag on the appropriate edge

   e) Make window fill screen   **v)** Drag on corner

Quiz answers appear in Appendix A, Lab 13.1

L A B 13.2

COMMON X PROGRAMS

LAB OBJECTIVES

After this lab, you will be able to:

✓ Start an X Program

✓ Start xterm

✓ Use xkill

✓ Use xeyes

This lab introduces some basic X-client programs. Any X program you start will be an X client, but (whether you know it or not), you're also running an X server.

X Windows programs are broken down into two different types of programs: "clients" and "servers." Rather than have every program contain all of the software for drawing pictures (that would make them all huge!), one program (the server) draws all the pictures on your screen. All other programs you run (such as the calculator program, or the xterm program, or a drawing program) ask the server to draw pictures for them while they do the rest of the job.

If your system doesn't run X Windows now but you want to try it, you may need to start an X11 display server program on your system before you can run X programs. Ask your system administrator or read your system documentation.

Besides the display server, you need to run another program in order to run X programs, the *window manager*. The display server (also called a display manager) is responsible for actually putting pictures up on the screen, but the window manager is responsible for coordinating all those windows on the screen. After the window manager handles which window is supposed to be where and who's on top (and similar details), the display server draws them. So the window manager handles moving windows, and changing their sizes, and making them go away. Because these are all handled by pictures attached to the window (as was shown in the last lab), the window manager is also responsible for how the windows are "decorated."

The window manager basically defines the "look and feel" of your X system. If you use the Motif Window Manager program, your windows will look one way; if you use the OpenLook program, they will look different. If you use the Tab Window Manager, your windows will look different again.

By the way, a window manager is just another client, like xterm or xcalc. Remember there are only two applications here, either a client or a server. If it's not a server (the thing that actually draws the pictures on the screen) then it's a client. The window manager client is just a client that controls how the other clients look.

One program (such as xterm) will behave the same no matter which window manager you use, but the decorations will be different. With a different window manager, there will be different ways to move the window, shrink it, or resize it.

LAB 13.2 EXERCISES

13.2.1 START AN X PROGRAM

a) Should you run an X program in the background or foreground?

_____

_____

b) How are options to X programs different from the other options you've seen?

_____

_____

13.2.2 USE *xterm*

Enter the following command:

```
$ xterm &
```

a) What directory do you start in?

_____

_____

Enter the following command:

```
$ xterm -fn 10x20
```

b) What effect does the `-fn 10x20` option have?

_____

_____

13.2.3 USE *XKILL*

Start an `xterm` session. In a different `xterm` session, enter this command:

```
$ xkill
```

a) What happens to the pointer? What message is displayed in the `xterm`?

_____

_____

b) What happens when you click on the `xterm` window?

_____

_____

c) What happens when you click on the root window?

_____

_____

13.2.4 USE *XEYES*

Enter the following command:

```
$ xeyes &
```

a) What happens as you move the mouse pointer?

_____

_____

LAB 13.2 EXERCISE ANSWERS

This section gives you some suggested answers to the questions in Lab 13.2, with discussions related to those answers. Your answers may vary, but the most important thing is whether or not your answers work. Use these discussions to analyze differences between your answers and those presented here.

**LAB
13.2**

If you have alternative answers to the questions in these exercises, you are encouraged to post your answers and discuss them at the companion Web site for this book, located at:

`http://www.phptr.com/phptrinteractive/`

13.2.1 ANSWERS

a) Should you run an X program in the background or foreground?

Answer: You should run X programs in the background.

You usually want to run more than one X program at a time. If you run the command in the foreground, you cannot start another program until the first program is done. If you start `xclock` in the foreground, you cannot start (for example) an `xterm` until you exit the `xclock` program.

For X programs that do a single brief task (such as `xkill` or `xwd`), it's fine to run them in the foreground.

b) How are options to X programs different from the other options you've seen?

Answer: The options to X programs are more than a single letter and cannot be grouped.

This was a design decision made by the original X programmers. Options to X programs are words such as `-geometry` and `-display`. Most options can be abbreviated; for instance, most commands will accept `-g` instead of `-geometry`. (If the command has another option that begins with "g" you need to include enough letters so the program can determine which option you mean.)

13.2.2 ANSWERS

Enter the following command:

```
$xterm &
```

a) What directory do you start in?

Answer: You start in the directory you were already in.

The xterm command starts a shell for you, and you start in your current directory. However, there's an important difference between logging in and starting xterm: a shell in an xterm doesn't normally read your start-up files. While this may not be significant now, it will be important after you've started modifying your start-up files.

To get the xterm shell to read your start-up files, include the option -ls in the command line. (The -ls stands for "log-in shell"). This option will also start your xterm session in your home directory.

b) What effect does the -fn 10x20 option have?

Answer: The option changes the size of the font and the size of the window.

X Windows provides a large number of fonts. The -fn (or -font) option lets you specify a particular font. In this case, you're specifying a font named "10x20." Some fonts have short names (as this one does); others have long names describing The font "5x7" is very small. Be careful when selecting fonts, as some fonts are constant width fonts and some are variable width fonts. While a variable might look great when reading a document (like this), it's really not very pretty when trying to run shell scripts or running command-line utilities.

You can list the fonts on your system with the command xlsfonts. (Pipe the output into a pager such as more or pg.) You can display the characters of a font or fonts by using the xfontsel (X font select) program.

Although there are a lot of fonts on the system, the xterm program will only use "fixed" fonts effectively. Fixed fonts are fonts where each character is the same width, unlike most of the fonts in this book, where an "i" is narrower than a "w."

A complete discussion of X Window System fonts and changing them would be too complex for this book.

13.2.3 ANSWERS

Start an xterm session. In a different xterm session, enter this command:

    xkill

a) What happens to the mouse pointer? What message is displayed in the xterm?

Answer: The mouse pointer changes shape and the xkill *program displays this text in the* xterm:

Select the window whose client you wish to kill with button 1....

The xkill command kills an X program, much the same as a kill command kills a program. (You can still kill X programs using kill, by the way; xkill provides a way to kill the program without looking up the process ID number.)

Without arguments, the xkill program lets you choose which X program you want to kill. The normal argument for the xkill program is the X resource number. You're unlikely to know (or care about) the resource number.

In the xterm window, give the xkill command again.

b) What happens when you click on the xclock window?

Answer: Clicking on the xclock *window kills the* xclock *program.*

There's really no difference between using xkill and selecting the "Close" entry from the window menu. However, xkill is useful for programs that have created windows without a window menu button.

Like kill, xkill *can remove programs you don't want removed. Use it with care.*

**LAB
13.2**

c) What happens when you click on the root window?

Answer:*The pointer changes back to its normal shape.*

This is a useful way to cancel an `xkill` command if you discover you don't really need it.

13.2.4 ANSWERS

Enter the following command:

```
$xeyes &
```

a) What happens as you move the mouse pointer?

Answer:*The eyes follow the pointer.*

The `xeyes` program is just a small demonstration program—a toy. Table 13.1 lists some other X programs you may find useful or interesting.

Table 13.1 ■ Some Other X Programs

Program	Description
xcalc	A calculator.
xedit	A text editor.
xwd	Save a picture of an X window (called an "X window dump").
xwud	Display an X window dump saved with xwd.
xpr	Print an X window dump saved with xwd.

LAB 13.2 SELF-REVIEW QUESTIONS

To test your progress, you should be able to answer the following questions.

1) X programs should be run in the background if you want to launch
   another program from the same command line.
   a) _____True
   b) _____False

2) Which of these techniques can be used to end an X program?
   a) _____xkill
   b) _____kill
   c) _____The "Cancel" menu item
   d) _____A "Quit" menu item in the program itself
   e) _____All of the above
   f) _____None of the above

3) The X programs you run, such as xterm, are known as which of the
   following:
   a) _____X clients
   b) _____X servers

4) When you start xterm without any other options, which of the following is your starting directory?
   a) _____Your home directory
   b) _____The root directory
   c) _____The directory you were in when you started xterm.

5) Which of these techniques ends your X session?
   a) _____The "Quit..." menu item
   b) _____Start xkill and click on the root menu

   Quiz answers appear in Appendix A, Lab 13.2

L A B   13.3

CUSTOMIZING YOUR X WINDOW SYSTEM

LAB OBJECTIVES

After this lab, you will be able to:

✓ Set a Program's Window Size and Location

✓ Set a Program's Color

✓ Change the Background

✓ Add a Program to a Menu

The X Window System provides a number of ways to customize each X program. You can specify the size and location of the program's window. You can set the color of the window's background, its foreground, or its decorations. These are set by standard options for X programs. You can set your root window to a different color or image using the xsetroot command.

You can also customize the menus you use in MWM to start programs. This involves making changes to your MWM start-up file, .mwmrc in your home directory.

LAB 13.3 EXERCISES

13.3.1 SET A PROGRAM'S WINDOW SIZE AND LOCATION

Enter the following commands:

```
$ xclock &
$ xclock -geometry 100x200+100+200 &
$ xclock -geometry 200x100-200-100 &
```

a) What does the `-geometry` flag do?

_____

_____

b) What do the parts of the argument to `-geometry` mean?

_____

_____

13.3.2 SET A PROGRAM'S COLOR

Enter the following command:

```
$ xclock -background yellow -foreground blue &
```

a) What do the `-background` and `-foreground` options do?

_____

_____

13.3.3 CHANGE THE BACKGROUND

Enter the following command:

```
$ xsetroot -solid black
```

a) What happens to your display?

_____

_____

Enter the following command:

```
$ xsetroot
```

b) What happens to your display?

_____

_____

13.3.4 ADD A PROGRAM TO A MENU

In your home directory, create a backup file of your `.mwmrc` file with this command:

```
cp .mwmrc .mwmrc.backup
```

Open the file `.mwmrc` with an editor. Locate the block of lines that begin with `Menu DefaultRootMenu`. Using a text editor, add the following line before the line that begins "Restart…"

```
"Clock sample"f.exec "xclock -geom 100x100-100+100 &"
```

Save and exit the file.

a) Does the new menu item appear on the root menu? If not, why not?

_____

_____

From the root menu, select "Restart…" and then check the root menu again.

b) How did the new line change the root menu?

_____

_____

LAB 13.3 EXERCISE ANSWERS

 This section gives you some suggested answers to the questions in Lab 13.3, with discussions related to those answers. Your answers may vary, but the most important thing is whether or not your answers work. Use these discussions to analyze differences between your answers and those presented here.

If you have alternative answers to the questions in these exercises, you are encouraged to post your answers and discuss them at the companion Web site for this book, located at:

```
http://www.phptr.com/phptrinteractive
```

13.3.1 ANSWERS

Enter the following commands:

```
$xclock &
$xclock -geometry 100x200+100+200 &
$xclock -geometry 200x100-200-100 &
```

a) What does the -geometry flag do?

Answer: The -geometry _flag specifies where on the screen the program window appears._

You can abbreviate it to -geom instead of typing the entire option name.

Where the program appears _without_ the -geometry flag depends on your system's current setup. (This is handled by the window manager program.) On some systems, each new window is slightly offset from the pre-

LAB 13.3

vious window, so new windows appear in different positions on the screen. On other systems, all new windows show up in the same location.

b) What do the parts of the argument to `-geometry` mean?

Answer: *The argument is in two pairs of numbers:*
widthxheight+horizontal_offset+vertical_offset

The actual numbers represent pixels (screen dots). The value 100x200 represents a width of 100 pixels and a height of 200 pixels. The value +200+100 means 200 pixels from the left side of the screen and 100 pixels from the top.

You can leave off either of the pairs, but you cannot supply half of a pair of numbers. The option `-geom 10x10` supplies a window that's 10 pixels by 10 pixels in the default location. The option `-geom -20+30` creates a window that's the default size, but is 20 pixels from the right side of the screen and 30 pixels from the top.

13.3.2 ANSWERS

a) What do the `-background` and `-foreground` options do?

Answer: *The* `-background` *option sets the background color in the window; the* `-foreground` *option sets the foreground color (text or other images).*

You can specify colors as numbers or as names. Some of the valid names are listed in Table 13.2. Different systems use different names; these are taken from my system. This is not all of the names; for example, my system has over a hundred shades of gray, and four different shades of sienna (named sienna1, sienna2, sienna3, and sienna4).

Table 13.2 ■ Some X Window System Color Names

Black	Gray	Grey	Blue	Salmon	Violet
Cyan	SkyBlue	SteelBlue	Green	Gold	SeaGreen
Magenta	Goldenrod	Orchid	Red	Pink	SlateBlue
White	Snow	Antique-White	Yellow	Aquama-rine	NavyBlue

You can vary many of these colors by adding "light" or "dark" or "medium" to the name (such as Blue, LightBlue, MediumBlue, and Dark-Blue).

For a complete list of the colors supported on your system, use the xco program, which displays the list of colors and names.

These names can be used anywhere an X option requires a color.

Of course, you must have a color display if you want to see colors. Many older X terminals are black and white only. They may show a number of shades of gray, however.

The -foreground option can be shortened to -fg and the -background option can be shortened to -bg.

If you want to set default colors for your X programs, you can do it by configuring your .Xdefaults file, the configuration file for your X display. Discussing the .Xdefaults file would add substantially to the length of this chapter. If you want to learn more about the .Xdefaults file, you can check the web site associated with this book, located at:

    http://www.phptr.com/phptrinteractive/

You can also try reading the X man page to learn about X resources. The .Xdefaults file contains a list of X resource descriptions.

13.3.3 ANSWERS

a) What happens to your display?

Answer: The background image turns black.

The xsetroot command controls the value of the root image. The useful options are -solid, -gray, and -mod. The meanings of the options are described in Table 13.3.

Table 13.3 ■ Options to xsetroot

Option	Meaning
-solid *color*	Set the background color to *color* in a solid block.
-gray	Set the background to solid gray. (This is not the same color as the default background.)
-mod *x y*	Set the background to plaid, with vertical line *x* units apart and horizontal lines *y* units apart. The *x* and *y* can be numbers between 1 and 16; choosing 1 for either number will give you a solid color because the lines are right next to one another. To change the color of the lines, also use -fg; to change the color of the background, also use -bg.

Again, you need a color display to actually see the colors.

b) What happens to your display?

Answer: The background image returns to the default shade of gray.

The xsetroot command without arguments sets the background image to the *default value*, which is a shade of gray. This is useful after experimenting with the root image.

If you want the root image to be a picture, there's no standard way to do it. There are several utilities that will set the root image, but the one I recommend is xv. It may already be installed on your system. If it isn't, you can ask your system administrator to install it. For more information about the latest version of xv, your system administrator can check the anonymous ftp directory at ftp.cis.upenn.edu, in pub/xv. (Don't worry if you don't understand; your system administrator will.)

If you want to set the root image every time you start up, you need to put the xsetroot command in the appropriate start-up file.

13.3.4 ANSWERS

a)   Does the new menu item appear on the root menu? If not, why not?

Answer: The `.mwmrc` *file is read by MWM when it starts up. The MWM program doesn't know about changes to the file after it starts up.*

Because the file changed after the Motif Window Manager was started, the program doesn't contain the new information.

**LAB
13.3**

Notice that before you changed the configuration file, you made a backup of the original file. If you make a mistake changing the configuration file, you'll want an easy way to go back to the old version. I cannot count the number of times that I've made a "simple" change and made a mistake. Nobody ever regrets making a backup copy, and sooner or later you will regret *not* making one.

   Before you change any configuration files, make a backup copy!

From the root menu, select "Restart..."

b)   How did the new line change the root menu?

Answer: The root menu now contains a menu entry reading "Clock sample" that can be selected to start the `xclock` *program.*

The `.mwmrc` file contains start-up information for the Motif Window Manager. The start-up file deals with menus, mouse buttons, and keys.

We won't deal with keys and mouse buttons here (although all of the information is in the mwm man page, under "mwm Resource Description File Syntax").

All menus are gathered in menu descriptions. A menu description starts with:

```
Menu nameofmenu
{
    title    f.title
```

```
        no-labelf.separator
        label    function
    }
```

The part `Menu` *nameofmenu* and the text in { } describes the menu. Every line in the braces is a menu item, with a *label* (the text that appears in the menu) and a *function* (a description of what the menu item should do).

Table 13.4 lists four functions you can use in menus. There are lots more; see the MWM man page for a list.

Table 13.4 ■ Some MWM Menu Functions

Function	Syntax	Description
f.title	f.title	Displays the *label* as the title of the menu.
f.separator	f.separator	Displays a separator line between the previous menu item and the next one. The label is ignored, but everybody types "no-label" just to make sure that's clear in the file.
f.exec	f.exec "com-mand"	Run *command* when this menu item is selected. In the exercise, you used the command "xclock -geom 100x100-100+100 &". If the command contains spaces, it must be put in quotation marks. You can use "!" as the function name instead of f.exec if you want to save some space. Make sure that you put an & at the end of the command, otherwise mwm will stop working until the app you just started exits!
f.menu	f.menu menuname	Open a new menu. Somewhere later in this .mwmwrc file there must be another menu description where *nameofmenu* is the name given here, *menuname*.

The *title* text is just the title at the top of the menu; no menu needs a title, but it's useful. A title is indicated by `f.title` as the second part of the line.

■ *FOR EXAMPLE:*

The very first menu might look like this:

```
! This is the starting menu:
Menu RootMenu
{
    "Root Menu"     f.title
    "Clock"         f.exec "xclock -geom -1-1 &"
    "New Windows"   f.menu NewWindows
    no-label        f.separator
    "Restart..."    f.restart
    "Quit..."       f.quit_mwm
}
```

Even though this looks complicated, it's not very difficult. Any line that *starts* with "!" is a comment; MWM ignores that line. The rest of this block describes one menu, with the title "Root Menu" (the `f.title` function.) The last *three* items in the menu are a separator (`f.separator`), and the Restart and Quit menu options. These have their own functions, but you will probably never write a menu containing them. You should just be aware that they're important, and they're in the first menu.

The "Clock" item is just like the one you created in the exercise.

The "New Windows" item creates a new menu. Somewhere in this file there should be another menu description with the menu name `NewWindows`.

■ *FOR EXAMPLE:*

This meu description would work:

```
! Create some new xterm windows
Menu NewWindows
{
```

```
        "New Window"          f.title
        no-label              f.separator
        "Small window"!       "xterm -ls -fn 5x7 &"
        "Medium window"!      "xterm -ls &"
        "Large window"!       "xterm -ls -fn 10x20 &"
    }
```

This creates a submenu with a title and three menu options. To be accurate, `f.menu` creates the title that points to the new menu, and this block or "stanza" is what actually creates the menu.

Remember that "!" means a comment line *only* if it's the first character on the line, and it stands for `f.exec` *only* if it's in the function position on a menu option line.

LAB 13.3 SELF-REVIEW QUESTIONS

To test your progress, you should be able to answer the following questions.

1) The start-up file for the Motif Window Manager is `.Xdefaults`
    a) True _____
    b) False _____

2) If the changes to the resource file are simple, you should make them without creating a backup copy.
    a) _____True
    b) _____False

3) Select the correct `-geometry` option to start a program in the lower right corner of the screen.
    a) _____ `-geometry +0+0`
    b) _____ `-geometry +0-0`
    c) _____ `-geometry -0-0`
    d) _____ `-geometry -0+0`

4) Which line in an MWM resource file creates a pointer to a new menu?
    a) _____ "Windows" f.title
    b) _____ "Windows" f.separator
    c) _____ "Windows" f.exec "xterm &"
    d) _____ "Windows" f.menu Windows

Quiz answers appear in Appendix A, Lab 13.3

C H A P T E R 13

TEST YOUR THINKING

The projects in this section are meant to have you utilize all of the skills that you have acquired throughout this chapter. The answers to these projects can be found at the companion Web site to this book, located at:

`http://www.phptr.com/phptrinteractive`

Visit the Web site periodically to share and discuss your answers.

You want to redesign your menus. The section of the new `.mwmrc` looks like this, but it doesn't work correctly. The "New Window" item doesn't display:

```
Menu DefaultRootMenu
{
        "Root Menu"             f.title
        New Window              f.exec "xterm -ls"
        "Refresh"               f.refresh
        "Edit .mwmrc"           f.exec "xedit ~/.mwmrc &"
        no-label                f.separator
        "Restart..."            f.restart
        "Quit..."               f.quit_mwm
}
```

1) What is wrong with the "New Window" item?

2) How would you add a "games" menu that runs the games xtetris, xeyes, and puzzle?

3) Consider adding the following:

   a) An `xterm` that appears in the lower-right corner of the screen.

   b) A command for saving and printing a screen capture (check the `xpr` and `xwd` man pages for the exact command).

   c) A selection of background colors. (Check the `xsetroot` man page.)

   d) How will you organize these new additions? Is there one answer or will it depend upon how your MWM menus and entries are already set up?

APPENDIX A

ANSWERS TO SELF-REVIEW QUESTIONS

CHAPTER I

Lab 1.1 ■ Self-Review Answers

Question	Answer	Comments
1)	b	Your log-in name identifies you on your system. You are the only user who has that name.
2)	a	The name of the terminal type is often stored in the TERM environment variable, and you can see it by typing `echo $TERM`.
3)	b	A user doesn't have to have a password. For security reasons, all users should have passwords.

Lab 1.2 ■ Self-Review Answers

Question	Answer	Comments
1)	a	Your log-in name must be unique, but not your password.
2)	b	Only the superuser (root) can change another user's password.

Lab 1.3 ■ Self-Review Answers

Question	Answer	Comments
1)	b	You need a shell program. It may not look like the command-line shell described in this book, however; some graphic user interfaces are shells.
2)	a	

Lab 1.3 ■ Self-Review Answers (Continued)

Question	Answer	Comments
3)	a	
4)	a-ii b-iv c-i d-iii	

Lab 1.4 ■ Self-Review Answers

Question	Answer	Comments
1)	b	Shutting down your shell is the most of the process of logging out. Your shell may run one or two commands before it finishes logging you out, though.
2)	b	Most systems are configured to log out with Control-D also.

CHAPTER 2

Lab 2.1 ■ Self-Review Answers

Question	Answer	Comments
1)	a	The first word in a command is always the command name.
2)	c	Some synopses will show two lines instead, one synopsis with -ab and the other with -ac.
3)	c	

Lab 2.2 ■ Self-Review Answers

Question	Answer	Comments
1)	a	The three files (more accurately, three file *descriptors*) are standard input, standard output, and standard error.
2)	b	A filter command doesn't need to change its input. The cat command does not, for example.
3)	a-v b-i c-ii d-iii e-iv	

CHAPTER 3

Lab 3.1 ■ Self-Review Answers

Question	Answer	Comments
1)	c	Siblings are both children of the same parent. In this example, only `guides` and `reference` have the same parent (`/pubs`).
2)	b	The `guides` directory contains the `user` directory.
3)	b	The child comes immediately to the right of the next / character.
4)	b	It's a relative path name. Apply each component of `../../reference` in sequence to change it into `/pubs/reference`: `../` (`/pubs/guides`), `../` (`/pubs`), reference (`/pubs/reference`).

Lab 3.2 ■ Self-Review Answers

Question	Answer	Comments
1)	e	Because / separates parts of a path name, it cannot be in a file's name.
2)	b	A file name beginning with dot can contain other dots, but it cannot be either of the names . (dot) or .. (dot-dot), because those are already taken.
3)	b	Different systems have different maximum lengths for file names.
4)	a	The `getconf` command returns information about system limits.
5)	b	The name .. (dot-dot) is reserved, because it always stands for "the parent of the current directory."

Lab 3.3 ■ Self-Review Answers

Question	Answer	Comments
1)	b	Users can belong to more than one group.
2)	a	You cannot make a hard link to a directory. You can, however, make a soft or symbolic link to a directory.
3)	b	Other options to `ls` can show the access time and the change time.
4)	a-iii b-i c-ii d-iv	

Lab 3.4 ■ Self-Review Answers

Question	Answer	Comments
1)	a	You need execute permission to cd into a directory, and read permission to list its contents.
2)	b	
3)	b	Only the owner (or the superuser) can chmod a file
4)	d	The = operator sets the mode to exactly the permissions in the chmod command. The users (u) permission is the first of the three numbers, and rw is 4+2, or 6. The permissions for the group and others are 0 and 0. Therefore, 600.

CHAPTER 4

Lab 4.1 ■ Self-Review Answers

Question	Answer	Comments
1)	a	True: In an ASCII sort, uppercase letters sort before lowercase letters.
2)	d	The -a option lists hidden files, and the -t option sorts by time.
3)	a	The -r option lists files in reverse order and the -p option indicates directories.

Lab 4.2 ■ Self-Review Answers

Question	Answer	Comments
1)	b	The wildcard pattern * does *not* match the / character in file names.
2)	a-i, ii (Andor, AM)	Matches all files beginning with A.
	b-iii (.env)	Matches a file name that is four characters long and starts with dot.
	c-i, iv, vi (Andor, Guide, diatribe)	Matches any nonhidden name that contains a character that isn't an uppercase letter.
	d-i, iv, vi (Andor, Guide,dia- tribe)	Matches any nonhidden name that ends in a lowercase letter.

Lab 4.2 ■ Self-Review Answers (Continued)

Question	Answer	Comments
	e-v (.environ)	Matches any name starting with dot followed by at least four letters.
	(f) *no match*	Matches any nonhidden name that contains a dot in it.
3)	c	

Lab 4.3 ■ Self-Review Answers

Question	Answer	Comments
1)	a	On Solaris, this is true. It may not be true on other systems.
2)	c	

Lab 4.4 ■ Self-Review Answers

Question	Answer	Comments
1)	a	
2)	b	False; the -m option to mkdir allows you to specify the permissions on the directory you're creating.
3)	a	True, but all of the directories must be empty.

Lab 4.5 ■ Self-Review Answers

Question	Answer	Comments
1)	a	
2)	a	An alternate name is called a link.
3)	b	False; only if the last argument is a *directory* can there be more than two file names in the command.
4)	a	
5)	d	The cp command will not copy a directory unless either the -r or -R option is given.

Lab 4.6 ■ Self-Review Answers

Question	Answer	Comments
1)	b	A moved file keeps its permissions.
2)	a	True; you're really just changing where in the file system it can be found.

CHAPTER 5

Lab 5.1 ■ Self-Review Answers

Question	Answer	Comments
1)	a	This is the default behavior, although you can change it by setting the PAGER environment variable.
2)	b	You can quit by pressing the q key.
3)	b	The operand might be a file name or some other topic.
4)	b	The man command searches all of the sections and stops as soon as it finds a match.
5)	a	

Lab 5.2 ■ Self-Review Answers

Question	Answer	Comments
1)	b	The man -k command searches the whatis files, not the man pages themselves. Since it only looks in directories named in your MANPATH environment variable, it may not even look at all of the whatis files on your system.
2)	a	

Lab 5.3 ■ Self-Review Answers

Question	Answer	Comments
1)	a	The xman command uses the MANPATH command, just like the man command.
2)	b	The xman command can be used on any UNIX system running the X Window System.
3)	b	You cannot quit an xman session by pressing the q key while reading a man page. You must select Quit from the menu (or select Close from the window menu, as described in Chapter 13, "X Window System").
4)	a	The xman command does display all of the section 1 man pages from all of the directories it searches.

Chapter 6

Lab 6.1 ■ Self-Review Answers

Question	Answer	Comments
1)	a	The characters ' and " are shell metacharacters.
2)	a	The shell uses a different prompt to indicate a command that continues onto a new line.
3)	d	If the entire command line is surrounded by apostrophes, the command will probably just fail.

Lab 6.2 ■ Self-Review Answers

Question	Answer	Comments
1)	b	Trick question. To find a command, the shell first checks its list of built-in commands. If it doesn't find the command, then it searches the PATH.
2)	a	Not everyone has the same PATH.
3)	a	Some commands, such as `type`, are built into the shell.

Lab 6.3 ■ Self-Review Answers

Question	Answer	Comments
1)	a	Control-C interrupts programs running at the terminal.
2)	b	Control-C does not interrupt programs running in the background; it can only interrupt programs running in the foreground. You must use `kill` to interrupt a background process.
3)	b	If three different people are running the same program, there are three different processes. There are also commands which start other commands, so they could be considered to be running more than one process.

Lab 6.4 ■ Self-Review Answers

Question	Answer	Comments
1)	b	The Control-L command doesn't always clear the screen. It does in some applications, such as `vi` or `more`.
2)	b	The `stty sane` command resets the terminal attributes, but it doesn't clear the screen.
3)	a	The `stty` command sets the characteristics or attributes of your terminal.

Lab 6.5 ■ Self-Review Answers

Question	Answer	Comments
1)	a	A signal such as interrupt or kill can be assigned to any key or key-combination.
2)	a	The signal to backspace is called "delete."
3)	a	The signal such as interrupt works when the program has set the terminal in cooked mode.
4)	a	Control-C is used by some programs as a command, not as an interrupt signal.

Lab 6.6 ■ Self-Review Answers

Question	Answer	Comments
1)	b	The only files stored on backups are those the administrator decides to store on backups.
2)	a	You must ask the system administrator to help you restore a backed up file.
3)	a	One disadvantage of the trashcan strategy is that you won't be able to "undelete" files if you move to a different UNIX system, unless you adopt the same strategy there.

CHAPTER 7

Lab 7.1 ■ Self-Review Answers

Question	Answer	Comments
1)	a	The grep command searches files or standard input.
2)	b	The grep command can search for patterns that begin with '-' but only if you use the -e option to indicate the beginning of the pattern. (On Solaris, the -e option is only available if you use the alternative grep, /usr/xpg4/bin/grep.)
3)	a	The fgrep command searches for words ("fixed strings") instead of patterns.
4)	b	When you specify two patterns in a grep command, grep displays all lines that have either one of the patterns. (On Solaris, you can search for two patterns only if you use the alternative grep, /usr/xpg4/bin/grep.)

Lab 7.2 ■ Self-Review Answers

Question	Answer	Comments
1)	b	The find command performs its tests in the order they appear on the command line. If -print comes before the other tests, each file name will get printed, whether it matches the rest of the tests or not.
2)	a	The ls -R command does a recursive directory listing.
3)	a	You only need parentheses to group find tests if there are choices (either this test is true or that test is true). You don't need parentheses if you want both tests to apply; that's what find does by default.
4)	a	The option -mtime +180 assumes that 6 months is exactly 180 days. That's probably close enough.

CHAPTER 8

Lab 8.1 ■ Self-Review Answers

Question	Answer	Comments
1)	c	The * character normally means "zero or more of the preceding character"—but when there is no preceding character, it matches an * character.
2)	c	The pattern "^[^^]" means "all lines that begin with a character that is *not* a ^ character." Because the lines must contain at least one character, the empty lines don't match.
3)	b	The pattern describes a single z, surrounded by non-z characters before it to the beginning of the line and non-z characters after it to the end of the line. All of the other patterns allow another z somewhere on the line, because they don't describe the whole line.

Lab 8.2 ■ Self-Review Answers

Question	Answer	Comments
1)	b	False. Remember that the (character has a special meaning in extended regular expressions.
2)	d	The others may find lines that contain "w".
3)	c	Most of them also find Anne Finch. This one finds any word before the colon that starts in an A and ends in a comma, or that starts in an A and ends in a colon.

CHAPTER 9

Lab 9.1 ■ Self-Review Answers

Question	Answer	Comments
1)	a	The vi editor has modes.
2)	b	No matter how many times you press Escape, you'll end up in command mode.
3)	d	
4)	a	The colon commands must be completed by pressing Enter.
5)	b	Although there is a :wq command, it's not short for anything.

Lab 9.2 ■ Self-Review Answers

Question	Answer	Comments
1)	a	In some versions of vi, the cursor does change shape to tell you you're in input mode.
2)	a	Each of the commands to enter text input mode inserts the text in a different place.
3)	a-iv b-ii c-i d-iii	Check the command summary in Lab 9.2 if you had problems.

Lab 9.3 ■ Self-Review Answers

Question	Answer	Comments
1)	a	For all of the movement commands described in this section, starting them with a number causes them to be repeated that many times.
2)	a-iv b-iii c-i d-ii	Since writing the chapter, I've learned that on the terminals that were used at Berkeley when vi was written, the h-j-k-l keys *were* the arrow keys.
3)	a-ii b-iv c-i d-iii	
4)	c	
5)	a	The Control-G command displays the name of the file, whether it's read-only, the current line, how many lines are in the file, and where the cursor is as a percentage of the file's length.

Lab 9.4 ■ Self-Review Answers

Question	Answer	Comments
1)	b	The D command deletes from the cursor to the end of the line. The d command deletes lines.
2)	a	A command that can be followed by a movement (like d) affects the entire current line if you double it.
3)	a-iii b-i c-iv d-ii	
4)	a-ii b-iv c-i d-iii	
5)	a	The first and third times undo the command, the second and fourth undo the undo.

Lab 9.5 ■ Self-Review Answers

Question	Answer	Comments
1)	a	Even if you save a file under a new name, vi keeps using the original name.
2)	a-iii b-i c-ii	
3)	a	To write over an existing file that isn't being edited, use the ! after the :w command. You still need permission to write the file.

Lab 9.6 ■ Self-Review Answers

Question	Answer	Comments
1)	a	vi uses basic regular expressions, with some additions.
2)	a-i b-iii c-ii d-iv	
3)	a-iii b-iv c-iii d-i	
4)	a	The command /z would search for the letter z; you need the second / to close the search pattern and tell the command that the z means "put the matching line on the first line of the screen."

Lab 9.7 ■ Self-Review Answers

Question	Answer	Comments
1)	a	The :s command is short for :substitute.
2)	a	Each repetition of the :s command replaces the first occurrence of the pattern.
3)	a-iii b-ii c-iv d-i	

Lab 9.8 ■ Self-Review Answers

Question	Answer	Comments
1)	a	The p command puts deleted or yanked text back into the file.
2)	a	The y command behaves like the d command, except it doesn't delete text, it only copies it.
3)	a	The :r command inserts a file into the buffer.

CHAPTER 10

Lab 10.1 ■ Self-Review Answers

Question	Answer	Comments
1)	a	All of the uppercase letters come before the lowercase letters.
2)	a-iii b-iv c-i d-ii	
3)	b	A space does count as part of the record.
4)	d	
5)	d	

Lab 10.2 ■ Self-Review Answers

Question	Answer	Comments
1)	a	
2)	a	An empty file has no words in it.
3)	b	Because the -m option counts multibyte characters and the -c option counts bytes, it's likely that the file contains multibyte characters, each of which may take up more than one byte.
4)	c	The -l option counts lines.

Lab 10.3 ■ Self-Review Answers

Question	Answer	Comments
1)	a	Any spell-checker relies on its dictionary.
2)	b	You should sort them before adding them to the dictionary. It will make `sort` run faster.
3)	a	The -b option checks British spelling.

Lab 10.4 ■ Self-Review Answers

Question	Answer	Comments
1)	b	The `fold` command will break words in the middle, unless you use the -s option.
2)	c	The default line length for `fmt` on Solaris is 72 characters.
3)	d	

CHAPTER 11

Lab 11.1 ■ Self-Review Answers

Question	Answer	Comments
1)	b	The `lp` command sends a print request; the printer daemon actually sends the file to the printer.
2)	b	The printer daemon waits for print requests; it doesn't look for files to print.
3)	b	The `nobanner` is an argument to the -o option.
4)	c	The -c option makes a copy of the file at the time you give the `lp` command. Even if you delete the file before it actually prints, it will have no effect on the printed copy.

Lab 11.2 ■ Self-Review Answers

Question	Answer	Comments
1)	a	The `pr` command formats files for printing.
2)	c	By default, `pr` assumes the page is 66 lines long.
3)	a	The command `pr -l 20` sets the page length to 20 lines.

Lab 11.3 ■ Self-Review Answers

Question	Answer	Comments
1)	a	The lpstat command shows you printer status.
2)	a-iii b-i c-ii d-iv	
3)	a	The -u option specifies the user and the -o option specifies a list of printers.

CHAPTER 12

Lab 12.1 ■ Self-Review Answers

Question	Answer	Comments
1)	a	The ; character marks the end of a command, just as Enter does.
2)	d	The result of `cat files` is the contents of the file files, which are used as the arguments to ls -l
3)	c	

Lab 12.2 ■ Self-Review Answers

Question	Answer	Comments
1)	a	A variable is a named temporary storage place for information.
2)	c	The apostrophes or single quotation marks prevent the $name from being converted into "jack."
3)	b	The variable name is not part of the environment for child processes until it is exported.
4)	e	It's confusing, but you can set a variable so it has no value. That's different from unsetting the variable, when the variable no longer exists at all.
5)	a	The unset command removes the variable entirely.

Lab 12.3 ■ Self-Review Answers

Question	Answer	Comments
1)	b	Only one command can run in the foreground.
2)	b	The Control-Z key combination suspends a command, which is different from running in the background.
3)	c	

Lab 12.4 ■ Self-Review Answers

Question	Answer	Comments
1)	a	The at and batch commands both schedule jobs to be run later.
2)	b	Jobs run with at and batch are run using the Bourne or POSIX shell.
3)	c	The command runs at the *next* noon, plus 2 hours, 3:00 PM tomorrow.

CHAPTER 13

Lab 13.1 ■ Self-Review Answers

Question	Answer	Comments
1)	a	The display server actually draws the pictures.
2)	c	The window manager program is responsible for the look and feel of your X session.
3)	c	You can run commands without the DISPLAY environment variable set, but you must provide the display name as an option to every command.
4)	a-v b-i c-iv d-ii e-iii	

Lab 13.2 ■ Self-Review Answers

Question	Answer	Comments
1)	a	X programs should be run in the background if you want to launch another program from the same command line.
2)	a	All of (a), (b), (c), and (d) can be used to kill an X program.
3)	a	The X programs you run, such as xterm, are X clients.
4)	c	Unless you provide the -ls log-in shell option.
5)	a	To end your X session, select the "Quit..." menu item

Lab 13.3 ■ Self-Review Answers

Question	Answer	Comments
1)	b	The start-up file for the Motif Window Manager is .mwmrc
2)	b	Always create a backup copy before changing an important start-up file.

Lab 13.3 ■ Self-Review Answers (Continued)

Question	Answer	Comments
3)	a	The + symbol causes the numbers to mean the opposite edge, so +0+0 is the lower right corner instead of upper left (-0-0).
4)	d	The f.menu line is the important one.

APPENDIX B

COMMANDS

T his appendix contains descriptions for most of the commands in this book. Each command synopsis is listed, along with a brief description of the command and a summary of the options. There have been omissions: Options that only the system administrator can use have been left out.

This list is meant as a convenience, not a definitive reference; see your man pages if the description doesn't apply to your version of the program. Where there are several different versions of a program, the one described is the standard version on Solaris. The shell described is the Korn Shell.

Some important commands (the X clients) are not described here, mostly for reasons of space.

AT—RUN JOB AT A CERTAIN TIME

```
at [-cms][-f file] time [date] [+increment]
at [-l|-r] [jobID...]
```

The first form of this command is used to schedule a command or commands to be run at a later time. The second form is used to list or remove jobs from the schedule.

In the first form, you provide a *time* when the job is to be run. Then you enter the commands that make up the job (unless you used the -f option), and end input with end-of-file (usually Ctrl-D).

-c	Run the job using the C shell instead of the default (the value of your SHELL environment variable, or /bin/sh if SHELL is not set.
-k	Run the job using the Korn Shell instead of the default.
-f *file*	Take the commands to be run from *file* instead of requiring you to type them in.
-l	List all jobs currently queued.
-m	Send mail to you when the job is finished. The mail will contain the results of the job and any output.
-q *queue*	Queue the job in the specified *queue*. There are twenty-six queues, a-z. The default queue is queue a; queue b is for batch jobs; queue c is reserved for cron jobs (so cannot be used with at).
-r	Remove the job specified by *jobID*. If no *jobID* is specified, remove all of your jobs.
-s	Run the job using the Bourne shell.

The *time* specification consists of a *time*, an optional *date*, and an optional *increment* (or delay).

time	One, two, or four digits indicating the hour in a 24-hour clock; or an hours:minutes time followed by AM or PM; or one of the words midnight, noon, or now.
date	A month name and a day or one of the words today or tomorrow. The date is optional.
increment	A + sign followed by a number and a unit of time (minute, hour, day, week, month). at understands the single and plural forms. Instead of + 1, you can use the word next.

BATCH—RUN JOBS WHEN SYSTEM ISN'T BUSY

```
batch
```

The batch command accepts jobs on standard input, just as at does, but doesn't allow you to schedule them. Instead, the job is scheduled by the system.

BG—MOVE COMMAND TO BACKGROUND

    bg [*jobID*]

The bg command moves the job indicated by *jobID* into the background. The *jobID* can be either a process ID number or a job number (as given by the jobs command). Job numbers must start with "%".

CANCEL—STOP PRINT JOB

    cancel *printID* | *printer...*

The cancel command cancels a print job sent using the lp command. You can specify a print job to be canceled either by the print job ID number, *printID*, or by giving the name of the printer. (Use lpstat to learn which printer a job is on or what its *printID* number is.) You must specify either a *printID* number or a *printer*.

See Chapter 11, "Printing Text Files."

CAT—COPY STANDARD INPUT TO STANDARD OUTPUT

    cat [-benstuv] [*file* ...]

The cat command copies its standard input to its standard output. It can be used to join text files together or to copy files to standard output.

-b	Number lines (like -n) but don't number blank lines.
-e	Print $ at end of each line; only with -v.
-n	Print line numbers before lines.
-s	Suppress error messages. In the BSD version, it squeezes out extra blank lines.
-t	Print tab characters as ^I and formfeed characters as ^L; only with -v
-u	Print output unbuffered. Normally cat saves output until there is a certain amount; this prints each character as it becomes available.
-v	Display nonprinting characters, such as control characters.

CD—CHANGE DIRECTORIES

```
cd [directory]
cd -
cd [old new]
```

The `cd` command changes your current working directory. If you don't provide any arguments, you move to your home directory (the directory named by the HOME environment variable). If you do name a *directory*, that directory becomes your current directory. The *directory* name can be an absolute path name or a relative path name.

If you give the argument -, you go back to your *previous* directory.

One feature of the Korn Shell not discussed in the book is the ability to move to a sibling directory. If you specify two arguments, the `cd` command replaces *old* in your current directory with *new*, and changes you to that directory. For example, if you are in the directory `/tmp/work`, and you give the command `cd tmp projects`, the `cd` command puts you in the directory `/projects/work`. It creates the name of the target directory by replacing the first argument (in the current directory) with the second argument.

See Chapter 1, "Your First Session."

CHMOD—CHANGE FILE PERMISSIONS

```
chmod [-R] mode file ...
```

The `chmod` command changes the permissions on a file. You can only change permissions on a file you own.

-R	If any of the *files* is a directory, recursively apply the change in *mode* to all files and subdirectories in that directory.

The *mode* can be specified as a symbolic mode or as a numeric mode.

A symbolic mode can *add*, *subtract*, or *assign* permissions to the user, group, or other, in the form `[ugoa][+-=][rwx]`.

Symbol	Meaning
u	User permissions
g	Group permissions
o	Other permissions
a	All (user, group, and other)
+	Add the specified permissions to the specified category
-	Subtract the specified permissions from the specified category
=	Assign exactly the specified permissions to the specified category
r	Read permission
w	Write permission
x	Execute permission

Symbolic modes may be joined by commas, so the mode `u+x,g=rw,o-wx` adds execute permission for the owner, sets the group permissions to read and write (exactly), and subtracts write and execute permission from the other permissions.

In a numeric mode, the numbers assign all of the permissions. The number is three digits, with the first digit being the owner's permissions, the second digit being the group's permissions, and the third digit being everyone else's permissions

Number	Permission meaning
0	No permissions
1	Execute permission only
2	Write permission only
3	Write and execute permissions
4	Read permission only
5	Read and execute permission only
6	Read and write permissions
7	Read, write, and execute permissions

See Chapter 3, "About Files and Directories."

COMMAND—RUN A SIMPLE COMMAND

```
command [-pvV] command
```

This is a Korn Shell built-in. Normally it runs the *command* line given as an argument, but it *never* runs an alias or a shell function (that is, if you have a shell function named 1s and a program named 1s, the command `command 1s` will always run the program).

-p	Find the *command* using a special default PATH instead of the PATH currently set.
-v	Don't run the *command* but display information about where the command is and what type of command it is.
-V	Like -v, but with more words.

See Chapter 5, "Finding Help."

CP—COPY A FILE

```
cp [-ipr] old new
cp [-ipr] file … directory
```

The cp command copies files and directories. There are two forms. In the first form, you specify the name of the file or directory (*old*) and the name of the new copy (*new*). In the second form, you name one or more files or directories that will be copied into another *directory*.

-i	Prompt for confirmation before overwriting a file
-p	Preserve times and modes on the copied file.
-r	Recursively copy a directory.

See Chapter 4, "Files and Directories."

CRONTAB—MANAGE CRONTAB FILE

```
crontab [-elr] [file]
```

The crontab command lets you schedule jobs using cron. If you start crontab without options, you can enter jobs to be scheduled from the keyboard; end input with end-of-file (normally Ctrl-D). If you give a *file* name, that file is copied into the directory where users' crontab files are stored, and becomes your new crontab file.

There are other options, which allow you to edit, list, or remove your crontab file.

-e	Edit the crontab file using an editor.
-l	List the contents of the crontab file.
-r	Remove the crontab file.

The format of the entries in the crontab file is well-defined. Each line is one job to be scheduled; a line has six fields separated by spaces or tabs. The first five fields describe *when* the command is to be run, and the sixth field is the actual command. The fields are, in order:

The minute of the hour the command is to be run, a number from 0–59.

The hour of the day the command is to be run, a number from 0–23.

The day of the month the command is to be run, a number from 1–31.

The month of the year the command is to be run, a number from 1–12.

The day of the week the command is to be run, a number from 0–6 and 0 means Sunday.

You can specify a range by using two numbers with a minus sign between them (Monday through Friday would be 1–5), or you can specify *all* values with an asterisk (*).

Although the crontab line must fit on one line, you can insert multiple line commands by using a % character in the command. The cron service interprets % as meaning a new line. To include an actual per cent character in a command, use \%.

Lines that begin with # are ignored.

See Chapter 12, "Commands and Job Control."

ECHO—REPEAT ARGUMENTS

```
echo [-n] [arguments...]
```

The `echo` command is a shell built-in that repeats its arguments on standard output. It's useful in shell scripts or for discovering how the shell interprets a command line or finding the value of a shell variable or parameter. It is almost the same as the Korn Shell built-in command `print`.

-n	Don't print a newline at the end of the arguments. This will cause the *next* line to run on after the end of the `echo` arguments.

The `echo` command interprets certain backslash sequences as special. Remember that the backslash is *also* special to the shell, so you'll have to escape the \ in these sequences.

\b	A backspace character.
\c	No ending newline (like the -n option).
\f	Formfeed character.
\n	Newline character (for printing two or more lines of output with a single `echo` command).
\r	Carriage return.
\t	Tab character.
\\	Backslash.
\0*nnn*	An ASCII character represented by *nnn*, where *nnn* is an octal character.

EGREP, FGREP, GREP—SEARCH FILES FOR REGULAR EXPRESSIONS

```
egrep [-bchilnsv] [eregexp] [file ...]
fgrep [-bchilnvx] [-f file] string [file ...]
grep [-bchilnvw] [regexp] [file ...]
```

The `grep` commands search files (or standard input) for a pattern. The `fgrep` command searches for a string, `grep` searches for a basic regular expression, and `egrep` command searches for an extended regular expression.

`-b`	Before each matching line, print the block number (of the disk) where it was found.
`-c`	Print the number of lines that match instead of printing the lines themselves.
`-e` *pattern*	Search for *pattern*; this is used only when the string begins with `-`.
`-f` *file*	Take the list of strings to match from *file*.
`-h`	Don't print the file name when printing the matching line.
`-i`	Ignore the difference between upper and lowercase letters.
`-l`	Print (list) only the names of files that contain matching lines.
`-n`	Before each line that matches, print its line number (first line is 1).
`-s`	Suppress error message.
`-v`	Print all lines *except* the ones that match the pattern.
`-w`	Treat the expression as if it were a word (in `vi`, as if it were surrounded by `\<` and `\>`). Only `egrep` and `grep`.
`-x`	Print only lines that match only the pattern and have no extra characters. Only `fgrep`.

See Chapter 7, "Finding Files" and Chapter 8, "Regular Expressions."

ENV—SET AND DISPLAY ENVIRONMENT

```
env [-] [variable=value...] [command]
```

Without arguments, the `env` command displays the current environment. With arguments, it sets the *variable* to the *value* and runs the *command* with that *variable* added to the environment.

- Ignore the current environment entirely. Normally, the env command adds the new variables to the current environment. With this option, you cause it to build an entirely new environment for the *command*.

EXEC—RUN A COMMAND

```
exec [command]
```

The exec command replaces the current process (usually the shell) with the command given as *command*. Used in this book to try out new shells, it's most often used in shell scripts as a way of manipulating file descriptors such as standard error and standard input. See the exec man page for more details.

EXIT—LOGOUT OF A SHELL

```
exit [n]
```

Exit a shell. When used in a shell script, it returns the return code of *n*, where *n* is an integer number. (If you don't provide *n*, the return code is the return code of the last command run in the script before exit.)

See Chapter 1, "Your First Session."

EXPORT—MAKE A SHELL VARIABLE VISIBLE TO OTHER PROGRAMS

```
export [variables]
export [name=[value]]
```

This is a shell built-in. Makes the shell variables *variables* (or *name*) visible to other programs, such as subshells. The first form exports variables that have already been set, while the second form assigns a value to *name* and exports it. If no arguments are given, the export command lists all variables that are currently exported.

FG—MOVE FILE TO FOREGROUND

```
fg [jobID]
```

The `fg` command moves the process specified by *jobID* to the foreground. If no *jobID* is specified, the most recent background command is used.

See Chapter 12, "Commands and Job Control."

FILE—GUESS FILE'S TYPE

```
file [-ch] [-flist] [-mfile] file ...
```

The `file` command examines *file* and attempts to determine what type of file it is (executable, data file for a particular program, graphic image, shell script, and so on). It does this by comparing the beginning of the file against a list of "magic numbers" in a database, called the "magic file."

`-c`	Check the magic file for errors.
`-flist`	Take the list of files to be checked from *list*.
`-h`	Don't follow symbolic links.
`-mfile`	Use *file* as the file database.

FIND—FIND FILES BY ATTRIBUTES

```
find path... conditions
```

The `find` command searches all files and directories under a specified *path* or *paths* for files that meet certain *conditions*. (The first argument that starts with -, (, or ! is taken to be the beginning of the conditions.) The conditions are tested in the order they occur on the command line.

When there's a time in the `find` command, it's in days. You can specify it as +n (more than *n*), n (exactly *n*), or -n (less than n). Condition expressions can be grouped with parentheses (), negated with !, joined in a logical and with -a and joined in a logical or with -o.

`-atime n`	True if the file was accessed *n* days ago.
`-cpio device`	Always true. Copies the file to *device* in cpio format.
`-ctime n`	True if file information was last changed *n* days ago.

`-depth`	Always true. Do a depth-first search, doing everything in a directory before doing the directory itself.
`-exec command`	Always true. Run the *command* on the file; the placeholder {} can be used to represent the file's name. The command must end with a semi-colon, which may need to be escaped for the shell.
`-follow`	Always true. Follow symbolic links.
`-fstype type`	True if the file system is of the specified *type*.
`-group name`	True if the file belongs to the group *name*.
`-inum n`	True if the file has inode number *n*.
`-links n`	True if the file has *n* links to it.
`-local`	True if the file is on a local file system.
`-ls`	Always true. Print the file's name and its statistics (much like `ls -l`).
`-mount`	Always true. Don't search past a directory containing a mounted file system.
`-mtime n`	True if the file was last modified *n* days ago.
`-name pattern`	True if the file's name matches *pattern*. If the pattern contains wild cards, you will have to escape them to avoid interpretation by the shell.
`-ncpio device`	Always true. Copies the file to *device* in `cpio -c` format.
`-newer file`	True if the file is newer than the named *file*.
`-nogroup`	True if the file belongs to an unknown group (one that isn't in the file `/etc/groups`).
`-nouser`	True if the file belongs to an unknown user (one that isn't in the file `/etc/passwd`).
`-ok command`	Always true. Like `-exec`, this runs *command* on the file, but first it asks you if you want the command run. To run the *command*, type y.
`-perm [-]mode`	True if the file's permissions are the specified *mode*. The *mode* is symbolic.

-operm [-]*mode*	True if the file's permissions are the specified numeric *mode*.
-print	Always true. Print the file's name, relative to *path*.
-prune	Always true. Don't go into subdirectories below *pattern*. Given after a -name *pattern* condition.
-size *n*[c]	True if the file is *n* blocks long, or *n* bytes long if the number is followed by a c.
-type *c*	True if the file is of the specified *type*. The types are b (block special file), c (character special file), d (directory), l (symbolic link), p (named pipe), or f (plain file).
-user *name*	True if the file belongs to the user named *name*.

FMT—FORMAT TEXT FILE

```
fmt [-w n] [file...]
```

The fmt command formats paragraphs of text. By default, it makes lines 72 characters wide or less, breaking the line at the last space or tab before the limit. It joins shorter lines into longer lines, until a new paragraph starts.

The fmt command considers a new paragraph to start after a change in indentation, an empty line, or lines that start with a dot (.).

-w *n*	Format the file for lines *n* characters wide. If you're using a BSD system, the command line synopsis for fmt is very different.

See Chapter 10, "Working with Text Files."

FOLD—SHORTEN TEXT LINES

```
fold [-bs][-w n] [file ...]
```

The fold command shortens lines in a text file (or standard input), inserting line breaks. The default line length is 80 characters.

-w n	Fold all lines longer than *n* characters wide.
-b	Use bytes rather than character positions to calculate the width of the line.
-s	Fold at spaces instead of at the exact column position.

See Chapter 10, "Working with Text Files."

GETCONF—DISPLAY SYSTEM CONFIGURATION INFORMATION

```
getconf system_variable
getconf pathname path_variable
```

The getconf command displays information about the system configuration. There are two forms: the first form displays the value of a *system_variable*, and the second form displays the value of a *path_variable* for a given file or directory. (The second form is necessary because some values can change when you move onto a mounted file system.)

The variables that can be listed include the maximum length for a file name, for a path name, and the maximum number of arguments allowed on a line. See your system's documentation for the complete list of variables.

JOBS—DISPLAY CURRENT JOBS

```
jobs [-l|-n|-p] [jobID...]
```

Displays a list of all running or stopped jobs, or just those specified by one or more *jobID*s. Processes are gathered together into process groups. If your shell has job control turned on (see set), background jobs belong to different process groups than foreground jobs.

-l	List the job IDs and the process group IDs.
-n	List only the jobs with a different status than the last time the shell notified you.
-p	List only process group ID numbers.

See Chapter 12, "Commands and Job Control."

KILL—END A PROCESS

```
kill -l
kill -signal processID
```

Technically, the `kill` command sends a signal to a process. In practice, this command is almost always used to end a process by sending the `kill` signal. The *processID* is the process ID number (from `ps`) or a job ID number (from `jobs`). If you use a job ID number, you must start it with a % character. The command to kill job 3 is `kill -9 %3`.

-l	List all signals. If your system lists the signals with SIG at the beginnings of their names; remove the SIG before using the signal name in a `kill` command. (The signal SIGKILL becomes -KILL.)
-signal	Send the specified *signal*. It can be given as a name (such as listed by `kill -l`) or as a number. The signal `-9` means "kill."

LN—LINK FILE

```
ln [-fns] old new
```

The `ln` command creates a new link (name) for the file *old*. Without options, `ln` creates a hard link. Hard links can only be created on a single file system; they cannot cross to another drive. Hard links cannot link directories. With the `-s` option, `ln` creates a symbolic link. Symbolic links can cross file systems and they can link directories.

-f	Force the link, don't prompt for permission to overwrite a file.
-n	Do not overwrite existing files; conflicts with `-f`.
-s	Create a symbolic link.

See Chapter 4, "Files and Directories."

LOGIN—LOGIN TO SYSTEM

```
login [name [variable=value]]
```

The `login` command logs a user into the system. Normally, `login` is started by the system administrator, without arguments. The command prompts for a user name and a password.

Once a user is identified and validated, `login` starts a user's shell and (optionally) sets one or more variables to the given values. (The values for the variables PATH and SHELL cannot be changed using this technique.)

See Chapter 1, "Your First Session."

LP—PRINT FILE

```
lp [-cmpsw] [-d dest | -d any] [-f name] [-H action] [-n
    num] [-o options] [-P list] [-q n] [-S name [-d any]] [-
    t title] [-T content [-r]] [-y mode] [file …]

lp -i printID … [-cmpsw] [-d dest | -d any] [-f name] [-
    H action] [-i printID] [-n num] [-o options] [-P list]
    [-q n] [-S name [-d any]] [-t title] [-T content [-r]]
    [-y mode]
```

The `lp` command queues up *files* for printing. If no printer is specified using -d, the `lp` command uses the printer named by the environment variable LPDEST. If LPDEST is not set, a default printer is used. When the request is queued, the `lp` command prints its print ID number on standard output.

The second form affects an existing print request or requests, identified by its print ID number, *printID*.

-c	Copy files to the print spooler, so changes made between giving this command and the print job do not show up in the printed copy.
-d *dest*	Print to the printer *dest*. You can specify a default printer by setting the value of the environment variable LPDEST to the name of the printer.
-d any	Used with -f and -S to cause the job to print on a printer that supports a specific print wheel or character set or a particular form.
-f *name*	Print on the form specified by *name*. The administrator must set up the *forms*.

-H *action*	Print but perform the specified *action*, which is one of hold (notify before printing), resume (turn off a hold action), or immediate (print now; only available to privileged users.
-i *printID*	Command affects print job identified by *printID*
-m	Send mail after the job has been printed.
-n *num*	Print *num* copies of the *file*.
-o *options*	Set a printer-specific *option*. Some standard options include nobanner (don't print a banner page) and length=n (print pages that are *n* long, where *n* is normally lines).
-P *list*	Print only the page numbers given in the *list*. The list consists of individual page numbers separated by commas or ranges separated by a - character. To print pages 1, 3, and 7 through 10, the option would be -P 1,3,7-10.
-q *n*	Print the request with a different priority. A priority of 39 is the lowest you can have.
-r	Reject the request if the printer cannot handle that sort of content. Used with -T.
-s	Suppress messages.
-S *name*	Use the print wheel or character set specified by *name*. This depends upon your printer and your system setup.
-t *title*	Use *title* on the banner page.
-T *content*	Send the job to a printer that supports the specified kind of *content*. The default kind of *content* is simple. An administrator can define kinds of content for a system; for example, an administrator might want to define "postscript" as a kind of content, so to print a PostScript file, you would include -T postscript with the lp command.
-w	Write a message to the terminal screen after the *file* is printed; uses mail if you're not logged on when it finishes.
-y *mode*	Print according to some locally-defined *mode*. Ask your system administrator.

See Chapter 11, "Printing Text Files."

LPSTAT—DISPLAY PRINTER STATUS

```
lpstat [-dDlrRst] [-a [list]] [-c [list]] [-f [list]]
       [-o [list]] [-p [list]] [-S [list]] [-u [list]] [-v
       [list]]
```

The lpstat command displays the status of printers on the system.

A *list* is a list of items, either separated by spaces (and therefore in quotation marks) or separated by commas. If you leave off the *list*, the default is "all."

-a [*list*]	Report whether the *list* of printers and printer classes are accepting print requests.
-c [*list*]	Print the *list* of all printer classes and the printers in them.
-d	Print the name of the default destination for print requests.
-D	Describe the printers listed as arguments to -p.
-f [*list*]	Verify that the forms named in *list* are handled by lp.
-l	List the possible forms or character sets. Used with -f and -S.
-o [*list*]	Display the current status of output requests on the *list* of printers.
-p [*list*]	Display the status of the printers in the *list*.
-P	List the types of paper supported
-r	Display the current status of the actual lp scheduling program.
-R	Show numbers describing where each job is in the queue.
-s	Show a status summary, including the output of the -o and -p options.
-S [*list*]	Verify that the character sets or print wheels in *list* are handled by lp.
-t	Display all status information, including that given by -s and the idle status of all printers.

-u [*list*]	Display the status information for the users whose log-in names are in the *list*. The log-in names can be in the form *login*, *system*!*login* (for a user on a remote system), *system*!all (for all users on the remote system), or all (for all users on this system).
-v [*list*]	Display the names of printers in *list* and the path names of their associated devices.

See Chapter 11, "Printing Text Files."

LS—LIST FILES

```
ls [-abcCdfFgilLmnopqrRstuvx1] [file …]
```

The ls command lists files and directories. If no *files* are given on the command line, ls lists the contents of the current directory.

-a	List all files, including hidden files and the directories dot (.) and dot-dot (..).
-A	List all entries, including those that begin with a dot but do *not* list dot (.) and dot-dot (..).
-b	Show nonprinting characters as octal numbers.
-c	Use the time that the file information (the inode) was last changed instead of file modification time.
-C	Print multicolumn output. When printing to a terminal, this is the default.
-d	If the *file* is a directory, print its name and not its contents.
-f	Force each argument to be interpreted as a directory. This turns off the -1, -t, -s, and -r, options (and turns on -a) and causes files to be listed in the order they appear in the directory, not in ASCII sorted order.
-F	Indicate the file types by printing a character after each file name. A regular character gets no indicator, a directory gets a slash (/), an executable file gets an asterisk (*), and a symbolic link gets an at-sign (@).
-g	Long output like -1, but don't print the owner's name.

-i	For each file, print the inode number.
-l	Show long listing; see below for the description of the output.
-L	If *file* is a symbolic link, list the file it points to instead of the name of the link itself.
-m	List files on a single line, separated by commas.
-n	Long output like -l but print the numeric values (UID and GID) for the owner and group.
-o	Long output like -l, but don't print the group's name.
-p	Indicate directories by a trailing slash (/).
-q	Print nonprinting characters as a question mark (?).
-r	Print files in reverse order.
-R	List recursively, including all subdirectories.
-s	Give size in blocks, not bytes.
-t	Sort by time (most recent first) instead of name. By default, modification time is used (but -c and -u change this).
-u	Use the time the file was last accessed instead of modification time.
-x	Print multicolumn output sorted across the line, not down.
-1	Print one entry per line in the output.

When the -l option is given, ls prints long-format output.

```
-rwxrwxrwx    2 susan   r+d      80252   Mar 23 13:28
racing_form
```

The first block of 10 characters in a line are the file's *type* and its *permissions*, for the user, group, and other. The following indicate the file types:

d	directory
l	symbolic link
b	block special file

c	character special file
p	fifo (or "named pipe") special file
-	ordinary file
|	FIFO

The permissions are read, write, and execute. The next number is the number of hard *links* to the file (2 in this case). After that come the *owner's* log-in name (susan) and *group* (r+d). Following that are the *size* of the file in bytes (80252), the *time* of last modification (March 23, 13:28) and the file's *name*.

See Chapter 4, "Files and Directories."

MAN—DISPLAY MAN PAGE

```
man [-] [-adFlrt] [-M path] [-T troff-macro] [-s sec-
    tion] topic ...
man [-M path] -k keyword ...
man [-M path] -f topic ...
```

The man command prints information about topics in the system documentation, or "man pages." There are three forms: the first displays information about a *topic* (usually a command name), the second searches for a one-line summary of a man page that contains *keyword*, and the third searches for the one-line summary for a particular *topic*.

Normally, the man command searches for directories matching the patterns man? and cat? under /usr/share/man or /usr/man/man, but if the environment MANPATH is set to a colon-separated list of paths, it will search those instead. Paths supplied with the -M option will be used instead of the MANPATH or the default path, if the -M option is given.

-	Display the file using cat instead of more -s. (The man command also displays using cat when the standard output is not a terminal.)
-a	Show all man pages that match *topic*. Normally, man stops with the first matching file it finds.

`-d`	Display debugging information.
`-f` *topic*	Display the one-line summary relating to *topic*.
`-F`	Force man to search the directories instead of using a database file. This is useful if the database isn't up to date.
`-k` *keyword*	Print all the one-line summaries that contain *keyword*.
`-l`	List all the man pages that match *topic* in the search path.
`-M` *paths*	Use the colon-separated list of search paths *paths* instead of the value of MANPATH or the default value.
`-r`	Reformat the page but do not display it.
`-s` *section*	Search only the specified *section*. The section can be a digit or a letter. You can specify multiple sections by separating them with commas.
`-t`	Format and print the page using `troff` (or some other system-dependent processor).
`-T` *troff-macro*	Format the page with the specified *troff-macro* package (the default is the `troff` option -man, which represents the file `/usr/share/lib/tmac/an`).

See Chapter 5, "Finding Help."

MKDIR—CREATE A DIRECTORY

```
mkdir  [-p]  [-m mode]  dir...
```

The `mkdir` command creates one or more directories.

`-m` *mode*	Create the directory with the specified *mode*.
`-p`	If necessary, create any intermediate directories in the path name *dir*.

MORE—DISPLAY TEXT ONE SCREEN AT A TIME

```
more  [-cdflrsuw]  [-lines]  [+linenumber]  [+/pattern]
     [file ...]
```

The `more` command is a pager that displays a file or its standard input on standard output, one screen at a time.

`-lines`	Display only lines lines of text.
`+linenum-` `ber`	Start displaying text in the first file at line linenumber.
`+/pattern`	Start displaying text two lines before the first occurrence of the regular expression *pattern*.
`-c`	Clear the screen before displaying text.
`-d`	Display error messages instead of ringing the terminal bell.
`-f`	Do not fold long lines.
`-l`	Do not treat formfeed characters (Ctrl-L) as page breaks.
`-r`	Display control characters as a ^ followed by a letter. By default, control characters aren't displayed.
`-s`	Replace (squeeze) multiple blank lines with a single blank line.
`-u`	Don't generate underline sequences; this is used if the terminal can understand underline sequences instead of `more` generating its own.
`-w`	Wait at the end of the file for some key to be pressed, then exit. By default, `more` exits as soon as it gets to the end of the file.

The `more` command has its own internal commands for movement. Some of the commands are given here. For more, see the official documentation. Most commands can be prefixed by a number of repetitions, shown here by *n*; if no number is given, the command occurs once.

*n*Space	Display another screen of text.
*n*Enter	Display another line of text.
*n*b	Move backward *n* screenfuls and then display one.
*n*d	Move forward by *n* lines or a half screenful. If *n* is given, that becomes the default for d and u commands.
*n*f	Move forward by *n* screenfuls and then display one.

h	Print help information.
Ctrl-L	Redraw the screen.
q	Quit.
Q	Quit.
=	Display current line number.
n/pattern	Search forward for the *n*th occurrence of the regular expression *pattern*. The *pattern* will be displayed on the third line of the screen.
:f	Display current file name and line number.
n:n	Show the *n*th next file. Only has an effect if more than one file was named on the command line.

MV—MOVE A FILE OR DIRECTORY

```
mv [-fi] oldfile newfile
mv [-fi] file … directory
```

The `mv` command is used to move or rename a file or directory. There are two forms: The first moves a single file (or directory) to a new name or location. The second moves one or more files into a directory without changing the file names.

-f	Forcefully move files; don't ask if a file should be overwritten.
-i	Ask before overwriting a file.

See Chapter 4, "Files and Directories."

PASSWD—SET OR CHANGE YOUR PASSWORD

```
passwd
```

The `passwd` command sets or changes your password. After giving the command, the `password` command asks for your current password (if there is one), then asks for a new password, then asks for the new password to be repeated.

See Chapter 1, "Your First Session."

PG—DISPLAY TEXT ONE SCREEN AT A TIME

```
pg  [-num]  [-cefnrs]  [-p str]  [+line]  [+/pattern/]
    [filename ... ]
```

The pg command is a file pager that displays a file or its standard input on standard output, one screen at a time. Unlike most versions of more, it allows you to back up and view past text. Its internal commands are different from more. Unlike more, the pg man page refers to screens of text as "pages."

-num	Use *num* lines to display text. (Normally, it uses one line less than the screen has.)
+line	Start displaying text at line number *line*.
+/pattern/	Start displaying text at the first line containing the regular expression *patt*.
-c	If possible, move the cursor to the top left corner and clear the screen before displaying a page.
-e	Do *not* pause at the end of the file. (By default, pg does pause.)
-f	Do *not* split (fold) long lines. You might want to do this if there is a lot of underlining on a line; folding the line looks bad.
-n	Don't wait for Enter after a command; run the command as soon as the letter is typed. Even with this option, you must press Enter after the search commands.
-p *str*	Use *str* as the prompt. Normally, the prompt is ":". A %d in the prompt shows up as the current page number.
-r	Run in restricted mode.
-s	Print all prompts and messages in standard output mode, which is usually reverse video.

The movement commands can take a preceding number. If the number is positive, the command moves forward that distance; if the number is negative, the command move backward that distance.

Some of the internal commands for `pg` are:

*n*Enter	Display another page of text, or skip ahead *n* pages.
*n*d	Move by *n* half pages.
*n*f	Skip *n* pages of text
$	Display the last page of text in the file.
h	Display help.
Ctrl-L	Redraw the screen.
s *file*	Save the file under the name *file*.
q	Quit.
Q	Quit.
n/*pattern*/	Search forward for the *n*th occurrence of the regular expression *pattern*. The *pattern* will be displayed on the first line of the screen.
n?*pattern*?	Search backward for the *n*th occurrence of the regular expression *pattern*. The *pattern* will be displayed on the first line of the screen.
*n*n	Show the *n*th next file. Only has an effect if more than one file was named on the command line.
*n*p	Show the *n*th previous file. Only has an effect if more than one file was named on the command line and you have already given an n command.

PR—FORMAT FILES FOR PRINTING

```
pr [+page]  [-column]  [-adFmprt]  [-e[char][gap]]  [-h
    header]      [-i[char][gap]]      [-l    lines]      [-
    n[char][width]] [-o offset] [-s[char]] [-w width] [-
    fp] [file...]
```

The `pr` command formats files for printing. Normally, this involves breaking the file into appropriately-sized chunks separated by a header (two blank lines, a line containing the date and the name of the file, and two more blank lines) and a trailer (five blank lines). The formatted file is printed on standard output. If no *file* is specified, `pr` reads its standard input.

`+page`	Begin output on page *page*.
`-column`	Print in *column* number of columns. The default is one.
`-a`	When printing columns, print them across the page, rather than up and down.
`-d`	Double space output.
`-e[char][gap]]`	Set tab characters (or the character specified by *char*) to expand with the specified *gap*. A tab character expands to the next column that is a multiple of *gap* plus 1. If no *gap* is specified or it's 0, then it is calculated as 8. That is, tabs go to columns 9, 17, 25, and so on.
`-f`	Use a formfeed character (Ctrl-L) for new pages instead of inserting newlines as needed.
`-h header`	Use the string *header* in the page header instead of the file's name.
`-l lines`	Set the page length to be *lines* long; default is 66 lines.
`-m`	Merge files. Each file gets its own column, instead of printing multiple *file* arguments after one another.
`-n[char][width]]`	Number lines of output; the space given for the number is normally 5 characters but can be set by *width*. After the number, `pr` normally prints a tab character, but that can be changed to the *char* character provided.
`-o offset`	Offset output by *offset* characters. Used to provide a left margin.
`-p`	When writing to a terminal, pause before beginning each page. Continue after Enter is pressed.
`-s[char]`	Separate text columns by a tab (or the character *char*) instead of by a number of spaces.
`-t`	Don't print the header or the trailer. On the last page, don't space to the bottom of the page.
`-w width`	For multiple columns, set the width of the page's line to *width* columns. Default is a width of 72 characters.

See Chapter 11, "Printing Text Files."

PS—SHOW PROCESS STATUS

```
ps [-aAcdefjl] [-g grplist] [[-o format] ...] [-p pro-
   clist] [-t term] [-u uidlist] [-U uidlist]
```

The `ps` commands display information about current processes. There are several output formats; you can also specify the information you want printed by using the `-o` option. By default, it displays the process ID, the name of the terminal device, the time spent executing so far, and the command name.

A number of options have been omitted from this summary. If you need information about session leaders (for example), see your system's `ps` man page.

Options that accept lists as arguments (such as `-o`) accept the lists either quoted and separated by spaces or commas, or just separated by commas. (If separated by spaces, the argument must be quoted.)

`-a`	Print information about almost all processes.
`-A`	Print information about all processes.
`-c`	Print in a way that shows process priority information as well.
`-d`	Print about all processes except session leaders.
`-e`	Print information about every process now running.
`-f`	Print a full listing.
`-g grplist`	Print only processes belonging to the groups listed in *grplist*.
`-j`	Print session ID and process group ID numbers.
`-l`	Print a long listing.
`-o format`	Print information according to the *format*. Each item in the *format* list is information to be printed. Each item has a default title, but you can specify a new title with *item=title*. The column is always at least as wide as the title text. (If there is no *title*, no title is printed but the column is as wide as the default title.)
`-p proclist`	Print information only about the processes listed in *proclist*.

-t *term*	Print information only about the processes associated with the terminal *term*. The terminal is in the form reported by the `tty` command.
-u *uidlist*	Print information only about processes with an effective user ID in *uidlist*.
-U *uidlist*	Print information only about processes with a real user ID in *uidlist*.

The full listing prints the following information. The left column is the header that appears on the screen.

UID	The user's log-in name.
PID	The process ID.
PPID	The process ID of the parent process, the process that started this one.
C	Scheduling information; not printed when -c is given.
CLS	Scheduling class; printed when -c is given.
PRI	Process priority; printed when -c is given.
STIME	The starting time of the process in hours, minutes, and seconds.
TTY	The controlling terminal, or ? if there is no controlling terminal.
TIME	The total execution time so far.
CMD	The command name.

The long listing prints the following information.

F	Flag information.
S	The state of the process. This could include O (process is running), S (process is sleeping), Z (process is a zombie), or T (process has been stopped). Other states are possible.
UID	The effective user ID of the process.
PID	The process ID.

PPID	The process ID of the parent process, the process that started this one.
C	Scheduling information; not printed when -c is given.
CLS	Scheduling class; printed when -c is given.
PRI	Process priority.
NI	Nice value, used for calculating priorities. Not printed when -c is given.
ADDR	The memory address of the process.
SZ	The size of the process in memory.
WCHAN	If the process is sleeping, this is the address of the event the process is waiting for. If the process is running, this is blank.
TTY	The controlling terminal, or ? if there is no controlling terminal.
TIME	The total execution time so far.
CMD	The command name.

The -o option allows you to specify the information in the display. Versions of ps that conform to the POSIX standard recognize at least these, and may recognize others:

args	The command and its arguments.
comm	The command name.
etime	Elapsed time since the process started, in *days:hours:minutes:seconds*.
group	Effective group ID.
nice	System's scheduling priority; a positive value gets less priority (it's "nice" to the other processes).
pcpu	Percentage of CPU time used by the process.
pgid	Process group ID.
pid	Process ID.
ppid	Process ID of the parent process.

`rgroup`	Real group ID.
`ruser`	Real user ID.
`time`	Total CPU time used by the process, in *days:hours:minutes:seconds*.
`tty`	Name of the controlling terminal
`user`	Effective user ID.
`vsz`	Size of the process, in kilobytes, in virtual memory.

See Chapter 6, "Emergency Recovery."

PWD—DISPLAY CURRENT WORKING DIRECTORY

`pwd`

The `pwd` command prints your working directory. It is a shell built-in command. In the Korn Shell, this is an alias for `print -r - $PWD`.

See Chapter 1, "Your First Session."

RM—REMOVE A FILE OR DIRECTORY

```
rm [-fi] file...
rm -rR [-f] [-i] dirname...[file...]
```

The `rm` command removes a link to a file or directory. When all of the links are gone, the file is gone from the system. If the *file* is a symbolic link, the link will be removed but the original (linked) file won't be affected.

To remove a directory, use `rmdir` or the `-r` or `-R` options.

`-f`	Force the removal of the file; don't prompt for confirmation if you do not have write permission on the file.
`-i`	Prompt for confirmation before removing a file.
`-r`	Recursively remove directories. You cannot use this option to remove a non-empty write-protected directory.
`-R`	Same as `-r`.

See Chapter 4, "Files and Directories."

RMDIR—REMOVE A DIRECTORY

```
rmdir [-ps] directory ...
```

The `rmdir` command removes an empty directory. (With the -p option, the directory can contain an empty directory, named in the argument.)

-p	Remove the entire path specified by *directory*, if possible. Each child has to be the only child of its parent directory for all of them to be removed. The `rmdir` command prints a message on the standard error telling whether the whole directory path or only part of it was removed.
-s	When -p is used, suppress messages to the standard error.

See Chapter 4, "Files and Directories."

SLEEP - DO NOTHING FOR A WHILE

```
sleep seconds
```

The `sleep` command does nothing for a number of *seconds*.

SORT - SORT A FILE

```
sort [-cmu] [-o file] [-bdfiMnr] [-t char] [-T dir]
[-k keydef] [file...]
```

The `sort` command sorts text input. By default, it sorts in ASCII order on the entire line (called a record in the man page). It can also sort based on several keys, specified with -k. The options [-dfiMnr] can be given in a key (in which case they affect only that key, or they can be used to modify the entire sort.

-b	Ignore leading blank characters when figuring out where a sort key starts.
-c	Check that the file is sorted according to the command arguments. Set the return code appropriately. On Solaris systems, `sort` prints a message if the file is not correctly sorted.

-d	Use a dictionary sort, counting only letters, digits, and blank characters for comparison.
-f	Fold lowercase letters into uppercase ones.
-i	Ignore nonprinting characters.
-k *keydef*	Sort based on the keys defined in *keydef*. Keys are sorted in the order they appear on the command line.

A key definition has this syntax:

start[type][,end[type]]

The *start* and *end* describe the number of the field (starting with field 1) to be used as a key and an optional offset. (For example, 1.3 is the third character of field one.) The *type* is any or all of the options bdfiMnr.

-m	Merge two sorted files.
-M	Compare keys as though they were months, so "JAN" sorts before "FEB." Lowercase is treated as if it were uppercase.
-n	Only pay attention to numbers in the sort key, and treat it as a number. A key without digits in it is treated as zero.
-u	Remove duplicates so that each line in the sorted file is unique.
-o *file*	Store output in *file*, instead of writing to standard output.
-t *char*	Use the character *char* as the field separator.
-T *dir*	Store temporary files in the named directory.

See Chapter 10, "Working with Text Files."

SPELL—CHECK SPELLING IN A FILE

```
spell [-bivx] [+local_file] [file]...
```

The spell command compares each word in a *file* against its dictionary. If the word is not in the dictionary, spell may try to determine if the word is plausible (for example, by creating a plural from a known dictionary word). If the word isn't plausible, spell prints the word to standard output.

`+local_file`	Also check against the words in *local_file*, which is a sorted file with one word to a line.
`-b`	Use the British spelling dictionary instead of the American one.
`-i`	Normally the file is run through a command called `deroff` to eliminate any `troff` commands. The `-i` option causes `deroff` to ignore the `troff` commands `.so` and `.nx`. If your system doesn't have `deroff`, this option does nothing.
`-v`	Print all words that aren't actually in the spelling list, and indicate plausible words.
`-x`	Display every plausible word-stem, one on a line, preceded by `=`.

See Chapter 10, "Working with Text Files."

STTY—SET TERMINAL CHARACTERISTICS

```
stty [-a] [-g]
stty setting ...
```

The `stty` command displays or sets information about the terminal. Without arguments, it prints an abbreviated list of the settings.

`-a`	Display all settings
`-g`	Display settings in a form that can be used as arguments to the `stty` command.

See Chapter 6, "Emergency Recovery."

TYPE—IDENTIFY UNIX COMMANDS, SHELL FUNCTIONS, OR SHELL BUILT-INS

```
type commands
```

The `type` command reports on the type of each argument, if it were used as a command. It identifies the argument as one of a shell built-in, function, alias, hashed command, or keyword; if the argument is a file, it will display the path name.

See Chapter 6, "Emergency Recovery."

UMASK—SET OR DISPLAY USER FILE MASK

```
umask [-S] [nnn]
```

Without an argument, it displays the current user file creation mask. With an argument, it sets the value to that argument. The argument is a file mode and specifies which bits are turned *off*.

In the Korn Shell, the -S option causes umask to display the current umask symbolically.

See Chapter 3, "About Files and Directories."

VI—TEXT EDITOR

```
vi [- | -s] [-ClLRvV] [-r [filename]] [-t tag] [-wn]
   [+command | -c command] filename...
```

The vi editor is the standard text editor on most UNIX systems. For information about the commands used in vi, see Chapter 9, "The vi Editor." This merely summarizes the options, which were not discussed in the chapter.

-	Run a script instead of running interactively. The script is provided on standard input.
+command	Run the *command* as soon as vi starts. Not all commands can be run, but search and positioning commands can be given.
-c command	The same as +command,
-C	Encryption option. For security, vi asks you for an encryption key and codes all text (even in temporary files) using that key. Very similar to -x, except that -C assumes the file you're reading in was already encrypted, and will give very strange results if it wasn't.

`-l`	Set tabs, autoindent, and so forth for editing programs written in the LISP programming language.
`-L`	List the name of all files saved when the system or the editor crashed.
`-r [filename]`	Recover the file *filename* that was being edited when the system or the editor crashed.
`-R`	Run in read-only mode, so the file cannot be overwritten.
`-s`	Run a script instead of running interactively, the same as -. The script is provided on standard input.
`-t tag`	Edit the file that contains the programming construct *tag*. This works for directories containing source code files where the file ctags has created an index of source code files.
`-v`	Start in vi mode (as opposed to ex mode). This is redundant if you typed vi to start the command.
`-V`	Be verbose. Echo nonterminal input on standard error. This can be useful when running editor scripts with -s.
`-wn`	Set the window size to *n* lines high. This is useful when working over slow systems or connections.
`-x`	Encryption option. For security, vi asks you for an encryption key and codes all text (even in temporary files) using that key. Very similar to -C, except that -x tries to guess if the file you're reading in was already encrypted, and won't try to "unencrypt" it if the file wasn't encrypted.

The following vi commands are described in this book:

Command	Meaning
Escape	Leave text input mode and enter command mode.
Control-C	Interrupt current command; also leaves text input mode.
`:quit`	Quit if there are no unsaved changes. Can be abbreviated :q
`:quit!`	Quit even if there are unsaved changes. Can be abbreviated :q!

Command	Meaning
`:write` [*name*]	Write current text into the file *name*. Can be abbreviated `:w` [*name*]
`:write!` [*name*]	Write current text into the file *name*, even if it's not the file you're currently editing. Can be abbreviated `:w!` [*name*]
`:wq`	Write the file and quit
`:next`	Go to next file in the argument list if there are no unsaved changes. Can be abbreviated `:n`
`:next!`	Go to the next file in the argument list even if there are no unsaved changes. Can be abbreviated `:n!`

`vi` Commands to Enter Input Mode

`a`	Insert the text after the current cursor position
`A`	Insert the text at the end of the current line
`i`	Insert the text at the current cursor position
`I`	Insert the text at the beginning of the current line
`o`	Insert the text on a new line before the current line
`O`	Insert the text on a new line after the current line

Movement Commands in `vi`

[*n*]`j`	Move cursor down *n* lines (default 1).
[*n*]`k`	Move cursor up *n* lines (default 1).
[*n*]`l`	Move cursor right *n* characters (default 1).
[*n*]`h`	Move cursor left *n* characters (default 1).
[*n*]Enter	Same as `j`.
[*n*]Space	Same as `l`.
[*n*]Backspace	Same as `h`.
`$`	Move cursor to right end of line.

^	Move cursor to first non-blank character on left of line.
0	Move cursor to first row of line.
[n]G	Move cursor to line *n* of file (default is end of file).
[n]w	Move cursor to beginning of *n*th next word (default 1)
[n]b	Move cursor to *n*th previous word beginning (default 1)
[n])	Move cursor to beginning of *n*th next sentence (default 1).
[n] (	Move cursor to *n*th previous sentence beginning (default 1).
[n]}	Move cursor to beginning of *n*th next paragraph (default 1).
[n]{	Move cursor to *n*th previous paragraph beginning (default 1).
[n]Control-F	Move cursor forward *n* screenfuls of lines (default 1).
[n]Control-B	Move cursor backward *n* screenfuls of lines (default 1).
[n]Control-E	Move screen forward *n* lines without moving cursor (default 1).
[n]Control-Y	Move screen backward *n* lines without moving cursor (default 1).
H	Move cursor to top line of screen.
L	Move cursor to last line of screen.
M	Move cursor to middle line of screen.
z	Redraw screen so line with cursor is at top.

vi Deletion, Change and Undo Commands

[n]dd	Delete the next *n* lines, starting with the current line (default is 1 line).
[n]d[*movement*]	Delete from the current cursor position to the destination of the *movement* command.
:addrd[elete]	Delete the lines described in the ex-style *addr*.
[n]rc	Replace the next *n* characters with the character *c* (default 1).
R	Delete the rest of the line and enter input mode.
u	Undo the last command that changed the file.

vi Search Commands

f*c*	Search forward in line for character *c*.
F*c*	Search backward in line for character *c*.
t*c*	Search forward in line for character *c*, but put cursor one character before it.
T*c*	Search backward in line for character *c*, but put cursor one character before it.
/*regexp*	Search forward for *regexp*
?*regexp*	Search backward for *regexp*
/*regexp*/z	Search forward for *regexp*, and display screen so matching line is at top.
?*regexp*?z	Search backward for *regexp*, and display screen so matching line is at top.
/	Search forward for last *regexp* searched for.
?	Search backward for last *regexp* searched for.
n	Repeat last search.

vi Search-and-Replace Commands

:s/*regexp*/*replacement*/	Replace first occurrence of *regexp* on this line with *replacement*.
:s/*regexp*/*replacement*/g	Replace all occurrences of *regexp* on this line with *replacement*.
:%s/*regexp*/*replacement*/	Replace first occurrence of *regexp* on a line throughout file.
:%s/*regexp*/*replacement*/g	Replace all occurrences of *regexp* throughout file.

vi Text Copying and Moving Commands

[*n*]yy	"Yank" *n* lines of text for copying.
[*n*]p	Put the contents of the buffer *after* the cursor, *n* times (default 1).
[*n*]P	Put the contents of the buffer *before* the cursor, *n* times (default 1).
:r *file-name*	Read in the file *filename* on the line after the cursor.

See Chapter 9, "The vi Editor."

WC—COUNT LINES, WORDS, AND CHARACTERS

    wc [-c|-m|-C] [-lw] [file ...]

The wc command counts the number of newlines, words, and characters in a file. Without options, it prints the size of the file in that order: lines, words, and bytes. If more than one *file* is specified, it lists a total as well.

The options specify which information to print.

-c	Count bytes.
-C	Count characters.
-l	Count lines.
-m	Count characters.
-w	Count words.

See Chapter 10, "Working with Text Files."

INDEX

A

Absolute path name, 73-74, 80-81, 147
Account, 2-3
adam program, 183
Alternate file, 375
American Standard Code for Information
    Exchange (ASCII), 129
Arguments, 462
ASCII sort, 129
at command, 488-93, 551-52
Awk, 432

B

Background/foreground, 479-86
Back reference, 316
Backspace character, 245-46
Backspace key, during login, 4
Backups, files, 257-58
Basic commands, 20-32
batch command, 552
bg command, 483-84, 553
Block special file, 101
Bourne-Again Shell, 28
Bourne Shell, 28, 29, 75
Buffer, 394, 397
Built-in commands, 220
Bytes, 100

C

cal command, 51-52
cancel command, 553
Canonical mode, 232, 251
cat command, 55, 61-64, 215-16, 264, 553
cd;pwd command line, 463-65
cd command, 554
cd command directory names, 22
Character class, 139-40
Character special file, 101
Checking spelling, 419-24
chgrp command, 112
chmod command, 107, 113-16, 554-55
chown program, 113
Clearing the display, 237-44
    Control-L, 237, 241
    stty -a, 242

stty -opost, 241-42
    stty sane, 237-38, 241
Clear-line (kill) character, 245, 250, 252
COMD, 21
command command, 220, 222, 556
Command line, 37-70
    command inconsistency, 49-50
    command synopses, 37, 40-42
    file redirection/pipes, 53-69
    operands, 38, 39
    options, 39, 40, 47-49
    structure of a command, 38-52
Command mode, **vi** editor, 331
Command pipe, defined, 64
Command prompt, 4
    cat command, 215-16
    echo command, 138, 216-19
    getting back to, 212-18
Commands, 219-26, 551-90
    and job control, 461-96
        foreground/background, 479-86
        multiple commands on a line,
            462-69
        scheduling jobs, 487-96
        setting environment variables, 470-
            78
Command substitution, 467
Command synopses, 37, 40-42
comm program, 431
Control-C, 227, 232, 245, 250, 339
Control characters, 130-31
    setting, 245-53
Control-D, 215-16, 245, 250, 264
Control-F, 357
Control-G, 131, 356-57
Control-H, 123, 246, 250
Control-L, 237, 241
Control-U, 250, 252
Control-Z, 483, 485
Cooked mode, 232, 251
Correct command, running, 219-26
Counting words, 415-18
cp command, 159, 164-65, 556
    -r option, 165-66
Crackers, 14-15
crontab command, 487, 556-57